A THEORY OF UNBORN LIFE

CONTENTS

For my mother

A THEORY OF UNBORN LIFE

From Abortion to Genetic
Manipulation

Anja J. Karnein

OXFORD
UNIVERSITY PRESS

OXFORD
UNIVERSITY PRESS

Oxford University Press, Inc., publishes works that further
Oxford University's objective of excellence
in research, scholarship, and education.

Oxford   New York
Auckland   Cape Town   Dar es Salaam   Hong Kong   Karachi
Kuala Lumpur   Madrid   Melbourne   Mexico City   Nairobi
New Delhi   Shanghai   Taipei   Toronto

With offices in
Argentina   Austria   Brazil   Chile   Czech Republic   France   Greece
Guatemala   Hungary   Italy   Japan   Poland   Portugal   Singapore
South Korea   Switzerland   Thailand   Turkey   Ukraine   Vietnam

Copyright © 2012 by Oxford University Press

Published by Oxford University Press, Inc.
198 Madison Avenue, New York, New York 10016

www.oup.com

Oxford is a registered trademark of Oxford University Press

Library of Congress Cataloging-in-Publication Data
Karnein, Anja J.
A theory of unborn life : from abortion to genetic manipulation / Anja J. Karnein.
   p.   cm.
Includes bibliographical references and index.
ISBN 978-0-19-978247-5
1. Unborn children (Law) 2. Genetic engineering—Law and legislation. 3. Bioethics.
4. Fetus—Legal status, laws, etc.—United States. 5. Fetus—Legal status, laws, etc.—Germany. I. Title.
K642.K37   2012
344.04'19—dc23   2011034080

9 8 7 6 5 4 3 2

Printed in the United States of America
on acid-free paper

ACKNOWLEDGMENTS

Here is where I tell the story of this book's unborn life and give credit to those who assisted in its creation. It began as my doctoral dissertation at Brandeis University but has, over the various years it took to mature, undergone many changes. I am grateful for having been given the chance to continue working on the manuscript as a visiting graduate fellow at the Edmond J. Safra Foundation Center for Ethics at Harvard University and as a postdoctoral fellow at the Center for Society and Genetics at the University of California, Los Angeles (UCLA). Generous funding from the Gerhard C. Starck Stiftung allowed me to further improve "A Theory of Unborn Life" in Germany and then to continue my work in the context of the research project "Bioethical Challenges to Normative Orders," directed by Rainer Forst, at the newly established Cluster of Excellence "The Formation of Normative Orders" at Johann Wolfgang Goethe-University Frankfurt. My subsequent junior faculty position at the Department of Social Sciences at Goethe-University gave me the opportunity to finish this book. Additionally, during my time in Germany, two visiting scholarships were of considerable help in putting together the arguments for why it is independence that we owe to future people: at the Center for Bioethics at New York University (NYU) and in the Law and Philosophy Program at UCLA. Finally, I am grateful to the Vereinigung von Freunden und Förderern der Johann Wolfgang Goethe-Universität for sponsoring my research in Los Angeles.

Within these institutions, I have to thank many people for supporting me: at Brandeis University, my supervisor Jeffrey Abramson, who was the one who inspired my interest in political philosophy and who taught me how to make texts come alive, as well as my other two committee members, Bernard Yack for his helpful advice and thought-provoking questions and Michael Sandel from whom I learned how to teach and think about heavy material lightly; at Harvard University, Frances Kamm, whose sharp-witted comments are always a delight, and Arthur Applbaum, whose weekly seminars were very enriching; at my first stay at UCLA, Sally Gibbons, whose kindness and warmth I will not forget,

Russell Korobkin for sponsoring and supporting my postdoctoral fellowship, and Seana Shiffrin for sponsoring my later visiting fellowship; at NYU, William Ruddick and J. David Velleman, who both offered comments and advice I am deeply indebted to; in Frankfurt, I am especially grateful to Rainer Forst for his support during very difficult times and for giving me the opportunity to finish this book.

I also want to thank Steve Teles for his encouragement and helpful advice in getting this book published. I am grateful to both anonymous reviewers at Oxford University Press for their incredibly useful and constructive criticism and to David McBride for his efficiency, patience, and good humor during the completion of the manuscript.

I have benefited from conversations with and written comments by Ayelet Banai, Ben Chan, Stefan Gosepath, Matthew Hanser, Markus Rothhaar, Martin Saar, and Marcus Willaschek. I also greatly profited from stimulating discussions with and questions from audiences at several meetings of the American Political Science Association, New York University, Columbia University, the University of California, Santa Barbara, the University of Cambridge, and the University of Oxford. Moreover, I want to express my appreciation for the various critical and helpful comments from the participants of an international workshop the Cluster of Excellence enabled me to organize in Frankfurt on "What We Owe to Future People" in February 2008.

I owe very special thanks to Jürgen Habermas for so generously commenting on and supporting my manuscript. My discussions with Mattias Iser have been of invaluable help. He has been my keenest reader, fiercest critic, and greatest supporter. Without him I could not have finished this book. Finally, I want to thank my parents, Alfred Karnein and Susan Stern, for just about everything. It was because of my father that I initially became interested in the ethical questions surrounding stem cell research. My mother's constant support and rigorous editorial help were vital for completing my dissertation. She was a great writer and had much to teach worth learning. I only wish I had been a better student. This book is dedicated to her.

A THEORY OF UNBORN LIFE

INTRODUCTION

"I Wish either my father or my mother, or indeed both of them, as they were in duty both equally bound to it, had minded what they were about when they begot me" (Sterne 1760, 1). Thus begin Tristram Shandy's bitter complaints about the circumstances of his conception. He is dismayed about his father's momentary distraction (by something Tristram's mother was saying to him about winding up the clock) in the precise instant the sperm that was to make Tristram left his body and started its voyage to the egg. Tristram is gravely concerned "that, through terror of it, natural to so young a traveler my little gentleman had got to his journey's end miserably spent; his muscular strength and virility worn down to a thread; his own animal spirits ruffled beyond description, and that in this sad disordered state of nerves, he had laid down a prey to suddenly start, or a series of melancholy dreams and fancies for nine long, long months together" (p. 3). Tristram is incensed about the consequences of this unfortunate beginning, which he considers to be beyond repair. "I tremble to think what a foundation had been laid for a thousand weaknesses both of body and mind, which no skill of the physician or the philosopher could ever afterwards have set thoroughly to rights" (p. 3).

The humor in these passages stems—in part at least—from the misattribution of cause and effect, namely that Tristram believes that his father's momentous disturbance at the moment of ejaculation would have such terrible and everlasting consequences for young Tristram. Despite the absurdity, there is of course a kernel of truth about what Tristram's father has to say about these fateful events, namely that "My Tristram's misfortunes began nine months before he ever came to this world" (p. 3). The beginning of an individual's life is always and inevitably also the beginning of that person's luck and misfortunes.

What we should take seriously about Tristram's lamentation is that it matters to persons what happened to the embryo from which they developed. In that sense, when Sterne broke with the tradition of epic narrative (which began in medias res and provided some of the background through flashbacks) and took beginning with the beginning to its extreme (i.e., *ab ovo*), he expressed a truth, namely that life does not begin at birth and that many events even long before can make a crucial difference to the resulting child and adult. This having been said, it does not follow that life before birth matters if there is no resulting person to care about it. Had Tristram not been born, there would have been no one to object to the circumstances of his conception from a first-person perspective. Thus, two things seem to be true at the same time. First, people care about what happened to the embryos from which they developed. Second, it does not matter to anyone from a first-person perspective what happens to embryos that do not develop into persons.

These two insights form the core of my theory of unborn life. This theory provides a solution for the problems that haunt debates on abortion but also, and with particular force, controversies arising in the context of new biomedical technologies, including stem cell research, preimplantation genetic diagnosis (PGD), and genetic manipulation. Stem cell research requires the destruction of embryos in order to derive human embryonic stem cells that promise to be important for scientific research and medical advance.[1] PGD allows parents to genetically select embryos because of certain traits in vitro. Genetic manipulation might soon enable parents to cure fatal or otherwise serious genetic defects in their embryos, or to physically or mentally enhance them to the point of changing the (human) nature of their future children entirely. The latter two technologies (i.e., PGD and genetic manipulation) are sometimes subsumed under the category of "reprogenetics."[2] This is because they constitute ways in which genetic technologies are used in combination with reproductive technologies to create persons who have either been selected on account of certain traits or genetically manipulated so that they have certain traits (or not). In the course of this book, I occasionally use this term as shorthand to describe PGD and genetic manipulation.

These new technologies present two kinds of challenges. The first relates to justifying practices that involve the destruction of embryos. Although this issue is familiar from the abortion controversy, in that debate it was possible to successfully circumvent questions about what we owe to embryos. A woman's right to end her pregnancy could always be defended with reference to her right to self-determination and bodily integrity. By contrast, when it comes to embryos created outside the female organism (i.e., embryos in vitro), there is no equally compelling interest to consider when the question arises of whether it is legitimate to destroy them for research and selection purposes.

The second challenge is genuinely new. It has to do with justifying practices that involve not the destruction but the genetic selection and manipulation of embryos that develop into persons. The problem is that the question about the way to conceive of our relationship to them has thus far not been carefully addressed. How should we treat embryos that mature into persons so that the persons they end up becoming will not have been wronged by our behavior?

In this book I develop a theory that provides answers to both kinds of challenges by spelling out the ways in which our normative commitments to persons should inform our treatment of embryos. The book is divided into two parts, each consisting of three chapters. The first part deals primarily with the challenge posed by technologies that involve destroying embryos. The second is concerned with the challenge presented by technologies intended to create genetically altered persons. In the following paragraphs, I briefly preview the arguments as they develop over the course of the individual chapters.

In the first part of the book (chapters 1 through 3), I claim that embryos that will develop into future persons should be treated in anticipation of the respect we owe to the persons they develop into. This is because it matters to born persons what happened to the embryo they emerged from. Thus, in chapter 1 I develop what I call the Personhood Dependent Principle, or PDP, which explains why we owe a special kind of protection to those embryos that will be persons. Although I am assuming a certain normative content to our commitment to persons, it is unclear who, descriptively, fits into this category and to what extent newborns or embryos can be part of it. I propose one possible way of construing personhood (acknowledging that there could be others equally befitting the theory), which includes all those capable of moral agency. It also includes, via secondary considerations, all those who are intimate parts of our social universe and of human descent. The unborn, I claim, cannot be subsumed under the category of "person." Because of their symbiotic connection to the body of a woman, they are structurally in a position in which they cannot be protected from destruction, that is, cannot be protected in a way persons would have to be.

Singling out embryos that develop into persons raises two questions. First, regarding how to know beforehand which embryos develop into persons and second, who has the authority to determine this. Obviously, we cannot know for certain which embryos end up becoming persons and which will not. However, as long as it is still the case that particular embryos could mature into persons, we should follow what I call the Principle of Precaution and treat them as if they will.

This having been said, as long as embryos are symbiotically connected to a woman's organism or, as it is the case with embryos in vitro, depend on such a connection for further existence, women can decide not to begin or not to continue their assistance. Thus, unless human beings find other ways of entering this world (e.g., through artificial wombs), it is ultimately always women on whose course of action it depends whether or not embryos grow into persons. I suggest that this should also make us rethink what we mean when we say that embryos are "potential" persons. Without particular women willing to carry individual embryos to term, there is no potential person to speak of. In cases in which there are women who consent to being pregnant the situation presents itself differently. Here I argue that respect for persons also implies an affirmative attitude toward their creation. This attitude may provide some reasons for allowing women to carry to term embryos leftover from fertility procedures (if they would like to do this), possibly even against the wish of these embryos' biological parents.

The final task of this chapter is to explain in more detail what it means to treat embryos in anticipation of the respect that is due to the persons they will come to be. I show that this does not create any obligation for women to continue their pregnancies. They need not ensure that new persons end up existing.

In chapters 2 and 3, I test the practicality of the theory thus proposed by looking at its attractiveness for two entirely different political and legal contexts, Germany and the United States, respectively. These are two countries with virtually opposite approaches to the moral value of embryos.

Chapter 2 is devoted to discussing Germany. This is an intriguing case because, to begin with, its official stance is remarkably protective of human embryos and for reasons that are predominantly secular. Germany went into the abortion debate with a recent history of atrocious medical abuses very much on its conscience. As a result and ever since, the notion of human dignity—which includes the dignity of the embryo—has been paramount. This experience has also led to the creation of a legal framework in which embryos in vivo are de jure protected from the moment of implantation and embryos in vitro from the moment of conception. However, especially in the case of embryos in vivo, the exceptions to the general rule of full protection are substantial—so substantial that Germany ends up with a fairly permissive abortion practice.

Many consider the German approach to abortion particularly hypocritical. But on all other issues pertaining to embryos, both in vivo and in vitro, it is equally inconsistent. A stranger, for instance, who negligently destroys a viable fetus (before birth) is not punished in the least according to criminal law (the same law that renders it illegal for a woman to have an abortion because embryos are considered to have human dignity and a right to life from the moment of implantation). While some embryos in vitro are more protected than embryos in vivo (the former are protected from the moment of conception, the latter can be destroyed before implantation), other embryos in vitro are not protected at all (embryos, for instance, that would have to be carried to term by someone other than their biological mothers).

I take these contradictions to be illuminating. They show that the existence of good and important reasons for protecting some embryos from the moment of conception does not imply that all should be equally protected. At the same time, and as instructive as it may be, I contend that Germany's stance on the embryo across various issues is not persuasive. This is primarily because the distinction between those embryos worth protecting and those that can be left to perish is made for arbitrary and sometimes prejudicial reasons. By "prejudicial" I mean reasons that are either based on problematic attitudes toward the role of women in the reproductive process or that discriminate against nontraditional family structures. This is where I suggest that the PDP could be of assistance. Given that Germany already treats different embryos differently, the PDP could help to make these distinctions less arbitrary, less prejudicial, and more coherent by distinguishing between those embryos that end up being persons and those that do not.

Chapter 3 discusses embryo protection in the United States. The latter presents an interesting comparative case to Germany as it approaches the moral value of embryos, especially early embryos, from a rather different point of view, namely by being agnostic toward it. Here, those in favor of women's right to end their pregnancies (so-called "pro-choice advocates") emerged from the abortion debate without having developed a coherent theory as to the moral value of (early) embryos. Moreover, there are no laws banning the destruction of embryos for research purposes or their genetic selection. Rather than creating an inconsistency, as in Germany, this situation is liable to producing a blind spot. It risks leaving embryos that will end up as persons unprotected. As it matters to persons what happened to their embryos, this is a troubling situation, rendering them extremely vulnerable to all kinds of harmful interventions by the previous generation prior to their becoming persons. The question is whether supporters of abortion and of technologies that involve the destruction of embryos have something (more than political strategy and rhetoric perhaps) at stake in thinking that there is no reason to treat at least some embryos with particular care from the moment of conception. I argue that there is nothing at stake for them and that therefore the PDP offers an attractive solution to avoid the blind spot. It provides a way to protect embryos that develop into persons while, at the same time, allowing women to abort their fetuses, parents to deselect embryos in the course of PGD, and scientists to use embryos for research purposes.

So far I have argued that women may decide, through their actions, *who* is born. This could suggest that they—or parents more generally—are also in a position to determine *how* future people enter this world; in other words, it may imply that parents can genetically manipulate their embryos according to what they consider to be "best" for their children. However, in the second part of the book (chapters 4 through 6), my central claim is that this is not the case, at least not without a number of strict limitations that follow from what it means to treat persons—including those of the future—as separately and equally important.

My suggestions in this regard run counter to the most prominent liberal approaches on issues pertaining to the genetic manipulation of future persons. I therefore begin the second part of this book, in chapter 4, by discussing three different such approaches. I start with John A. Robertson's (2003) claims that parents are entitled both to genetically select and to manipulate their future children due either to their reproductive liberties or to the privileges attached to raising a child. I then turn to a discussion of Ronald Dworkin's (2000) views on utilizing the new technologies in the name of moral and technical progress. Finally, I review the arguments of Allen Buchanan, Dan W. Brock, Norman Daniels, and Daniel Wikler (2000) in their coauthored book *From Chance to Choice. Genetics and Justice*, who support genetic interventions in the name of social justice.

Robertson puts major emphasis on the procreative or reproductive liberties of adults. He thinks that they have a right to use whatever technologies can assist them in their pursuit to transmit their genes to the next generation. Moreover, they can do so under their own conditions. Thus, if adults were to claim that they will have only children with certain genetic predispositions, their procreative liberties would entitle them to use genetic selection and also some forms of genetic manipulation to make it the case that their children end up with these predispositions. Those forms of genetic manipulation that fall outside the scope of reproductive liberties (i.e., certain forms of genetic enhancement) are protected by the general discretion afforded to parents in rearing their children. On Robertson's account, virtually the only way for adults to wrong the future persons they bring into existence would be to make them so much worse off than they would have otherwise been that they end up below the threshold of what constitutes a "normal" and healthy life. This, I claim, does not show the appropriate amount of respect for future persons. The latter are entitled, as persons, to be accepted the way they come into existence (i.e., without having been manipulated). They cannot be expected to be so grateful for having been born (i.e., having been spared nonexistence) that they should be glad to accept whatever conditions their parents may attach to bringing them to life.

Where Robertson takes the reproductive rights of adults too seriously, Dworkin overemphasizes the importance of not impeding scientific advance and the enhancement of the species. He endorses the new technologies to such an extent that he wants to throw overboard conventional moral concepts that stand in their way or that make their implementation questionable in certain cases. However, not only does it remain unclear what Dworkin means when he speaks of "conventional" moral concepts, but it is also puzzling why he wants to let the new technologies challenge our conventional concepts as opposed to using these concepts to rein them in. His approach fails to take seriously legitimate claims of all persons concerned, that is, those of women not to be subject to procedures that involve violating their physical integrity in the name of their embryos and those of future persons to be accepted for the separate individuals they come to be without having been genetically manipulated.

The most comprehensive and convincing account of those discussed here is provided by Buchanan et al. In the name of equal opportunity, they partly mandate and partly allow parents to perform a number of genetic alterations on their children both for treatment and for enhancement purposes. The chief problem with their approach is that they misunderstand what it means to respect future persons' right to an open future. They understand it to refer primarily to the absolute number of children's future options. They thereby fail to appreciate that children's right to an open future may also entail a right to have the particular future left open that would be theirs if no one had genetically interfered with them. In other words, they do not realize that an open future may not only have a quantitative dimension to it but a qualitative one as well. Moreover, Buchanan et al. overestimate what parents can possibly know about what would be "best" for their children. At the same time, the authors underestimate the difference between familiar ways of influencing children's development through socialization and genetically manipulating future persons. They do not realize that, while socialization occurs over years and is highly interactive, genetic manipulation is a one-time and completely noninteractive process.

Overall, my main criticism of liberal eugenicists is that they do not pay enough attention to the two conditions necessary to avoid situations of intergenerational domination. These are situations in which members of one generation can make decisions for members of another without adequately tracking their interests and without the latter being able to contest decisions so made. I argue that if liberal eugenicists were more perceptive of the threat of domination, they would notice how limited the possibilities of tracking future persons' interests really are (they would thus not suggest that parents can make a variety of alterations in the "best" interest of their children). Furthermore, they would acknowledge how important it is to leave intact the opportunity for future persons to contest their parents' choices (and thus not propose interventions that are merely "done" to future persons, as is genetic manipulation, and not communicated to them in some interactive way, as are socialization and education).

These thoughts lead me directly to chapter 5, in which I offer a detailed discussion of Jürgen Habermas's arguments. In the name of the same liberal values (i.e., freedom and equality) that the previously discussed authors use to endorse genetic selection and design, he rejects most ways in which these technologies can be used. Habermas believes in the importance of being subject to the natural lottery and not to the design of other persons. He is keenly aware of the problems that may arise from aggravating the already existing asymmetry between the generations. Thus, he is concerned that genetically manipulated individuals will no longer be able to perceive of themselves as undivided authors of their own lives and as equal to those who genetically altered them. The latter may, in turn, lose respect for the future persons they design and persons (including themselves) more generally. These psychological effects could undermine the ability of persons on both ends of genetic design to cooperate with each other in a moral community based on egalitarian universalist principles. I claim that Habermas is certainly onto something here: Humans have no business mingling in the genetic affairs of other humans, present or future. But I do not agree with Habermas that the principal concern is with the psychological effects on those who are genetically manipulated or the problematic attitudes of those who undertake genetic alterations on their offspring. Rather, the central problem is that genetic manipulation fails to express the appropriate amount of respect for the equal and separate importance of persons, regardless of when they are born.

Therefore, in chapter 6 I argue that the principal issue is normative, not psychological. Future persons are entitled to be treated in anticipation of the respect that is due to the actual persons they develop into. This, I claim, translates into an obligation to honor their independence from us and to restrict our genetic designs on them accordingly. Besides appreciating their other- and separateness from us, members of the previous generation, we should also make sure that it is possible for them to be reasonably independent from their peers. Respect for (future) persons' independence thus gives us two kinds of obligations, one negative and one positive. The negative obligation is to generally abstain from genetic interventions and to accept (future) persons the way they come into existence. I call this our duty to respect (future) persons' natural independence. The positive obligation is that in cases in which it cannot be guaranteed that persons will be born with the mental and physical endowment necessary to lead a minimally independent life, some genetic alterations are required. Minimally independent lives are ones in which persons are not permanently forced to depend on the charitable help of others and in which they can choose the kinds of relationships (of dependence) they want to be part of. I call this our duty to respect (future) persons' substantial independence.

I contend that both kinds of independence are necessary to avoid situations of domination. The first is geared at averting forms of domination that may result from one generation making genetic choices for the next. The second aims at preventing forms of domination that may occur due to being subject to relationships one cannot choose (to leave).

The two notions of independence may be thought to conflict with each other, one asking us to refrain from interfering with future persons' genomes and the other mandating alterations in certain situations. However, I understand substantial independence as a threshold notion. As soon as it has been ensured that future persons have the necessary mental and physical capacities to lead a minimally independent life, no further interventions may be undertaken. In cases in which future persons already have these capacities to begin with, all forms of genetic manipulation are rendered illegitimate.

I end this proposal by responding to five possible concerns regarding my account. These arise with respect to, first, its implications for persons with disabilities; second, its esteem for relationships of dependence more generally; third, the extent to which the notion of independence as I am defending it is different from claims about autonomy; fourth, the ways in which my approach is supposed to fare any better than those of liberal eugenicists, especially when it comes to imprinting offspring with the particular value judgments, prejudices, and tastes of previous generations; and fifth, whether and how my suggestions circumvent the potential problem of changing human nature having detrimental effects on morality.

In response, I show that my approach neither devalues persons with disabilities nor fails to appreciate the importance of relationships of dependence more generally. Instead, it merely seeks to ensure that persons, with or without disabilities, can choose the relationships (of dependence) they want to be part of. I also illustrate how independence differs in a slight but important way from autonomy, namely by protecting persons from being governed by other people as opposed to primarily protecting persons from being governed by their own impulses and desires. I also maintain that my proposal involves less particular and time-sensitive value judgments than the genetic interventions endorsed by liberal eugenicists. This is because independence is an absolute and not a relative notion and therefore less vulnerable to changing with continued and widespread use of genetic manipulation. In other words, according to my proposal, an IQ of 120 either allows a person to live independently or it does not (although it is of course also true that whether or not an IQ of 120 allows a person to live independently may depend on the stage of technological advance in a society and whether an IQ of 120 continues to be sufficient for independent functioning). By contrast, the criterion of removing opportunity-limiting hindrances that Buchanan et al. invoke, for instance, is bound to consider an IQ of 120 relative to the IQ of everyone else. So if most people eventually came to possess an IQ of at least 140, then having an IQ of 120 almost automatically becomes opportunity-limiting (without, however, necessarily rendering an independent life impossible). Finally, I maintain that because ensuring independence is not likely to alter human nature, any worries we might have about changing the anthropological foundations of morality are moot.

I conclude the general argument of the book with some thoughts about the identification of the "we" when I speak of "our" obligations to future persons or, in other words, who should bear the costs of "our" obligations. I argue that this is not necessarily those who are causally responsible for bringing future persons into existence (i.e., their biological parents). Rather, I claim that because individual reproduction is not only a means for personal flourishing but also largely serves social goals, it is society more generally that should be held responsible for fulfilling "our" obligations to future persons.

The purpose of my theory of unborn life is to ensure that the life of each person we create is made into the best kind of "gift" it can possibly be. As it is, it comes as a surprise to the persons thus called into existence and is replete with daunting challenges they never asked for. Therefore, as I argue in the first part of this book, those who have an interest in giving such dubious gifts need to make sure that those who will receive them are physically protected (i.e., not harmed) from the moment of their conception. Beyond that, my central concern in the second part is that, to the extent the new technologies enable us to, we must provide what nature cannot guarantee in terms of the proper physical and mental equipment for embryos to develop into independent persons. Any further genetic intervention, however, violates our normative commitment to persons who deserve to receive a "gift" that no other persons have left their imprint on or played around with.

CREATION AND DESTRUCTION

1 EMBRYOS AND FUTURE PERSONS

The abortion debate shows how difficult it is to arrive at any kind of consensus regarding the moral value of embryos.[1] It is especially challenging to respond to issues raised by technologies, such as stem cell research (and, to some extent, assisted reproductive technologies and preimplantation genetic diagnosis) involving the destruction of embryos. Whereas the abortion conflict could arguably be resolved by relying entirely on the value of women's right to self-determination (Thomson 1971), there is no way of settling questions concerning these technologies by referring solely to the value of newly competing interests to the embryo's claim to life. These interests include those that scientists (and future patients) might have in gaining further insights into embryonic development and in generating cures for hitherto fatal diseases. They also include interests that prospective parents might have in deselecting embryos with certain genetic disorders. Such interests arise in the context of very different kinds of relationships to embryos and are thus simply not comparable to those women can invoke. Embryos cannot develop unless women are willing to carry them to term. Therefore, a woman's choice concerning whether or not she wants to allow her embryo to continue its development is of particular significance. By contrast, no embryo depends for its continued existence on a scientist's pursuit of knowledge, a patient's desire to see cures developed, or a parent's wish to have a child with a particular genetic endowment—as legitimate as each of these endeavors may be. Thus, when it comes to evaluating a biomedical technology such as stem cell research, we need a way of tackling the question of whether and in what circumstances it is legitimate to destroy embryos, which does not rest solely on the interests competing with their claims to life.

This chapter seeks to provide exactly that—a way to conceive of embryos' moral value that accounts for our obligations toward them in all situations in which their health is at stake or their lives are threatened.[2] It does this by focusing on the moral claims of those we have a clear commitment to protecting, namely, persons. As imprecise and problematic many hold the concept of *person* to be,[3] I am assuming that we can identify clear normative commitments to whomever we deem to be a person.[4] Referring to individuals as persons in the normative sense signifies, for instance, that they may not be arbitrarily killed or made worse off relative to how well off they could have been independently of our actions.[5] As individual rights-holders, persons are usually considered to be nonsubstitutable. In general, our concern for persons compels us to take their interests seriously.

As I argue in more detail below (section 3), these interests also include the backward-oriented interests persons have in the well-being of the embryo from which they developed. Thus, I claim that we have good reasons to treat embryos that develop into persons in anticipation of the respect that is due to these persons. I call this the Personhood Dependent Principle (PDP). I maintain that our commitment to persons will not only tell us how to value and treat embryos that actually end up being persons but will also provide rough guidelines for how to think of embryos that stand a reasonable chance at becoming persons.

I develop this argument in four steps. First, I sketch one possible way to construe personhood. I maintain that, to begin with, this category is restricted to moral agents, by which I mean agents capable of being guided by moral reasons. I also propose, however, that there are secondary considerations that compel moral agents to widen the scope of personhood to include all born human beings.

I am offering what I take to be the most plausible way of defining personhood. Nevertheless, for the claim that we owe a certain kind of protection to embryos that develop into persons, nothing much depends on determining who exactly counts as a person or on when personhood begins. The only important assumptions are that there are persons to whom we have certain normative commitments and that personhood does not begin at conception but sometime thereafter (section 1).

The second step of the argument explains why embryos—human beings in their own right—are in morally significant ways unlike those human beings (persons) whom we are committed to protecting. I defend the claim that personhood begins at birth because it is only then that the fetus leaves its symbiotic attachment to the organism of a woman. Until a child is born the fetus is structurally in a position in which the woman carrying it can deny her assistance or refuse to give birth; unlike a newborn, therefore, a fetus cannot be protected as a person would have to be (section 2).

The third step shows why the protection we owe to persons should extend to the embryos from which they developed. In the course of spelling out the implications of this proposal, I address four concerns that may arise in response to it: first, the question of what this does or does not say about the nature of embryos; second, the epistemic problem of how to know the moral value of any particular embryo before it has actually developed into a person; third, the question of who has the legitimate authority to decide which embryos develop into persons and which do not; and fourth, the issue of what it means to treat an embryo like the person it develops into (section 3).

These first three steps of the argument spell out the assumption that we owe a certain kind of care and protection to persons. Moreover, they explain why we should treat embryos that end up becoming persons in anticipation of their later personhood from the moment of their conception. So far, nothing has been said about our obligations to embryos whose fate is not yet clear. Thus, in a fourth step I show why there is some value in creating persons. This means that when there are women willing to carry already existing embryos to term, we have no good reasons to prevent these women from doing so (section 4). Together, these four steps provide an argument for how to relate to embryos in all debates concerning the permissibility of their injury or destruction.

1. Protecting Persons

One prominent reason for thinking that we owe each other a special kind of respect as human beings is because typical members of the species are capable of (moral) agency. They are endowed with certain higher-order faculties that make them responsive to reasons and thus accountable for their actions. As the space of reasons includes moral ones, such agents are objects of moral praise and blame. Thus, only moral agents can be "subjects" of morality, that is, receptive to its demands and capable of acting accordingly. A hungry tiger can certainly not be stirred by the fact that the piece of living lunch before it is capable of moral agency that makes it more "special" than the squirrel the tiger had for breakfast. By the same token, only the subjects of morality can determine the "objects" of morality; in other words, they, unlike anyone else in the animal kingdom, can decide who is to be protected and in which way. This power to decide should, of course, be wielded in the light of good reasons.

It is this kind of agency—which makes morality possible in the first place—that is often thought to confer on those who have it a distinctive (intrinsic) moral status that is often identified as personhood. This status as a subject (and not only object) of moral considerations commands that they be treated as ends in themselves—and that they in turn treat all others (who share the same feature of moral agency) likewise. Arguably, individuals who have lost the moral agency they were once capable of due to sickness or old age are in-cluded in this category. The interests they once had (when they were moral agents) in their future well-being remain binding for all those who are pres-ently capable of moral agency.

Even if we find such a Kantian explanation of human dignity—that special moral status humans arguably possess—plausible, it creates a well-known problem. Not all human beings presently possess or once possessed the ca-pacities required for moral agency that would normatively distinguish them from other animals.[6] Small children, for instance, never had nor presently have these capacities. In some cases, they may be unable to ever develop them. It remains unclear how those who are capable of moral agency should relate to them or what it implies about the moral status of animals that have charac-teristics that are similar to those of small children.

Therefore, the scope of protection needs to be further elaborated on. Some argue that because "typical" members are capable of moral agency at some point in their lives, all members of the human species should be deserving of a distinctive kind of respect. Many reject this sort of reasoning, denouncing it as "speciesism" (an unjustified favoring of one's own kin). They argue that there is no reason to include all members of the human species if we are not also willing to include members of other species that may have capacities similar to those of human embryos or small children (neither of which have the capacity for moral agency). Moreover, if it turned out that members of other species or from other planets displayed the same (or perhaps even supe-rior) capacities for moral agency as some adults do today, then we would have to include them as well. We would have to hold them to the same standards and offer them the same kind of protection we grant to members of our own species. They, in turn, would have to act identically with regard to us.[7]

But the case for incorporating more human beings than are currently (or were, sometime in the past) capable of moral agency does not necessarily have to rely on the species-membership argument. There are other, secondary rea-sons for including those who are not themselves capable of moral agency. The intuition that gives rise to such secondary reasons is the following: There is something deeply disturbing about the thought that some of those who are intimately and inevitably part of the social universe of moral agents are treated with less concern just because they lack the capacity of moral agency. This is troubling especially if they are human-born. Let me elaborate on this for a moment.

Very young children may not themselves be capable of moral agency, but there are significant reasons to include them in the social universe of moral agents. To begin with, they are frequently expected to eventually develop into moral agents. Arguably, they can only do so if they are treated in anticipation of their later moral agency. Moreover, every moral agent was once a very young child. Thomas Scanlon (1998), who thinks that having judgment-sensitive attitudes is what gives rise to personhood, thus writes that "infants and young children are not separate kinds of creatures. Rather, infancy and childhood are, in normal cases, stages in the life of a being who will have the capacity for judgment-sensitive attitudes" (p. 185).

This line of reasoning seems to run into the problem that not all young children will mature into moral agents. Scanlon certainly assumes that "in normal cases" infants and young children will develop the capacities required for moral agency. However, he does not seem to consider it necessary that they actually, and in each instance, do so to be included within the "scope of morality." There are good reasons for this. Among them is that even infants who will not mature to be moral agents are frequently born to individuals capable of moral agency. In other words, they are intimately and inevitably part of the social universe those capable of moral agency inhabit. Scanlon (1998) argues that "the beings in question here are ones who are born to us or to others to whom we are bound by the requirements of justifiability" (p. 185). Thus, we are bound to the newborn by extension of our being obliged to the newborn's parents.

Moreover, what makes infants and young children part of their parents' intimate social universe also makes them part of the social universe of persons more generally. A relationship that is established by being born to someone is, at least, gestational[8] but usually implies a further kind of kinship. Scanlon (1998) himself maintains that the mere fact that a being is human-born "provides a strong reason for according it the same status as other humans" (p. 185). In other words, beyond our duties to the parents of newborns, we as moral agents have reasons to grant infants equal concern because they are of human descent.

Scanlon (1998) denies that it is mere speciesism (i.e., prejudice) to think that our relation to these beings gives us reason "to accept the requirement that our actions should be justifiable to them" (p. 185). The only way this is not mere speciesism, however, is if we have additional arguments for why being of human descent by itself should matter. One way to do this is to point out what I have said before, namely that all human beings should be regarded as inevitable parts of the social universe of moral agents. This is because it would be strange and disturbing if moral agents thought they could treat human beings who lack the capacity for moral agency with less moral concern than they would display toward themselves. Treating the very young and all others who may lack the capacity for moral agency (for now or forever) differently would mean that we would have to establish a moral class system within humanity (Ladwig 2007, 34). Establishing such a class system among humans would be troubling—much more so than establishing a system that morally distinguishes between humans and other animal species.[9]

Thus, the conception of personhood proposed here includes, in the first instance, all those human beings and all members of any other species who are actually capable of moral agency or who once were. It also includes, via secondary considerations, human newborns and infants who have never possessed, do not presently have, and may never acquire the capacities necessary for moral agency.

This claim bears further explanation with regard to embryos. From what has been said so far, it could be argued that embryos should also be considered to be persons by means of secondary considerations. They are certainly genetically human[10] and could be said to be part of at least some moral agents' social universe (presumably that of the women who are pregnant with them).[11] Moreover, some of them are expected to eventually develop into individuals capable of moral agency, just as the early infant is. Nevertheless, the unborn are not proper objects of the type of moral concern personhood gives rise to. Unlike a newborn, who exists as a separate entity and is no longer dependent for his or her survival on one irreplaceable person, a fetus is symbiotically attached to one nonsubstitutable other organism, namely that of the woman carrying it. The kind of assistance a woman is required to provide through her symbiotic attachment to her fetus regularly gives her a legitimate claim to end her support, even if that means the death of her unborn offspring.

In the following, I argue that it makes no sense to include in the category of personhood entities whose life support can regularly and legitimately be withdrawn by the person necessary for providing this support. This claim may appear to assume what needs to be established. Let me therefore explain it in more detail.

2. Why Birth Matters

I argue that embryos by themselves do not have the moral value of born human beings. Although a fetus just before birth is not much different from a newborn when it comes to its development and capacity for moral agency, I claim that the secondary reasons to extend personhood even to the newborn (discussed in the previous section) do not apply to fetuses before birth.

Thus far, I have proposed a conception of personhood that includes individuals who are not (yet) capable of moral agency if they intimately belong to the social universe of moral agents. But there is another important condition, which is that the entity in question must not inevitably rely for its continued existence on life support of a kind that can always be denied. As long as embryos are attached to a woman's organism, they are dependent for their existence on precisely such help. This means that embryos are structurally in a position in which they can be left to die or killed. I therefore contend it would be overstretching the concept of personhood to bestow it on embryos on secondary grounds.

I am relying for this claim on the argument that women have a right to detach themselves from their embryos. This would amount to a mere tautology if, for this to be true, we would have to already assume that embryos are not persons. But we need not make that assumption. Quite to the contrary, this case can compellingly be made by an analogy to two persons (Boonin 2003; Kamm 1992, Thomson 1971; critical McMahan 1993). It holds that even if embryos were persons, women could detach themselves in situations analogous to pregnancy. Judith Jarvis Thomson (1971), for instance, offers her much-cited example of the violinist. She asks us to imagine having been kidnapped by the Society of Music Lovers. Upon awakening we are told that we have been attached to a famous violinist who will need our life support for the next nine months. If we detach ourselves, the violinist will die. She argues that, even if embryos were persons, just as the violinist is a person, we would have a right to detach ourselves.

With this claim Thomson is not passing judgment on the moral value of the person whose life support can be denied. Rather, she thinks that it is the kind of help the violinist requires that allows us to end our assistance (Thomson 1971, 48). This help is too demanding and too intrusive for anyone to be compelled to provide it. Not only does it need to be given for a substantial amount of time (i.e., nine months), but it also causes significant discomfort in the best of circumstances. Moreover, even if pregnancies lasted only a few days and involved only minor aches, there is a further factor that makes the necessary assistance overly demanding. This is the quality of the help required, which involves a woman having to share her body with a symbiotically connected organism that develops inside her. Having to provide this kind of support is quite different from asking someone to pay a lot of money or to engage in hard labor to help other persons in need, although both of the latter kinds of aid may last for a substantial amount of time and may cause significant pain and discomfort.

Many will protest at this point that although random adults may not have a right to this kind of assistance, embryos do, at least in those cases in which women deliberately brought them into existence or did not take enough care to prevent their conception. In those cases, women are frequently held responsible for the embryo needing their help and thus are also considered responsible for providing it. Even Thomson (1971, 59) concedes that in some of these cases embryos may have a right to the use of their mother's body. However, and although women may, in this day and age (i.e., with the availability of various methods of birth control), be responsible for conceiving embryos, there is a limit to how responsible they can be for something that they would have to go out of their way to prevent. In other words, while persons can be asked to make significant sacrifices to save those they have deliberately pushed into the water, women cannot be asked to provide a substantial amount of assistance to someone who came into existence because they did not prevent a "natural" process from occurring. Women cannot be made responsible for the way human reproduction works.

Furthermore, unlike cases in which persons are responsible for others needing their help, pregnancy is a case in which those requiring assistance have no prior existence apart from the help they now need. In other words, Peter, who is pushed into the water by John, would have existed independently of John's action. Peter is thus made worse off than he would have been without John's deed. Embryos, by contrast, have no life prior to or independent of the action that causes them to require assistance. Denying assistance to embryos, therefore, arguably does not make them any worse off than they were before (Boonin 2003, 175).

Suppose one agrees that the kind of assistance required during pregnancy is not what women can be expected to provide. This still leaves open the question of why this would speak against including embryos in the realm of personhood via secondary considerations. The reason is that there is a principal difference between (i) being in exceptional circumstances in which one requires life support of a kind that can be denied and (ii) structurally being in such a situation. Assuming that the normative concept of personhood is, at its most basic level, geared at securing mutual protection (from each other) and care (for each other's continued existence), it would not make much sense to call entities "persons" that are structurally in a position in which the persons they crucially depend on are allowed to let them die or even kill them.

Newborns are, of course, also wholly dependent on other human beings for their survival, but they are not structurally in a position in which life support can be denied to them. This is because they are not unavoidably dependent on the assistance of only one specific and irreplaceable individual in a way that is both so intrusive and so demanding that no person can be asked to provide the required help. Their needs can be met extracorporeally and they could be raised and cared for by a variety of people. Therefore, the crucial feature preventing embryos from being protected in a personhood-specific way is their particular kind of structural dependence on one specific and irreplaceable person.

Of course, all of these things would radically change if there were artificial external wombs capable of carrying fetuses to term, so that the fetus was no longer dependent on a symbiotic connection to a woman's body. At that point, birth may no longer have the normative significance I am attributing to it. The moment of conception may take its place. Just as we cannot deny newborns, who are anything but self-sufficient, the love and care they need, we could also not deny those embryos in the artificial womb whatever was needed to keep the womb going (if that ended up being very costly we might have to think about creating fewer embryos). Thus, my argument about birth mattering rests entirely on the empirical observation that it currently marks the moment at which embryos no longer inevitably require the particular kind of assistance that can be denied to them.

At birth, humans usually become physically separate individuals. Why being a physically separate individual is so important for establishing personhood can be seen by considering the reasons frequently garnered in defense of the notion that conception should be the starting point of personhood. Many consider conception to be the only nonarbitrary moment at which something substantially new happens in the otherwise continual development of egg and sperm to adult. It marks such a distinguishing event for an illustrative reason: It signifies the beginning of a new, separate individual. Only because twinning is still possible until sometime between the fourteenth and the twenty-first day do some people think that personhood should begin at a slightly later date (than conception), namely as soon as it is clear whether there will be one, two, or more separate individuals. Every other stage of development from then onward is arguably hard to distinguish from its immediately preceding stage. One might wonder, of course, why it is so important to have a new, separate individual in the first place. We could imagine an argument saying that something else entirely matters for the beginning of personhood, for instance the mental conception of a child: Personhood could, plausibly, be established by the mere act of someone vividly picturing his or her future child. That not all children so conceived end up materializing into actual children cannot be a deterrent factor for such reasoning, because not all conceived embryos end up being children either (and many believe that embryos are persons).

The reason this thought has not struck a majority of people is probably because there is something about actual individuation and separateness that matters. The only difference is that I am arguing that the morally important instance of separation—at least when it comes to the conception of personhood defended here—is birth. That is when individuals leave their special kind of dependence on the organism of another and it becomes legitimate to ask all members of the moral community, including their gestational mothers, to care for their continued existence.

Arguing that personhood begins at birth in this way is quite different from claims that pin the beginning of personhood to the moment at which particular faculties or features are present in the embryo, newborn, or infant. Instead of relying on birth to denote a significant developmental incision, the account offered here depends only on there being a certain (separate) unit of concern so that personhood can be conferred on secondary grounds. I maintained that personhood should not be extended to include entities that are structurally in a situation in which they can be left to die or killed, as it is with embryos. Furthermore, for this account it is also important that entities are actually physically detached and not that they are only potentially physically separate. Thus, it matters that the child has been born. A viable fetus, although it could continue to exist outside the woman's organism, is nevertheless still inside the woman's body. It thus remains up to her whether she wants to continue her assistance and give birth to her child or not. She cannot be forced either way, as all courses of action will affect her physical integrity. This brings me to the question of how to assess the moral value of embryos that women eventually give birth to.

3. The Moral Value of Embryos That Will Be Born

Elizabeth Harman (1999) has proposed a similar account to the one I am offering here. I will briefly discuss her views and present my own, alternative approach in response to some of the problems faced by her argument. Harman, too, makes a case for morally distinguishing between embryos that will end up being persons and embryos that will not. According to what she refers to as the Actual Future Principle (AFP), an "early fetus that will become a person has some moral status. An early fetus that will die while it is still an early fetus has no moral status" (p. 311). She assumes that embryos by themselves do not have the intrinsic properties that are required for establishing personhood (p. 310). Embryos that end up being persons have some moral status because "a thing's present nature is solely determined by the intrinsic properties it ever has" (p. 318). According to Harman, it is thus the actual fate of any particular embryo that determines its moral status.

There are four problems with Harman's argument. The first is ontological, the second is epistemic, the third concerns the question of legitimate authority, and the fourth arises from a certain degree of indeterminacy regarding the notion that embryos that actually develop into persons have "some" moral status. First, the ontological difficulty lies in how Harman identifies the "nature" of the fetus. She argues, as cited above, that the present nature of the fetus is solely determined by the intrinsic properties it ever has. To make sense of this, much depends on Harman's understanding of a thing's "nature." Traditionally, for instance, it was assumed that it is in the nature of an acorn to grow into an oak tree. This is obviously not what Harman takes a thing's nature to mean. Her alternative to this could be understood in three ways.

First, she might want to say that the nature of a particular acorn that fails to grow into an oak tree lies in becoming whatever else might end up happening to this particular acorn, such as being run over by a truck. By this she might imply that the possibility of being run over by a truck is inherent in the nature of an acorn: it is possible for acorns to be run over by a truck. This interpretation would strip the notion of a thing's "nature" of its teleological content but it would, nevertheless, be descriptively true. This having been said, it would not help us to distinguish between some acorns and others according to what actually happens to them, as the possibility of being crushed by trucks is inherent in the nature of every acorn (and indeed of many other things). What is more, it would apply before any particular acorn was actually run over by a truck.

Second, Harman might be suggesting that it is descriptively (retrospectively) true of a particular acorn that it was run over by a truck or that a fetus actually developed into a person. That, however, tells us something about a particular acorn or fetus only after the fact. It thereby fails to reveal anything about the respective "natures" of an acorn or a fetus. Thus, if "nature" is to be of any help here, it surely cannot refer to something that may (or may not) suddenly come into being due to entirely accidental and unforeseeable events.

Third, when it comes to the fetus, Harman might, of course, want to point out that becoming a person is not an entirely accidental and unforeseeable event (such as being run over by a truck probably is, in most cases, for an acorn). But the explanation for this would have to be that there is something inherent in a fetus that makes it not only possible but perhaps also rather likely that a fetus develops into a person (because, she might be pressed to add, this is what fetuses-as-such frequently do). In that case, however, Harman would have said something about all fetuses alike and not just about some.

Thus, I see no persuasive way to determine the present nature of a fetus by what actually happens to it (or by the intrinsic properties it ever has). However, the central argument distinguishing between fetuses that actually develop into persons and fetuses that do not can be made without reference to the nature of one or more fetuses. I therefore suggest that we should do without such reference.

The more plausible way to explain why fetuses that end up being persons matter normatively is to assign this significance to them derivatively—derived from what they mean to those we have a standing commitment to protecting, namely persons. I am arguing that personhood is not a property that is already inherent in future persons. But once someone is a person, the previous stages of this person's existence matter. Therefore, we have good reasons to treat fetuses that develop into persons in anticipation of the persons they will develop into. I call this the Personhood Dependent Principle (PDP). Rather than determining the nature of a fetus according to what actually happens to it (like the AFP does), the PDP makes our normative commitment to the fetus dependent on whether this fetus's fate ends up mattering to a person from a first-person perspective.

The PDP, nonetheless, immediately gives rise to an epistemic concern identical to the one that is the second problem with Harman's (1999) AFP. This is that Harman does not satisfactorily answer how we know beforehand which fetuses will develop into persons. Harman (1999, 318) rejects the proposal that the moral value of any particular fetus should be determined by what a woman expects to do by arguing against the Mother's Intention Principle. Her worry is that if an embryo's moral value was determined by what a woman intends to do, then it might change by the hour, day, or week. The embryo would be one thing in those moments the woman actually intended to have a child and another in all those moments the woman had serious doubts about carrying her fetus to term (p. 318).[12] Harman thus maintains that although women can make it the case that the embryo turns out not to have had moral value by aborting, their intentions at any moment do not count. This is persuasive. It certainly does not matter what women intend to do; it matters what they actually do. But the immediately following question is how we are supposed to know beforehand what women will actually do.

Harman denies that this is much of a practical difficulty as "we often do know a fetus's overwhelmingly likely future" (p. 319). This does not solve the problem, however: We might get it wrong and, in contrast to what Harman makes it out to be, getting it wrong is serious. Harman argues that when a pregnant woman makes a mistake (by thinking she will abort, then harming the fetus but then ultimately being unable to obtain an abortion), she should not be forced to end her pregnancy. Whatever harm was done to the embryo in this way should be judged akin to had some accident occurred (p. 319, note 8). This is not convincing. Our commitment to protecting persons is stronger than this solution suggests and violations thereof more serious. This is especially true if the independence of the later adult is at stake. Therefore, if a pregnant woman causes substantial harm based on the (mistaken) conviction that there will be no person there to harm, then, although she cannot be asked to end her pregnancy, she may indeed stand morally obliged to make sure that the harm is remedied if that is possible (through surgical or any other kind of intervention, for instance). I return to a more detailed discussion of this issue later on in chapter 3, section 3.

To avoid or at least significantly lessen such serious mistakes, I propose an additional principle, namely the Principle of Precaution, to moderate the epistemic problem. This principle asks us to err on the side of caution and to treat all embryos (and stem cells, for that matter) as if they were going to become persons—at least until we have made it the case that they will not, by, for instance, having an abortion or rendering stem cells in a petri dish unable to develop into viable embryos. That way, we reduce the likelihood of harming an entity that might still turn into a person. The obvious difficulty with this suggestion is that it is unclear how to treat fetuses as if they were going to be persons and then still permissibly destroy them.[13] But according to the view proposed in this book and as I will explain in more detail below, we do not stand under any obligation to treat embryos as if they already were the persons they might (or might not) turn into. We do not, for instance, have to care for their continued existence. Our obligations to embryos arise retrospectively (once they have become persons). They are applied in a forward-looking manner only via speculation (as to an embryo's future) and as a matter of caution so that we avoid violating our (retrospective) obligations. We have no obligation to make our speculation true. Thus, while the PDP makes destroying fetuses unproblematic at all times, it renders harming future persons wrong. The Principle of Precaution makes it generally problematic to harm fetuses, even where it is not clear what their future development will be.

This brings me to a third problem with Harman's account. Connected at least in part to the epistemic concern is the question of legitimate authority, that is, about who should have the power to decide which embryos are permitted to continue their development and which are not (and thus can be destroyed). The question is whether women are the only ones who have this authority or if others, too, can make it the case that some embryos do not develop into persons. Harman's account seems to imply that everyone can, by destroying embryos, determine their moral value. This, I think, fails to take seriously that, from the perspective of valuing persons, some appreciation for their creation follows. In other words, there is some value attached to not preventing embryos from developing into persons if they have the chance of being carried to term by a woman (who has the desire to be pregnant and give birth). If there is such value attached to the creation of persons, however, then it matters not only whether embryos actually develop into persons (as Harman's Actual Future Principle suggests) but also who gets to decide this issue and for what reasons. Let me explain.

Consider, for instance, a number of in vitro embryos that are destroyed because someone comes into the laboratory and, for the fun of it, throws the petri dish holding the embryos into the trash. According to Harman's principle, embryos that do not actually end up being persons have no moral significance. Thus, as long as there is no reason to think that it matters one way or the other (i.e., whether or not embryos actually develop into persons), the intruder will have legitimately made it the case that these embryos are of no moral importance. If, by contrast, there is some value attached to the creation of persons, then not just any disposal of embryos by just anyone is automatically permissible.

There is, after all, a special reason why women can refuse to have embryos implanted or to continue their life support for those they are already carrying. This reason has to do with the quality of help that is required of them in both cases, which entails having a fetus develop inside their bodies that is symbiotically attached to them, causing a substantial amount of discomfort for a significant period of time. It is that particular quality of help that they can legitimately refuse. If, however, the only reason women are entitled not to have embryos implanted or to end their support for the embryos they are carrying is because of the very particular features of their relationship with their embryos, then not just any person (who does not aid the fetus in the same way) has the right to do the same.[14] I have much more to say about this in section 4 below. But first let us address the final problem Harman's approach encounters.

When Harman argues that embryos that will be born have "some" moral status, she leaves underdetermined what "some" moral status amounts to. This could mean three different things. First, it could imply that we can do whatever we want to the embryo as long as our actions do not lead to the birth of a person in a wrongful state (a).

It could also mean that we should treat the embryo in anticipation of its later personhood. This, in turn, can be interpreted in two ways: It could suggest that we have to treat embryos exactly like the persons they develop into. This would make it difficult to justify a woman's choice to terminate her pregnancy for reasons that are not exceptionally serious and include grave peril to her own life (b). Alternatively, it could imply that we must treat embryos in anticipation of the respect that is due to persons. This would indicate that although persons have a claim to great care being displayed toward the embryos from which they emerge, no one is treated disrespectfully if embryos perish. Such reasoning would not affect a woman's entitlement to deny her life support for the fetus (c).

(a) Frances Kamm (2005) agrees that embryos that will develop into persons should be treated with more respect than embryos that do not (which—in her view—in turn should be treated with more respect than embryos that do not even have the potential to develop into persons). However, she maintains that we stand under no obligation to act as if embryos were like the persons they develop into (p. 301). Rather, she suggests that we ought to treat those embryos in a way that the future person is not born in a wrongful state, that is, in a state that lies below the threshold of what we owe to future persons by way, for instance, of ensuring for them some minimal conditions for a decent life.[15] But if the embryo had some features that by far exceeded what would be necessary for the future person not to be born in a bad state, it would be permissible to reduce or even take away some of the features that go beyond what is required.

Kamm (2005) compares the situation to one in which person A deposits money in a bank intending to give it to person B the next day. Kamm thinks that if A changes her mind and decides to take that money away again before the next day, no harm will be done: As long as B is not owed this money by A, not receiving it has the same effect as if A had never put it in the bank account in the first place. So if A is under no obligation to give this money to B, she can take it away again any time before it ends up being in B's possession. Analogously, Kamm argues that "a fetus is not the sort of being that is entitled to keep a characteristic that it has, such as a genetic makeup that will generate a 160 IQ. This is because it is not the sort of being that can be the bearer of rights (to retain anything). It lacks moral status (...) and lacks additional properties that would make it a rights-bearer, in part, because it is not sentient or conscious" (p. 301). Kamm maintains that embryos do not own their properties, whereas persons do. This, I think, is mistaken.

Consider, for instance, a valuable object that only queens can possess. Suppose, in some particular instance, the queen passes away early and leaves only a toddler to inherit her throne. For the several years it takes the toddler to grow up, there is no one yet who could rightfully claim the valuable object. But it would be wrong for someone to take this object or to use it (so that its value is changed or decreased) during the time of the toddler's maturation. This is because whoever takes or uses it would violate his or her obligation to the future queen, who is the rightful owner of this object. It is the same with embryos that will develop into persons: Whatever they "have" they slowly develop for the later persons to rightfully possess. Taking anything away from the embryo would amount to taking something away from the later person.

In that way, already-existent future persons are different from nonexistent future persons. We do not have a duty to bring about the latter in any particular state (as long as this state is not below the threshold of capacities the provision of which we owe to future persons quite generally). This means that if we had a choice to procreate on day 1, and thereby bring about an embryo with the potential of developing an IQ of 160, or to procreate on day 2, when we are more likely to produce an embryo with the potential of developing an IQ of "only" 130, then we are under no obligation to procreate on day 1. The nonexistent future person is clearly not an entity that can be entitled to any specific set of traits beyond a certain threshold that ensures a minimally decent life (assuming, again, that we owe it to future persons to bring them into this world above such a threshold). But this is different in the case of the already-existing future person. If an embryo that will develop into a person has the potential to develop an IQ of 160, we may not do anything to lower this potential, even if the resulting person would still be left with an above-average IQ. Therefore, to say that embryos ought to be treated in a certain way by virtue of actually developing into persons asks of all concerned to be respectful "safe-keepers" of the later persons' (biological) possessions.

Again, this leaves open the question of how exactly the later person's (biological) possessions should be treated: can they be used in some way, for instance, and then returned to the rightful owner just before she can actually appropriate them? Let us return for a moment to the example of the queen and her valuable object. Suppose the object was taken, played around with, and used in all kinds of ways that were not respectful of the future queen's property. However, for some reason, this way of handling the object fails to leave a mark. Arguably, as long as this disrespectful use leaves no sign, it might be deemed permissible. Or suppose that the disrespectful behavior does leave marks but that these can be repaired somehow to restore the valuable object to its original state. Here again, one could say that as long as the queen ends up being presented with the (repaired) object, such actions are permissible.

But once the queen claims possession of this valuable object, it might very well matter to her what happened to it while the world around her was entrusted to respect her future entitlement. Likewise, and perhaps even more strongly, it matters to persons what happened to the embryo they developed out of. Suppose persons were told that their embryos had been subjected to scientific experimentation that had exposed them to tremendous amounts of heat over a period of time. These persons were also informed that the scientific experiments had caused no lasting damage. Alternatively, consider that another group of persons were told that their embryos had been kidnapped and subjected to electric shocks for a week while in a petri dish. They had been retrieved just in time to be implanted into their mothers—again without this having had any effect on the later persons. The reason these stories are likely to make a difference to the resulting persons is not because some intrinsic value of embryos was violated. Rather, just as persons have future-directed interests, they have an interest in their past—their entire past, as Tristram Shandy's complaints about the circumstances of his conception, which are recalled at the outset of this book, so humorously remind us. It is in this way—that is, in the way it affects the past-directed interests of persons—that it matters that their embryos were treated in anticipation of the respect due to the later persons. This respect should express itself chiefly by treating embryos with care and by regarding them for "who" they are genetically encoded to be, that is, without other people interfering with their endowment and certainly without other people taking anything away from them.

This still leaves open the question of whether the Personhood Dependent Principle requires treating embryos "like" the persons they develop into, as in (b) above, or "merely" in anticipation of the respect we owe to persons they develop into, as in (c). If embryos were treated "like" the persons they develop into, it would be impermissible to destroy them. However, I am claiming that embryos have no right to continued existence, precisely because they are not "like" persons. Therefore, our treatment of embryos cannot be "like" the persons they develop into. Rather, by depending on whether they develop into persons, the way we treat embryos can merely reflect our anticipation of the respect owed to the persons who will emerge. This respect does not entail a right of the fetus to be born against the wish of the woman carrying it, that is, it does not entail a right to become a person. Thus, statement (b) has to be rejected.

So far, I have argued that there is a moral difference between embryos that end up being born and those that do not. Moreover, I have maintained that although there is no duty to continue life support for embryos (i.e., no duty to prevent them from dying or even to refrain from killing them), those embryos that will be born should be treated in anticipation of the respect that is owed to the persons they grow into. I have said little about what this amounts to. It certainly implies that we have to protect and may not harm embryos in the sense of altering or taking away features that they "hold in trust" for the persons who will develop from them. In the second part of the book I argue that this also means that we may not intervene to add to the endowment the embryo brings with it. But first some further questions need to be answered regarding embryos (in vitro) whose fate is not yet clear, as they could develop into persons if there were women willing to have them implanted and carry them to term. May they be used for stem cell or other kinds of research?

4. The Value of Creating Persons

Harman (1999) suggests that it would not be wrong to destroy embryos that do not end up being persons as "their deaths simply do not matter morally" (p. 311). In the following, I would like to agree in principle but qualify this claim in one important respect. I argue there are no good reasons for denying embryos the opportunity to be implanted in women's wombs if particular women would like to become pregnant with them. This might be taken to imply that I am saying something about the embryo's moral value in and of itself. But this is not the case. In the following, I critically discuss various ways to conceive of the embryo's moral value. I show that only the combination of an embryo that can further develop and a woman willing to carry it to term create a kind of potential that has some value.

I begin by describing an account of why we should treat all human embryos with a certain amount of respect, because not doing so may have detrimental effects on moral agents and the normative system they subscribe to (a). Second, I discuss a variety of arguments—very much in contrast to the one I am proposing—about why it would be inconsistent to treat embryos any differently from how we treat moral agents because they are in some morally significant way indistinguishable. Some argue that this is because there is a continuous development from embryos to individuals capable of moral agency. Others insist that embryos and individuals capable of moral agency are in crucial ways identical to each other. Again others consider embryos to be potential moral agents (b).

I reject both ways of defending the claim that all embryos have the same moral value (maybe even akin to that of moral agents). In other words, I deny that (a) and (b) are persuasive in the forms they are frequently presented. I claim instead that only the combination of being an embryo that could develop further and having a woman willing to be pregnant with it may provide reasons not to deny such an embryo a chance at being given birth to. These considerations require modifying the practice of destroying embryos (c).

(a) One reason to think that we should treat unborn life with a certain amount of respect has to do with possible detrimental consequences it may have on us, as moral agents, if we act differently. Jürgen Habermas (2003), for instance, has argued that dealing with human life carelessly may have the effect of blunting our moral sensibilities.[16] He maintains that it is this sensibility that enables us to recognize the perversity involved in practices of "using" human life to suit our preferences (p. 20). It is not immediately obvious what Habermas means, as this "blunting" effect could occur in two different ways.

First, in analogy to why Immanuel Kant (1797, 6:442) believes it wrong to abuse animals, mistreating embryos could dull our sensibility if it required accepting the consequences of causing pain for and injury to another being whose suffering is similar to that of persons. The numbing effect would be the result of becoming accustomed to seeing such suffering. But unlike various (born) animals, embryos do not suffer in the same way persons do. At least during the early stages of development, they are unable to feel pain. Moreover, the human embryo has about the same resemblance to persons as any mouse embryo has. Therefore, using the latter for research purposes would have to have the same numbing effect on our moral sensibilities as mistreating the former. In any case, at least early embryos are not sufficiently "like" born individuals for their mistreatment to affect our moral sensibility in the way this kind of argument envisions it.

However, there is a second way this blunting effect could result, which is likely to be the one Habermas actually has in mind. He would probably consider the remarks just made to be beside the point and maintain instead that the dulling effect derives from the symbolic value embryos have for us due to their being instances of human life. According to this reasoning, there is no need for us to recognize any kind of likeness between embryos and ourselves. We must only respect human life and acknowledge that embryos are embodiments thereof. The question is what makes embryos so special, given that there are certainly many forms of human life that we do not treat with much respect: for example, the hair and skin cells every person loses in abundance each day, sperm, egg cells, the placenta, the foreskin, or other pieces of human tissue removed during operations. Thus, it seems that it is not being human or a human cell per se that warrants respect. Some additional feature must be present—something about the embryo that makes it a symbol of human life of the kind that we are committed to protecting. This feature is presumably that the embryo genetically encodes an entire person (and sometimes even more than one). As such, it harbors such "stuff" as persons are made of. This having been said, embryos are not persons. In other words, they are not yet the distinct human life form we value in a particular way. They encode it, yes, but so does any human cell. Therefore, it is somewhat of a stretch to consider embryos to be symbols of the kind of human life we have to revere in order not to numb our moral sensibilities.

(b) This brings me to the next set of arguments. Thinking that the embryo may be a symbol of the kind of human life we value stems from the descriptive truth that human embryos may develop into persons. Thus, many people claim that it would be inconsistent to regard embryos differently from persons. They do this for one of three reasons (or a combination thereof): because they emphasize the uninterrupted continuity between embryos and the persons they develop into, focus on the numerical identity between embryos and persons, or consider embryos to be potential persons. I discuss these three claims in turn.

First, some contend that human development is a continuous process and that conception is the only nonarbitrary point in human development to draw a line. But even if we think (and this itself remains debatable) that conception is the only nonarbitrary moment where we *can* draw a line, this does not imply that this is where, all else considered, we *should* draw one. We may have good reasons for drawing a line at some other moment, even if that other moment is a less clearly distinct one (see also Boonin 2003, 39f.). From the perspective offered in this book, for instance, according to which physical separateness is an important aspect of personhood, birth is a perfectly sensible point to draw a line.

The second argument in defense of treating embryos like persons although they are not maintains that the two are numerically identical. This is of course true of embryos that develop into persons. It is, however, in some obvious way not true of embryos that do not. Thus, as long as embryos do not develop into persons, they are not numerically identical to any persons for whose sake we would be committed to treating their embryos with particular care.

Third, some maintain that we should treat embryos like persons because they are potential persons. "Potentiality" can mean several things.[17] Frequently, it is understood as implying a disposition. This means that, to the extent embryos have all that is required for developing the capacities for moral agency, they are "potential" persons. The only thing distinguishing those embryos from persons is that they are not persons *yet*.[18] From this reasoning, some want to draw the conclusion that all potential persons ought to be treated like persons. This would make abortion and all other "uses" of embryos (that have the capacity to develop into persons) impermissible. There are generally two objections to this. First, and as I am not the first to point out, it is not clear that any specific normative entitlement follows from being a "potential" person. Just because someone could become president of the United States does not already entitle her to the privileges that such a position would bring. Second, and more important, calling embryos "potential persons" assumes that they have a "natural" disposition that can be assessed on its own. But for embryos to develop into persons, they require being carried to term by women. As women are (presently) indispensible for an embryo's "nature" to unfold, embryos alone have no "natural" disposition to develop into persons.

Nevertheless, that embryos could make it to birth if women choose to become pregnant with them or to continue their pregnancies may constitute a kind of potential that warrants some normative concern. A potential president of the United States (all natural-born U.S. citizens) may not be entitled to be treated like the president of the United States. But once a person becomes a presidential candidate, our esteem for the position of president may lead us to treat her in anticipation of the possibility that she might be the next president. The combination of having a viable embryo and a woman who would like to carry it to term gives the embryo a serious chance of developing into a person. Although there is certainly no commitment to create more persons, we might think that, because of the way we value persons, there is something valuable about letting such a development occur, at least if there is no important reason to stop it. In other words, we should take an affirmative attitude toward the creation of persons. For practical purposes this means that we have reasons for allowing women to become pregnant with embryos left over from other persons' fertility procedures. Thus, in cases in which there are such leftover embryos or in which viable embryos are produced for research purposes, we might, as a matter of policy, want to encourage those responsible to make this fact public for a certain amount of time. They could then see whether any women wanted to carry these embryos to term. In cases in which no one wanted to, the embryos in question could be discarded or used for research purposes.

There are two possible kinds of objections to this argument. First, allowing women to have leftover embryos implanted may conflict with the interests of the embryos' biological parents, who might, for some reason, not want to or be unable to carry their embryos to term themselves. Second, there could be a practical concern about encouraging women to carry to term orphaned embryos. I discuss both of these objections in turn.

First, one might think that the genetic parents of the embryo should be the ones to decide whether "their" embryos develop into persons and that they are thus entitled to object to other persons having them implanted. It is certainly plausible to think that once "their" embryos are created, biological parents should have the first say about which of them they want to become pregnant with. But unlike other entities of "some" value such as oak trees and beautiful paintings, embryos are no one's property. Unlike any organ we may wish to keep or give away, embryos do not "belong" to anyone. That they require the assistance of one particular organism to develop into independent persons allows their gestational mother to refuse her assistance but does not give her property rights. Thus, embryos are, from the beginning, their own entities. As Joel Feinberg (1979) notes: "If fetuses were property, we would find nothing odd in the notion that they can be bought and sold, rented out, leased, used as collateral on loans, and so on" (p. 59). If embryos are no one's property, however, then biological parents have no grounds for opposing the wish of someone else to carry their leftover embryos to term.

One might of course worry that a policy allowing others to implant the embryos leftover from fertility procedures may deter many people from seeking reproductive help and from donating their embryos to research. This, however, is no reason against the practice itself. If genetic parents were seriously opposed to other persons adopting the embryos they created but do not want to use, they could always restrict the number of embryos they bring into existence per cycle to that amount they are willing to implant. Such, we will see, is the general policy in Germany, for instance (chapter 2, section 4).

The second kind of objection arises in connection with the vast number of leftover embryos. Having to "offer" all these embryos for adoption before they can be used for other purposes may lead to a situation in which the wish of one researcher to use embryos leads to multiple births and the wish of a couple for one child to the birth of multiple siblings. People might fear a massive demand for leftover embryos by women who cannot themselves produce them. There certainly might be reasons, quite generally, why it would seem advisable to restrict the number of future persons,[19] but there is no conceivable reason for denying the existence of particular future persons. There is even less reason for thinking that women who need reproductive assistance are less entitled to become pregnant than women who need not rely on such help (Karnein 2012). Thus, if there turned out to be a "run" on these embryos, this would only show that we might currently not be doing enough to help infertile persons fulfill their reproductive wishes.[20]

None of this is to suggest that there is some kind of moral obligation to carry these embryos to term. Moreover, someone might wonder whether it follows from all that has been said so far that all women who agree to become pregnant with embryos in vitro (their own or someone else's) stand under a greater obligation to carry through with their pregnancies than women carrying embryos that never left their bodies. The argument could be that, by choosing to have these embryos implanted, women prevent them from being implanted into other women who might be willing to continue their life support.

As much as we might have some obligation to value the creation of persons, our responsibility does not go so far as to override a woman's prerogative to terminate her pregnancy whenever she chooses to do so. Embryos inside women's bodies have as little potential to become persons if women do not want to continue their assistance as do embryos by themselves without women wanting to carry them to term in the first place. The fact that they could have been carried to term had other women had them implanted changes nothing about this. This is not what happened and it was never owed to the embryos that they be given birth to. Rather, the respect owed to the creation of persons merely generates an obligation not to hinder the creation from taking place if all the parties primarily involved consent and continue to do so. Thus, women who "adopt" an embryo and then decide to discontinue their assistance can do so even if, by adopting the embryo, they may have prevented another woman from having it implanted who would have carried it to term. The only way to run afoul of the obligation to value the creation of persons is if someone not essentially involved in the creation of persons were to destroy embryos that would otherwise be given a chance at being carried to term.

5. Conclusion

The central argument defended in this chapter was that our moral commitment to persons implies a moral commitment to treating the embryos they develop from with anticipatory respect for their later personhood. I thus proposed the PDP. Although it is debatable on what grounds personhood is bestowed and when it begins, I maintained that the following proposal seems plausible. To begin with, all beings capable of moral agency are persons. In addition, there are secondary reasons for including all born human beings into this category, as it would be problematic to establish a moral class system within humanity. I claimed that these secondary reasons do not apply to the unborn. This is because an embryo is dependent for its further existence on the organism of one specific and irreplaceable woman in such a way that she can refuse to continue her assistance. I thus argued that it would not make sense to extend personhood to entities that are structurally in a position in which they can be left to die or even killed.

I went on to maintain that although personhood does not begin until birth, our respect for persons gives us reasons to protect the embryos from which they develop (PDP). This suggestion raises several questions, such as how we are supposed to know beforehand which embryos develop into persons and which will not, or what it means to treat embryos with anticipatory respect for their later personhood. In response to the epistemic question, I claimed that we should generally proceed according to the Principle of Precaution. This principle asks us to treat all embryos as if they are going to be persons until it has been made the case that they will not. In response to the question about what it means to treat embryos that develop into persons with anticipatory respect for their later personhood I contended that this implies that we are not entitled to take any of their properties away from them. This is because doing so would violate our obligations to the persons they will grow into. I also suggested that persons have a legitimate claim that the embryos from which they emerge have not been altered in any way. I will return to this in the second part of the book and qualify this statement somewhat by spelling out some kinds of (genetic) alterations that do not violate legitimate claims of persons but instead are part of what they are entitled to.

The chapter then proceeded to explore the value of creating persons. I argued that if women are willing to lend their assistance, we have no good reasons for hindering embryos from continuing their development. From this I concluded that we should have an affirmative attitude toward the creation of persons, which means that third parties ought not to deny embryos a chance at being carried to term (again, only if there are women who would like to do this). I thus proposed changing the practice of dealing with leftover embryos to one in which all viable ones are advertised for a certain period (to see whether there are women who would choose to carry them to term) before being discarded or donated to research.

In the following two chapters, I look at how attractive my suggestions are for current policy in Germany and the United States—two countries with very different approaches to the moral value of the embryo and the kinds of protections afforded to it. If compared to individual topics, such as abortion, my proposal might seem strange and untranslatable in both cases. Whereas German legislation and jurisdiction display a strong commitment to protecting all embryos from the moment of conception, U.S. jurisdiction professes to remain value neutral on this question. However, as chapter 2 shows, if one takes a closer look at the reasons behind Germany's protection of the embryo and takes note of various inconsistencies across a range of issues, the apparent farfetchedness of my approach vanishes. Adopting the PDP might actually help to solve some of the internal inconsistencies in German law and jurisdiction.

In chapter 3 I claim that the same holds true for the United States, albeit for other reasons. Here the problems are not so much located in internal inconsistencies as in the continued political explosiveness of *Roe v. Wade*, which has rendered debates on the moral value of embryos highly contentious and difficult. I argue that my proposal to protect those embryos that develop into persons is not in conflict with positions to which pro-choice advocates are deeply committed. Rather, adopting the PDP would help solve a major potential shortcoming pro-choice advocates are prone to, namely to leave embryos that end up being born largely unprotected. Moreover, I suggest that the PDP is also an attractive position for proponents of stem cell research. They may be expected to be even less inclined to agree that some embryos have moral significance. But they, too, need a way to protect those human embryos that will develop into persons.

2 THE HUMAN DIGNITY OF EMBRYOS?

THE GERMAN CASE

In Germany, biomedical technologies are developing amid a welter of restrictive laws and regulations. With some exceptions, stem cell research is prohibited. Preimplantation genetic diagnosis (PGD) can be performed only under certain narrowly defined conditions.[1] These restrictions, however, were not prompted by, or tailored to, the new biomedical technologies. In part as a response to the atrocious abuse of human life during the holocaust, strong legal protections for the human embryo were put in place when controversies over abortion and, later, assisted reproductive technologies (ARTs) made it necessary to reform existing law (as in the case of abortion), or to create new law (as in the case of ARTs). In both of its abortion decisions, the German Constitutional Court conferred upon the embryo constitutional protection under the Basic Law (German constitution) and declared its human dignity to be inviolable. This protection determined the moral, political, and legal framework of many of today's biomedical issues long before they ever arose.

As I show in this chapter, the protection of embryos in Germany is riddled with inconsistencies. In contrast to what various constitutional and statutory pronouncements suggest, not every embryo is protected equally in Germany. Rather, embryos are fully protected above all in those situations in which the conflicting interests are those of the women pregnant with them. Embryos can regularly be destroyed with impunity in criminal contexts apart from abortion. Embryos in vitro are created and protected only when they are likely to be carried to term and raised in traditional family contexts. Their lives can not only be discontinued when their further existence would challenge established notions of the family (e.g., by severing biological ties), but also in the normal course of assisted reproduction, where more embryos are implanted than are expected to survive.

The following account explores to what extent the Personhood Dependent Principle (PDP) could provide an attractive solution to

Germany's embryo protection puzzle. I argue that adopting the PDP would constitute no fundamental contradiction to the way embryos are already conceived of in Germany (namely, differently depending on the context). But the way Germany draws a distinction between various embryos, that is, on the basis of who destroys them, under what circumstances they are destroyed, and within what kind of family they are supposed to develop, is not convincing. Thus, not only is the PDP a principle Germany could adopt on the basis of its current practice, it is also one it should adopt so as to make the distinction between different embryos more persuasive.

The argument proceeds in four steps. First, I review the German abortion debate and the two Constitutional Court decisions on abortion. This shows that part of the reason for why embryos are constitutionally protected the way they are may have less to do with an interest in protecting unborn life per se and more to do with the Constitutional Court's stance on women and the family (section 1). Second, I explore embryo protection in the contexts of criminal and tort law. This highlights that, once the issue is no longer about abortion, unborn life is not treated as if having human dignity and a right to life translates into an obligation of the state to punish those responsible for its death. On the contrary, there are virtually no consequences for the negligent destruction of embryos in the context of a crime (section 2). Third, I review the Law for the Protection of the Embryo (*Embryonenschutzgesetz*, or ESchG). This reveals that the law is very protective only of some embryos from the moment of conception. Embryos that exist apart from traditional family contexts are not necessarily given an opportunity to continue their existence. In this context, I also discuss a court ruling from 2010 that allows the genetic (de)selection of embryos through PGD in certain circumstances (section 3). Fourth, I briefly review the so-called "Stem Cell Law." It spells out an important exception to the general prohibition to destroy embryos and explains under what conditions the import of human embryonic stem cells is permitted. This exposes the hypocrisy involved in disallowing the destruction of "local" embryos while being perfectly willing to profit from embryos destroyed elsewhere (section 4).

1. The German Abortion Debate

I begin with a brief review of the history of the German abortion debate (a). I then discuss the two Constitutional Court's abortion decisions, focusing in particular on its views on embryos (b), women (c), and its stance on the family and society (d). I close with a short portrayal of how the court's decision was implemented by the legislative process to arrive at the law that governs abortion today (e).

(a) A Brief Sketch of the Historical Background. The first time that any form of abortion was permitted in Germany was with the passing of a Nazi eugenics law in 1933, the so-called Law for the Prevention of Genetically Diseased Offspring.[2] This was a radical departure from earlier twentieth-century policy whereby abortion had been regarded as the killing of the "bodily fruit" (*Leibesfrucht*) and considered a capital offense.[3] The Nazi law continued to be in effect until well after the end of World War II, although abortion in general was still illegal and, on the statute books at least, punishable by death. However, the allies prohibited cruel or disproportionately harsh punishment, and thus the death penalty became a moot threat after 1945.[4]

In the early postwar period, although the laws on abortion were not entirely uniform in all of the West German federal states (*Bundesländer*), abortions for medical reasons were generally accepted throughout the Federal Republic.[5] Abortions for other than medical reasons continued to be treated as the killing of the bodily fruit and punished as a misdemeanor with up to five years in prison. This forced most women to either go abroad (which only the wealthy could afford), make a life-threatening attempt to self-induce an abortion, or pay a lot of money to medical quacks. According to one statistic, about 300 women were sentenced each year under the law, and it is estimated that between 75,000 and 300,000 illegal abortions were actually being performed annually. This has been taken as evidence that the law was thoroughly inefficient and simply made abortion unnecessarily dangerous, without reducing its occurrence (Eser 2001, 1727).

Although it had long been clear that imposing severe penalties was not an effective solution, the real political debate about the reform of the infamous § 218 StGB (the "abortion paragraph") did not start until the social-liberal coalition under Willy Brandt came to power in 1969. The taboo on abortion had begun to crumble.[6] What quickly developed into a large-scale abortion controversy turned on two competing models for how to deal with unwanted pregnancies. First, there was the model according to which women should be allowed to freely decide whether to terminate their pregnancy within the first trimester (*Fristenlösung*), though only after consultation with a doctor and on the condition that the abortion was performed by a doctor. The rationale for this model was that "the pregnant woman will undergo consultation because she has no fear and knows that she will be left free to make her own decision" (Eser 2001, 1727; my translation). I refer to this model as the "liberal solution."

The second model principally condemned abortion and held the practice to be illegal and punishable unless there were "justifying reasons"[7] referred to as "indications" (*Indikationslösung*). Justifying reasons in this sense included danger to the mother's life, rape as the cause of pregnancy, or genetic defects in the embryo. Variants of this model differed only with respect to the range of reasons that were accepted as justifying an abortion. For instance, in 1973 there was a proposal by members of parliament from the Social Democratic Party that envisioned a very wide range of justifying conditions. It accepted all reasons listed above, plus ethical reasons and other "emergencies." These could include a wide array of things, such as various problematic financial or social situations, often subsumed under the term "social indication." By contrast, proposals from the Christian-conservative parties (the Christian Democratic Party and the Christian Social Union) were far less permissive and allowed only medical reasons to count as sufficient to render an abortion free of punishment. The only other exception was that a judge could refrain from punishing a woman if she was under extreme distress at the time of the abortion procedure.[8] I refer to this model as the "restrictive solution."

The two models have an interesting history of *de facto* and *de jure* successes. On two occasions, after the liberal solution had received a majority vote in parliament, its conservative opponents petitioned the Constitutional Court to have the law declared unconstitutional.[9] This happened for the first time in 1975 and led to the initial Constitutional Court decision on abortion (BVerfGE 39, 1). The second decision occurred in 1993 in reaction to the legislation that was passed to find a common solution for a unified Germany (BVerfGE 88, 203). In both cases, the court found that the liberal solution the legislature had worked out did not properly honor the embryo's right to life as guaranteed by Article 2, Paragraph 2 of the Basic Law, read in connection with human dignity protected by Article 1, Paragraph 1. Each time, the court held that allowing the liberal solution would give the wrong impression that it was up to the pregnant woman to decide whether she wanted to continue her pregnancy or not. Women should never be allowed to "merely" choose an abortion; only in exceptional circumstances should they not be punished for ending their pregnancies.

(b) **The Constitutional Protection of the Embryo.** In both abortion decisions, the Constitutional Court declared that the human embryo has human dignity and a right to life. Although the court did not argue that embryos are persons, it adopted a version of the continuity thesis about the moral value of embryos (briefly discussed in chapter 1, section 4), insisting that they do not develop into human beings but *as* human beings (BVerfGE 88, 203 [252]).

In construing Article 2, Paragraph 2, Sentence 1, of the Basic Law, one should begin with its language: "Everyone has a right to life . . ." Life, in the sense of historical existence of a human individual, exists according to definite biological-physiological knowledge, in any case, from the 14th day after conception (nidation, individuation). (. . .) The process of development which has begun at that point is a continuing process which exhibits no sharp demarcation and does not allow a precise division of the various steps of development of the human life. (BVerfGE 39, 1 [37]; Jonas and Gorby 1976, 638)

As human beings, embryos should be treated as independent legal values that the state needs to protect, including against the women carrying them (BVerfGE 39, 1 [42]; Jonas and Gorby 1976, 642). This extensive protection of all human life was supposed to be a direct reaction to the horrendous abuses of human life during the Nazi regime. "The express incorporation into the Basic Law of the self-evident right to life—in contrast to the Weimar Constitution—may be explained principally as a reaction to the 'destruction of life unworthy of life,' to the 'final solution' and 'liquidations,' which were carried out by the National Socialistic Regime as measures of state" (BVerfGE 39, 1 [37]; Jonas and Gorby 1976, 637).

This reactive attitude to Germany's immediate past is, from many perspectives, important and laudable. But there is no obvious reason for why the answer to gross human rights violations is one of breadth—by including more instances of human life as potential addressees of human rights violations—rather than one of depth—by institutionally making sure that such abuses can no longer occur. In other words, there is no obvious or necessary link between including embryos in the realm of those who are constitutionally protected and ensuring greater safety from atrocious abuses of human rights.

Moreover, the kinds of abuses Germany arguably wants to prevent in the future (due to its past) are not ones that embryos are primarily subject to. It was born human beings whose human dignity was systematically violated. If we wanted to prevent the same kinds of human rights abuses, it is certainly not obvious why it would be embryos we should be looking out for first and foremost. This is true unless, of course, we think that embryos' human dignity is violated by women who choose to end their life support. This, however, as argued in chapter 1, is clearly not what occurs in abortion conflicts. Women do not disrespect the dignity of embryos by not wanting to continue their pregnancies. Instead, they assert a legitimate claim to self-determination and bodily integrity against an entity that can develop as a human being in the first place only if women volunteer their assistance, an act that they cannot be required to perform. From this perspective, an attempt to avoid past mistakes would arguably provide German judges with more reason to oppose a ruling that not only systematically denies women their right to self-determination, but also disrespects their physical and mental integrity.

Obviously, this is not the lesson the judges came away with. However, even if one chooses, as the judges did, to respond by granting embryos far-reaching constitutional protection, it still does not explain why abortion should in principle, and with only few exceptions, be declared illegal. Even if embryos are considered a form of human life that must be protected in a way that outweighs important rights of persons (to self-determination, for instance), there are situations besides medical emergencies and rape in which women could be thought to permissibly end their life support for their fetus. That the court found no place for such considerations can be explained only by the attitude it took toward (pregnant) women.

(c) **The Constitutional Court's Distrust of Women.** The basic attitude of the judges was that an abortion, even if it is in certain cases not punishable by law, is a reprehensible act, not comparable with a visit to the doctor for the treatment of an illness or with methods of birth control (BVerfGE 39, 1 [44]; Jonas and Gorby 1976, 644). Therefore, the woman's right to self-determination alone should not be able to justify an abortion, and she should not be allowed to make her own personal decision in that matter. In principle, it was held that it is the duty of the woman to carry to term her pregnancy and that abortion must be viewed as illegal.

> The legal order may not make the woman's right to self-determination the sole guideline of its rulemaking. The state must proceed, as a matter of principle, from a duty to carry the pregnancy to term and therefore to view, as a matter of principle, its interruption as an injustice. The condemnation of abortion must be clearly expressed in the legal order. (. . .) The state may not abdicate its responsibility even through the recognition of a "legally free area," by which the state abstains from the value judgment and abandons this judgment to the decision of the individual to be made on the basis of his own sense of responsibility. (BVerfGE 39, 1 [44]; Jonas and Gorby 1976, 644)

Generally, whenever the right to life and human dignity of the embryo stood against the right to self-determination of the woman, the former should outweigh the latter (BVerfGE 39, 1 [43]; Jonas and Gorby 1976, 643).

As already mentioned, the court allowed for certain exemptions from punishment if, for instance, the life and health of the mother were threatened, the child would be born with a severe disability, or the pregnancy was the result of rape.[10] Apart from such circumstances, however, both Constitutional Court decisions emphasized that a woman can be reasonably required to bear the burdens of any "normal pregnancy" (BVerfGE 39, 1 [49]; Jonas and Gorby 1976, 649; cf. BVerfGE 88, 203 [257]).[11] The court did not seem to think that whether any particular pregnancy could be reasonably required should be up to the respective women to decide. Rather, it argued that one cannot rely on women's (or men's) opinions on these matters, as that would "misjudge the reality in which men and women often take their own outlook on life too seriously and are not willing to subordinate it even if that would seem reasonable from an objective point of view" (BVerfGE 88, 203 [267]; my translation).

This depiction of a woman's reproductive duties stands in stark contrast to the one advocated in this book. Here, pregnancy is conceived of as a woman giving her assistance to unborn life that, first, could not exist without her and, second, relies entirely and irreplaceably on her for its development. The kind of help an embryo needs is of a kind, I am claiming, the woman can refuse, even if it is because it just happens not to agree with her personal outlook on life to be pregnant at this time. Only such a description takes women seriously and does not reduce them to their reproductive roles.

The Constitutional Court systematically failed to realize that women cannot be expected to tolerate the discomfort and pain involved in being pregnant and giving birth; it should have instead concluded that women who agree to do this should be thanked profusely. It would certainly be hard to establish that, just because women can, it is their duty to become mothers and bear the burdens this might entail. This is true even if the inconveniencies of pregnancy and birth may be deemed "normal" in the sense that all pregnancies come at a certain unavoidable cost and even if the human species needs future persons for its survival. I have more to say about procreative responsibilities in the final chapter of this book (chapter 6, section 3).

In some sense, the attitude displayed by the court toward women in both abortion decisions is surprising. The 1970s and certainly the 1990s were phases in which the court was far more progressive in other realms pertaining to gender equality than the abortion decisions would suggest (Sacksofsky 2009, 209). However, there is one thing that can be said in defense of the court on this matter: It drew consistent conclusions from its views that women should stay pregnant and give birth by encouraging social arrangements that would support and protect parents.

(d) The Constitutional Court's Views on the Family and Society. The court recognized that childbearing is not only a private matter but that it has a social dimension in two ways: First, as already mentioned, it viewed the embryo as a separate entity worthy of government protection against third-party intervention, including the intervention of the woman carrying it. Second, it understood that motherhood and child-rearing are not only in the interest of particular individuals but in the interest of the larger community as well. Therefore, it argued that society must show some recognition for reproductive labor (BVerfGE 88, 203 [259]). The court demanded, for instance, that the legislature make sure that women and men are not disadvantaged economically and socially by becoming parents. Jobs should be guaranteed during paternity or maternity leaves, there should be forms of financial aid, and parents of newborns should be protected from being evicted from their apartments (BVerfGE 88, 203 [259f]).

These directions show some consistency in the court's views on individual reproduction and society. If women have a general obligation to carry their children to term, then they should at least be supported in their endeavor to do so. Unfortunately, however, some of the provisions that are supposed to protect women tend to work to the detriment of gender equality in practice. For instance, due to the protections afforded to them, women who are at an age at which they are still "in danger" of becoming pregnant end up not being attractive to employers.

> Since an employer must reckon with the possibility that a woman will become pregnant (. . .) and take advantage of her legal rights, particularly child-raising leave, she is indeed an economic risk in a highly trained, highly paid position. Given the choice, most employers understandably prefer to hire a man, and there are always ways to circumvent the equal-opportunity laws. (Stern 1997, 11)

As the discussion so far has shown, my contention with the Constitutional Court's decisions is only partly grounded in its view on the embryo. Most of it has to do with its position on women and their role in the reproductive process. Once the court was forced to revise these views, there would not be much left of the argument for why women ought not to be entitled to end their life support for the embryos they are carrying. Abortion could then be more properly appreciated as an instance in which women legitimately express their rights to bodily integrity and self-determination toward entities that could neither exist nor survive on their own. Thus, the view I am suggesting the court to adopt is not a disrespectful attitude toward the embryo; rather, what I am proposing is an appropriately respectful attitude toward women.

(e) **Abortion Today.** According to the current § 218 StGB, abortion is illegal and punishable. However, § 218a StGB exempts a woman from punishment until the twelfth week of pregnancy under two conditions: first, she has to ask for an abortion and show that she underwent a consultation with a doctor at least three days prior to the procedure; second, the abortion must be performed by a doctor (§ 218a (1) StGB). It is legal for a woman to obtain an abortion within the first twelve weeks if her pregnancy is the result of rape (§ 218a (3) StGB). Even after that, § 218a StGB renders it legal for a woman to terminate her pregnancy if there are persuasive social or medical indications (§ 218a (2) StGB). [12] Without social or medical indications abortions until the twenty-second week remain free of punishment, but only for the pregnant woman herself and after she has undergone a consultation with a doctor; in other words, this exemption from punishment applies exclusively to the pregnant woman and does not include anyone else who might be involved in the abortion procedure, not even the doctor (§ 218a (4) 1 StGB). A woman is generally not punished if she was under extreme duress at the time of the procedure (§ 218a (4) 2 StGB).

Thus, although an abortion is only legal in Germany in those cases in which a woman has a medical or social emergency or her pregnancy is the result of rape and she terminates it within the first twelve weeks, the de facto abortion ruling in Germany ends up being quite liberal.[13] This is probably also why the heat of the initial abortion debate has cooled down much more than in the United States.[14] In Germany, everyone got a little of what they wanted: Women can abort, and embryos are still protected from the moment of implantation—on paper, at least. But this is a far cry from what women should want for themselves in Germany. What they should insist on is full recognition of their right to end their pregnancies for whatever reasons they may have.

Given that the court has expressed a clear commitment to treating the embryo as a human being with dignity and a right to life, it may come as a surprise that embryos are not generally considered to be very much like human beings with dignity and a right to life outside of the abortion context. This can be clearly seen when we turn our attention to criminal and tort law.

2. Embryo Protection in Criminal and Tort Law

According to § 1 of the civil code (*Bürgerliches Gesetzbuch*, or BGB) the fetus is not regarded as a person until birth. In other words, the capacity to be a subject of legal rights and duties begins with the completion of birth. According to § 212 (manslaughter—*Totschlag*) of the criminal code (*Strafgesetzbuch*), the fetus counts as a person already during the birthing process (BGHSt 10, 291; BGHSt 31, 348; BGHSt 32, 194). Thus, under criminal law, personhood begins a little before it does under civil law (i.e., starting with the first contractions as opposed to birth itself). The reason personhood commences a little earlier in criminal law is probably due to the nature of the cases it applies to: While the point at which personhood begins may not be quite as important with regard to when a newborn has rights and duties, it is very significant with regard to when its life must be protected like that of a born person. In 1983, for instance, a doctor was accused of having negligently killed a child (as opposed to having negligently performed an abortion, which would have been free of punishment). He had repeatedly failed to notice that a woman, who was complaining of severe cramps but denied being pregnant, was having contractions. He had thus prescribed several doses of a strong painkiller. This drew out the birthing process to such lengths (various days) that the fetus died from a lack of oxygen supply and was stillborn. As it could not be determined for certain that the contractions had already begun when the doctor first visited, the doctor was not convicted. But it was established that had the contractions already begun, he would have been guilty of having negligently killed a child as opposed to having negligently aborted a fetus (BGHSt 31, 348 [356]).

In the same year, another case was decided on similar grounds, this time convicting a man of murder not only of the pregnant woman he pushed over a cliff but also of the murder of the fetus she was carrying, since the contractions had clearly already set in at the time of his crime (BGHSt 32, 194). Thus, according to the Federal High Court for Criminal Justice, the beginning of the contractions mark the borderline between § 218 StGB (abortion) and § 222 StGB (negligent homicide) (BGH 31, 348 [350]).

What some consider to be most disturbing about this state of affairs is that, as a consequence, German criminal law is surprisingly lenient with fatal injuries done to a fetus by a third party outside of an (official) abortion context. If, for instance, a person other than the pregnant woman herself destroys the embryo or fetus before the first contractions have occurred but without intending to bring about an abortion, he or she is neither liable for manslaughter nor for any harm done besides the harm to the woman herself (BGHSt 10, 291; 31, 348; 32, 194). If someone harms an embryo any time before the first contraction and, as a result, an injured child is born, the child can, however, sue for damages (BGHZ 8, 243; 58, 48; 93, 351).

In some sense, it might seem troublesome that someone who injures a pregnant woman and thereby (negligently) kills her eight-month-old fetus would not be punished (while anyone who negligently killed a newborn would be) but that if the fetus survived until birth and was born in an injured state, the same person would be held liable for damages. At least initially, one might think that killing should be considered much worse than injuring and that it is therefore counterintuitive that injury would result in damages having to be paid while killing would result in no legal consequences at all (Kaufmann 1971, 570). However, although it certainly would seem that killing is worse than harming, the theory of the embryo laid out in chapter 1 shows why this must not always be the case. Injuring embryos at any stage of their development, in or outside the womb, is problematic only if these embryos develop into persons. If there are no future persons into which these embryos develop (because the embryos are destroyed before), then there are no persons who have been harmed from a first-person perspective.[15]

From the perspective of the women carrying these embryos, it may, of course, not be true that they perceive it as better that their embryos are destroyed rather than injured. For them, having an injured child may be preferable to losing their child altogether. But this only establishes that when a fetus a woman intends to carry to term is killed, as opposed to injured, we may have reasons to consider the harm done to the woman. This harm could be substantial, given that she will have lost the child she was expecting. Thus, it might indeed be warranted to ask persons who are responsible for negligently killing the fetus a woman wanted to carry to term to compensate her for the harm this will have caused her or even to punish them for their actions. I return to a more detailed discussion of this issue in the context of fetal manslaughter laws in the United States (chapter 3, section 3).

One problem with this account, for which the crucial question turns on *whether* a person is injured and not on *when* the injury took place, may be that it cannot be used to distinguish between whether the cause of the later injury was incurred during pregnancy or before. So, arguably, if it could be shown that some behavior of a person's grandmother, for example, caused the egg cells of this person's mother to be damaged, then the grandmother could be accused of bodily injury to her grandchild. Some think this would be overstretching the argument (Kaufmann 1971; Lüttger 1983).

But it is not clear why this should be a problem. Within reasonable bounds, one should probably try not to damage one's sperm or egg cells or those of another in view of potential damages to future persons. As no one is forced to reproduce, people certainly continue to have a choice of how to behave and to draw conclusions about the right thing to do in light of their past behavior. Therefore, if people choose to have offspring, it is not unreasonable to ask of them to make sure that they do nothing that they know is likely to lead to the creation of a future person born in a wrongful state (in whatever way "wrongful" is defined and however far removed the future person is who will be born in a wrongful state, i.e., irrespective of whether it is one's own child or one's grandchild).

In sum, counter to the impression left by the Constitutional Court's ruling on abortion, namely that the human dignity and right to life of embryos imply strong legal measures for their protection, it turns out that there are virtually no consequences for negligently killing them in contexts apart from abortion and only some for injuring them. Furthermore, the discussion showed that the apparent inconsistency of treating nonfatal injuries to the unborn more harshly than bringing about their demise can be made sense of only if it is taken to reflect a distinction such as that advocated in this book (i.e., between embryos that make it to birth and those that do not). Such a distinction helps explain why nonfatal harm to embryos that actually make it to birth should be redressed in all cases while fatal harm can be left unpunished in certain circumstances. I have argued that such circumstances obtain if the fatal harm is inflicted by the pregnant woman herself. By contrast, German criminal law implies that such circumstances obtain only if someone other than the pregnant woman inflicts fatal harm to an embryo outside an abortion context. Thus, while German criminal and tort law open the door for making the right sort of distinction, they apply it the wrong way. Instead of acquitting everyone else from fatally injuring a fetus, this distinction should be used to absolve women from any charge who choose to end their pregnancies.

The cases just discussed deal predominantly with rather late-stage fetuses in nonabortion contexts. The embryos at issue in the context of biomedical technologies, however, are usually only a few days old. Nothing in the abortion decisions or the criminal or tort law contexts has said anything about those. Therefore, to fill the gap in embryo protection that arose when ARTs became an issue, the Law for the Protection of the Embryo (*Embryonenschutzgesetz*, or ESchG) was passed in 1990. Judging from the Constitutional Court's decision about how to protect embryos, it could have been expected that when women's bodily integrity is not involved, the embryo would, and without exception, be protected from the very moment of conception due to its human dignity and right to life. In the following we see that this is not what happened. According to the embryo protection law, embryos can and even must, on occasion, be left to perish in the name of a variety of social and cultural values.

3. The Law for Protecting (Some) Embryos

Ever since ART procedures made the embryo available outside the woman's womb, the ambition was to bridge the "gap" regarding the protection of embryos between conception and implantation. This was to make sure that early embryonic life, now so readily available to scientists and doctors, would not be used in impermissible ways. For this purpose, the ESchG was passed to protect embryos in vitro from the moment of fertilization, that is, even before the law rendering abortions illegal (§ 218 StGB) recognizes that pregnancy has begun.

According to the definition used in the ESchG, the embryo is the fertilized, viable human egg cell from the moment its nucleus has fused with that of the sperm cell (zygote) and every totipotent stem cell[16] taken from a zygote (§ 8 (1) ESchG).[17] The law criminalizes the fertilization of an egg cell for any purpose other than to produce a pregnancy in the woman from whom the egg cell originates (§ 1 (1) 2 ESchG). It prohibits the implantation of more than three embryos into a woman during one cycle (§ 1 (1) 3 ESchG) and does not allow the fertilization of more than three eggs total during one cycle (§ 1 (1) 4 ESchG). The ESchG also forbids the fertilization of more eggs than will be implanted into a woman during one cycle (§ 1 (1) 5 ESchG), the transfer of an embryo that has been extracted from a woman prior to implantation to another woman or the use of such an embryo for purposes unrelated to its continued existence (§ 1 (1) 6), the transfer of embryos to or fertilization of women who are willing to give their child into the permanent care of a third party (§ 1 (1) 7), and the creation of embryos for any purpose other than to produce pregnancies in the women who contributed their egg cells to the creation of these embryos (§ 2). Furthermore, the law prohibits eugenic applications such as sex selection (with the explicit exception of sex selection for the prevention of certain sex-specific genetic diseases; § 3), germ-line intervention (§ 5), cloning (§ 6), and purely scientific and ethically problematic uses such as the creation of chimeras or hybrids (§ 7).

The embryo protection law was passed at a time when PGD was in its infancy and stem cell research barely on the horizon. But since no embryo may be created for any other purpose than to bring about a pregnancy (in the woman with whose egg cell the embryo was created), the legislation appears to preclude creating enough embryos to make selection feasible, discarding embryos that have been deselected, and using leftover embryos for research purposes (Kollek 2002, 202).

Judging by its name, it may seem as if the explicit purpose of a Law for the Protection of Embryos is to protect embryos. However, this is not the case.

To begin with, it entails no obligation to allow embryos to continue their existence outside the womb. By allowing more embryos to be implanted into a
woman's uterus than can be expected to successfully develop (to increase her
chances of becoming pregnant), it implicitly condones the sacrifice of some
embryos (§1 (1) 3). With its prohibition against transferring a cloned embryo
to a woman (§ 6 (2)) it actually even mandates the destruction of embryos. The
same is true of the prohibition against transferring hybrids or chimeras con-
taining human cells or embryos (§ 7 (2) 1) into the uterus of either animals or
humans. Failure to adhere to this interdiction is punished with up to five years
in prison.

Therefore, it is more accurate to say that the Law for the Protection of the
Embryo protects embryos not so much against destruction but against being
"misused" (Günther et al. 2008, 92). Such forms of "misuse" include those
mentioned above, such as implanting clones, chimeras, and hybrids into the
wombs of women or animals, but also giving reproductive assistance to those
who seek to sever the biological ties within a family. [18] Women who require the
donation of an egg cell or women who are willing to give their children up for
adoption, for instance, may not be assisted. Surrogacy is precluded by not
permitting the transfer of an embryo to a woman who would be willing to
carry to term a child for someone else.

These restrictions seem to indicate that an embryo that has been created
but whose biological mother is (for some reason) unable to carry it to term
would have to be destroyed rather than implanted into a biologically unrelated
woman (who would like to be pregnant with this embryo). This is certainly
true for embryos in vivo prior to implantation. They may not be extracted and
transferred to another woman (§ 1 (1) 6). When it comes to embryos in vitro the
law arguably tries not to prevent their transfer in such exceptional circumstances. This has been inferred from the fact that while the law threatens a
person with punishment who transfers a foreign nonfertilized egg cell to a
woman (§ 1 (1) 1) it does not explicitly prohibit the transfer of an embryo in
vitro (Günther et al. 2008, 111f.). However, it seems generally adequate to say
that the embryo protection law allows the creation of embryos only in traditional family contexts and does not protect all embryos. It silently accepts that
some will regularly perish on the way of producing a pregnancy. Moreover, it
mandates the destruction of embryos women may be willing to donate to other
women seeking to be pregnant.

The boundaries of the ESchG have been challenged in court and, with the
further advance of new reprogenetic technologies, will surely continue to be.[19]
In what follows, I concentrate on a challenge that has gained some prominence.

It occurred in 2010 and concerned the permissibility of performing PGD under the ESchG.

The issue of whether PGD is permissible under the ESchG arose because a fertility doctor who had performed PGD (in three instances) pressed charges against himself to solve the question of whether these actions he deemed necessary were lawful or not. The first time he used the procedure was on a couple with a known chromosomal abnormality that usually leads to the death of offspring. The only way for them to be sure to have a child that would survive was through PGD. The doctor thus tested three embryos and found only one without the genetic abnormality. He implanted the healthy embryo. The others were left to perish.

The second and third cases were similar in that both involved women who, due to chromosomal abnormalities on their part, had increased risks of having disabled children. In both cases the doctor used PGD to see which embryos were healthy, implanted the healthy one(s) he found, and left the other(s) to perish.

The doctor was acquitted of all charges. The main reason was that, according to the judges, the doctor had not violated the spirit of the ESchG since all his actions were geared at bringing about a successful pregnancy (BGH 5. StR 386/09 2010, Rndnr. 14, 30). The judges argued that PGD was used only as a means to this end (Rndnr. 19). Moreover, PGD was performed on pluri- and no longer totipotent cells. While the latter fall under the protection of the ESchG, the former do not (Rndnr. 23). The court maintained that the ESchG does not comprehensively protect embryos (Rndnr. 25). Moreover, it argued that § 3 sentence 2 of the ESchG (allowing gender selection if that would prevent the birth of a seriously disabled child) already suggests that embryo selection may occur if serious disabilities of future offspring are at stake (Rndnr. 25). The court also pointed out that the knowledge of carrying a disabled child is covered under the social-medical indication of the law on abortion, i.e., provides a reason not to punish a woman if she chooses to have an abortion in response (Rndnr. 26). However, the judges maintained that PGD can be permissible only when there is reason to believe that a couple's embryos will have serious genetic defects, not exclusively for gender selection or to choose an embryo with a certain immunity pattern (Rndnr. 29).

What makes this case significant is that, prior to this decision, many, including the author of this book, deemed it impossible that PGD would be allowed anytime soon in Germany.[20] The reason for this is quite simple: It appeared to be highly problematic to make an argument for the selection of "worthy" and the deselection of "unworthy" life in a country with Germany's history. The former German federal president, Johannes Rau, expressed this concisely in a speech he delivered in 2001: "Eugenics, euthanasia and selection: These are terms which are connected to terrible memories in Germany. They therefore—and rightly so—produce a reaction of emotional defense" (Rau 2001, 11, section XIV; my translation).

Thus, until this court case came to pass, it seemed close to committing political suicide to defend PGD. For a long time, PGD was used mainly as leverage to argue for stem cell research: Several of those in favor of loosening the regulations on stem cell research chose to make a big issue of rejecting PGD to be able to make the case *for* stem cell research. The then-federal minister of justice, Brigitte Zypris, for instance, emphasized how Germany had to affirm the protections granted to the embryo in the abortion decision, and how parents ought not to be allowed to subject their embryos to any form of quality control. At the same time, the reason stem cell research should be permitted was because, she argued, embryos in vitro have less potential than embryos in vivo to develop into born persons. Thus, she considered destroying them to be morally different from having an abortion (Zypries 2003, 6).[21]

Similarly, arguing against PGD (and stem cell research, for that matter) while continuing to support abortion, Jürgen Habermas (2003) cautions against engaging in a practice that commodifies embryos. He thinks that the intention of parents who subject their embryos to PGD is clearly to discard those embryos they consider to be less desirable. By allowing only those to continue their existence that meet certain quality criteria, parents fail to treat embryos as ends in themselves. In this way, he thinks PGD is very different from abortion (Habermas 2003, 30; see also Kollek 2002, 210). He views abortion as constituting an involuntarily caused conflict between the right of the mother to self-determination and the right of the embryo to life (Habermas 2003, 30). In this conflict, performing an abortion does not in principle treat the embryo as a commodity. On the contrary, the right of the embryo is weighed against the right of the woman, which, in his view, outweighs that of the embryo, at least until the end of the first trimester.

In various respects Habermas misrepresents the situation of abortion. First, on an empirical level, it is well known that women regularly abort for eugenic reasons. As the court rendering the judgment on PGD rightly saw, it is inconsistent to allow in vivo pregnancies on a "trial and error" basis (Renzikowski 2001, 2757) in the sense that women can have an abortion if they discover that their fetus has a genetic defect but not to permit in vitro pregnancies on similar terms. Second, and more important, it is not clear why anyone should have the right to judge the intentions of prospective parents.

There are all kinds of reasons for wanting children, and these are bad or good regardless of how the children are produced. In other words, it is just as likely that couples pursuing "natural" reproduction have a wish for a healthy child as couples subjecting their embryo to PGD. The fact that the former leave it to chance (for whatever reasons) does not make their original wish less suspicious than that of the latter.

Although this decision on PGD has partly resolved the discrepancy in treatment between embryos in vitro and embryos in vivo, some differences remain. As already mentioned, whereas the former may be created and continue their existence only under certain circumstances, there are no restrictions on how and why the latter are created. Moreover, their development may be interrupted only by way of exception. At the same time, embryos in vitro are protected from a much earlier point of their development than are embryos in vivo. Whereas § 218 StGB allows various forms of birth control that prevent the embryo from implanting, similar measures that destroy the early embryo are prohibited by the ESchG.[22]

Thus, although allowing some forms of PGD appears to be a turn to greater consistency, the permission to select unborn life shows once more that embryos are not comprehensively protected in Germany. Rather, it seems that many reasons suffice to override an embryo's right to life—most reasons, actually, except, it seems, those women have to offer in defense of their right to self-determination. The Stem Cell Law of 2002 provides further proof of this.

4. The Stem Cell Law

The final piece of the German embryo protection puzzle is the Stem Cell Law from 2002. In August of 2000, the neuropathologist Oliver Brüstle from the University of Bonn applied for a grant from Germany's largest nonprofit, independent research funding agency, the German Research Association (*Deutsche Forschungsgemeinschaft*, or DFG), for the use of embryonic stem cells to develop a cure for multiple sclerosis. The scientist had already successfully used the stem cells of mice to repair rat brains with the myelin deficiency that causes the disease. Since the ESchG prohibits any use of embryos other than to bring about a pregnancy, Brüstle proposed to import his cells from Israel. Given Brüstle's credentials and the likelihood that his project would be at the cutting edge of research, the DFG would ordinarily have enthusiastically sponsored his project. However, his application caused a controversy: Could he legally import the cells for his project? There was nothing in the ESchG that explicitly prohibited such an undertaking. Nevertheless, the DFG was not willing to run the risk of funding a research project that was based on a loophole in the law. It therefore turned to parliament for a decision on how to regulate the matter. But what needed to be regulated turned out to be no minor technicality. On the contrary, it became politically highly explosive. Formerly held principles suddenly clashed with new hopes. Many were excited by heady prospects such as finding the miracle cure for fatal ills or the secret to everlasting youth.

After a long and heated public debate, the so-called Stem Cell Law (*Stammzellengesetz*, or StZG) was passed by parliament in the spring of 2002, regulating the import of embryonic stem cells. It generally prohibits the import of stem cells but allows for a significant exception. A specially created Central Ethics Commission may permit the import of early human stem cells under three conditions: First, the scientific goal to be achieved has to be high-ranking. Second, the research must have been previously performed on animals and must have produced satisfactory results. Third, there must be reasons for why this particular research can be done only on human embryonic stem cells. To avoid the possibility of this law serving as an incentive to destroy embryos for the extraction of stem cells abroad, the law requires that the cells be derived before January 1, 2002, and that they are pluri- and no longer totipotent. In the meantime, however, parliament has passed a law that moves the date prior to which the cells have to be derived up to May 1, 2007.

This Stem Cell Law and its latest amendment are morally troubling in two respects: First, not allowing research on German embryos but at the same time permitting research—no matter how restricted—on imported embryos introduces a morally indefensible double standard. Second, permitting German scientists to conduct research on stem cells that are the product of an otherwise condemned action—the destruction of embryos—is problematic. Arguably, the first deadline (January 1, 2002) implicitly sanctioned the previous destruction. Moving the deadline forward, however, renders no longer credible any pretense of worrying about embryo destruction in principle.

The Stem Cell Law is further evidence of what should be clear by now: Only some embryos are protected in Germany. From the perspective of the PDP that, in itself, is not troubling. What is not convincing are the reasons for why some embryos are protected while others are not. I conclude with some suggestions of how the PDP could help make the various rules and regulations pertaining to the embryo in Germany more consistent and thus more plausible.

5. Conclusion

This chapter sought to explore whether the PDP is an attractive principle for a legal and political system, such as Germany, which is committed, at least de jure, to protecting the embryo's right to life and human dignity. It turns out that it is.

Currently, Germany's position on the embryo is inconsistent in various ways. To begin with, although the embryo's human dignity and right to life are constitutionally protected and regularly overrule women's right to self-determination in abortion conflicts (making many abortions illegal), embryos can be destroyed in criminal contexts with impunity. Moreover, of embryos created in vitro only some are given the opportunity to continue their existence, while others, which could be carried to term or raised by biologically nonrelated parents, are left to perish. Furthermore, a recent court case has suggested that one reason for letting embryos die is an unfavorable genetic disposition. Finally, it is permissible for German scientists to import stem cells that are derived from embryos previously destroyed elsewhere.

Thus, the picture that emerges is that although all human embryos are accorded human dignity and a right to life, only some embryos end up being protected. But the distinction between different embryos is made on grounds that are unpersuasive, such as whether they will be carried to term by their biological mothers or whether they are from Germany or elsewhere. A better and more consistent way to differentiate between embryos would follow from the PDP, according to which those embryos that will develop into persons should be protected from the moment of conception. Embryos that will not develop into persons (i.e., embryos that do not have women willing to be pregnant with them) can be used for research purposes or destroyed.

If the proposal of how to think of the moral value of embryos (both those that develop into persons and those that do not) offered in this book were to be adopted in full by German courts and the legislature, several current rulings could be made more coherent while other elements would have to change. There are at least three areas in German law that could be made more intelligible. The first concerns the differential treatment between harming and destroying embryos. Currently, it is hard to explain why, if all embryos equally share human dignity and a right to life, we should judge harming them more harshly than destroying them. According to the PDP, this is easily accounted for, as our chief concern is with persons and the embryos they developed from. Therefore, it is worse to injure an embryo that will be born than to destroy an embryo. When it comes to the latter, we thus have no reason to be concerned about its demise (unless the death was brought about by a third party. In that case, the woman carrying the embryo would have to be compensated for the loss she incurred).

Second, the differential treatment of embryos according to § 218 StGB and the ESchG would disappear. As discussed earlier, not only does the ESchG protect embryos starting from a much earlier period of their existence, it also is much stricter about the conditions under which they can be created and carried to term. For the PDP it does not matter whether embryos exist in vitro or in vivo. Both are equally protected from conception onward if they develop into persons. At the same time, both are equally unprotected if no woman wants to implant them or if women want to end their assistance. Moreover, both are supposed to be given equal opportunities to develop into persons, meaning that embryos in vitro are not denied a chance to continue their existence if there are women who are willing to carry them to term, regardless of whether they are the biological mothers or not.[23]

Finally, the treatment of stem cell research would become less hypocritical. This is because the cells used could, in principle at least, be derived from German embryos as well (certainly after the embryos in question have been offered up for adoption and no woman wants to carry them to term).

The most significant issue that would have to change would be the Constitutional Court's attitude toward women and their role in the reproductive process. Rather than expect women to honor the continuity in a human being's life (i.e., the human dignity and right to life of the embryo), it would have to acknowledge that embryos have no independent way of continuing their development as human beings. The court would have to realize that women have legitimate claims to refuse their assistance. Thus, rather than expect women to fulfill a duty to continue their pregnancies, the court (and society quite generally) should appreciate such acts as ones women cannot be required to perform. Women should thus be praised for carrying their children to term and not blamed for deciding not to.

Next I turn to a country that approaches the question of how to treat embryos quite differently. In the United States, pro-choice advocates like to bracket the question of when life begins. That, however, makes it more difficult for them to protect persons when they need protection the most, namely when they are still early embryos.

3 THE MORAL ANONYMITY OF EMBRYOS

THE AMERICAN CASE

In contrast to Germany, the United States has liberal abortion laws, an expanding market for in vitro fertilization (IVF), and routine performance of preimplantation genetic diagnosis (PGD) for a variety of genetic predispositions (including gender selection). Embryo research is thriving. The United States emerged from its abortion controversy having bracketed the question of when life begins. Embryos, therefore, have nothing like the constitutional protection they are accorded in Germany. Thus, as a political and legal matter, the moral value of embryos, especially early embryos, is still an unresolved and therefore highly contentious issue. In constant fear that women's right to self-determination will be scaled back, pro-choice advocates frequently find it difficult to make any clear statements concerning the moral value of embryos. The continued controversy makes them wary of anything that may look like "caving in" to their opponents' arguments.

This may appear to make it difficult for pro-choice advocates to endorse the protection of some embryos (i.e., those that end up being born) from the moment of conception. The reason it is important to protect these embryos will become most obvious in the second part of the book, when the issue is about legitimate forms of genetic manipulation. However, it is already apparent in the context of prenatal injury claims that even the most passionate defender of a woman's right to abortion needs to acknowledge that embryos that will be born warrant our moral consideration even at the earliest stages of their development. As the PDP offers a way not only to protect a woman's right to end her pregnancy but also to protect embryos from the moment of conception (for the sake of the persons they develop into), the central argument made in this chapter is that the PDP is very attractive for pro-choice advocates. Something similar is true for supporters of stem cell research. Although they obviously believe that early embryos can be destroyed for research purposes, they do not necessarily have anything at stake in believing that all embryos should end that way or that those continuing their development into persons should not be treated with care. Thus, there is nothing in principle standing in the way for stem cell supporters to allow for some embryos to be protected from the moment of conception. Endorsing the PDP would thus enable them to hold onto their view of the embryo (i.e., that it is of no or only little moral value) while protecting the interests of future persons.

In a way, the argument in this chapter must proceed in the opposite way from how it did in the chapter on Germany. To show that the PDP is a viable and helpful option in the German case, I had to demonstrate that a legal and political framework committed to protecting the human dignity and right to life of embryos is not necessarily also committed to protecting all embryos equally. In contrast, part of the challenge in the U.S. case is to show that a political and legal order committed to bracketing the question of when life begins can still protect some embryos from the moment of conception.

The argument unfolds in four steps. In a first step I briefly review the history of the abortion debate in the United States and the central Supreme Court ruling *Roe v. Wade* (1973). This shows that remaining agnostic about when life begins leaves pro-choice advocates with no firm commitment to the embryo's value and thus raises the question as to what extent they could endorse a principle that protects some embryos from the moment of conception, as the PDP does (section 1). In a second step I take a look at tort law, especially prenatal injury cases. This reveals that there is no difficulty, in principle, for those in favor of women's right to end their pregnancies to agree that injuries to embryos that end up being born should be avoided (section 2). In a third step I take a glimpse into criminal law. This illustrates that there should be no problem for pro-choice advocates to punish third parties for committing crimes against the unborn. A more challenging case arises when it is the mother herself who threatens the health of her fetus. But here again, I demonstrate that pro-choice advocates should be able to agree that it is morally desirable, in principle, that future children not be harmed (section 3). In a fourth step I explore to what extent the PDP would be acceptable for supporters of technologies that involve the destruction of embryos, such as assisted reproductive technologies (ARTs) and stem cell research. I show that even here there is no reason why proponents of such technologies should not be willing to protect some embryos (section 4).

1. The U.S. Abortion Debate

I begin the first step of the argument by providing a brief background to the U.S. abortion debate and the events that led up to *Roe v. Wade* (a). Then, a short discussion of *Roe v. Wade* shows that the abortion debate leaves pro-choice advocates ill-equipped for protecting embryos (b).

(a) A Brief Sketch of the Historical Background. Up until the 1960s, abortion was strictly prohibited in all states, the most common exception being to save or preserve the life of the mother. Two states (Alabama and the District of Columbia) went so far as to permit abortion if the health of the woman was endangered by the pregnancy; three other states (Massachusetts, New Jersey, and Pennsylvania) permitted abortions that were not "unlawfully performed" or not "without lawful justification," leaving the exact determination of these terms up to the courts.

The American Law Institute's Model Penal Code of 1962 suggested a liberalization of the criminal law on abortion. According to the Model Penal Code, an abortion was justified if a licensed physician "believes there is substantial risk that continuance of the pregnancy would gravely impair the physical or mental health of the mother or that the child would be born with grave physical or mental defect, or that the pregnancy resulted from rape, incest, or other felonious intercourse" (MPC, § 230.3 (2)). Colorado, California, and North Carolina were the first states to "pick up on" the new Model Penal Code and liberalize their abortion regulations. In 1970, New York, in turn, was the first state to allow abortion "on demand," which meant that women could elect to terminate their pregnancies until the 24th week. After that, abortion was considered homicide. This example was followed by Alaska, Hawaii, and Washington.

Shortly after its enactment, New York's new abortion statute was challenged by Robert Byrn, who was appointed guardian *ad litem* for the unborn child "Roe," and all other unborn infants facing a woman's choice to abort, in *Byrn v. New York City Health & Hospital Corp.* (1972). The law was upheld by the New York Court of Appeals. This is an interesting case for two reasons. First, it was an instance in which conservatives used the judiciary to challenge liberal legislation. Later, after *Roe*, this would turn out to be one of the great sources of criticism that conservatives launched against liberals: that by going through the Supreme Court, they took the issue out of the political process to superimpose their views.

Second, the *Byrn* decision highlights a pre-Roe liberal solution to dealing with the problem of establishing the moral status of the embryo. The Court started out by arguing that the embryo is, biologically speaking, an independent, live, potential human being that "has an autonomy of development and character although it is for the period of gestation *dependent* upon the mother" (*Byrn* 1972, 392; emphasis added). Interestingly, however, the Court decided that whatever may be true biologically does not determine the legal status of the embryo.

> Whether the law should accord legal personality is a policy question which in most instances devolves on the Legislature, subject again of course to the Constitution as it has been "legally" rendered. That the legislative action may be wise or unwise, even unjust and violative of principles beyond the law, does not change the legal issue or how it is to be resolved. The point is that it is a policy determination whether legal personality should attach and not a question of biological or "natural" correspondence. (*Byrn* 1972, 393)

Suggesting that the legislature should decide who is a person and who is not gives rise to a concern clearly expressed by the dissenting judge, Adrian Burke. He claimed that "to equate the judicial deference to the wiseness of a Legislature in a local zoning case with the case of the destruction of a child in embryo that is conceded to be 'human' and is 'unquestionably alive' is an acceptance of the thesis that the 'State is supreme,' and that 'live human beings' have no inalienable rights in this country" (*Byrn* 1972, 397).

The question of whether the legislature must respect some natural or preconventional "truth" about the moral status of the human embryo or may decide on its legal status, regardless of any such "truth," is highly intriguing. But the fierce debates about abortion that followed did not turn on this issue. For better or worse, the central issue connected to *Roe v. Wade* concerned the extent to which it is possible to devise policies that are truly neutral with regard to ethical questions (such as when human life begins) so that each person remains free to decide these issues for him or herself.

(b) Roe v. Wade. We saw that in Germany the need to liberalize abortion was clearly driven by a change of mores in society (see chapter 2, section 1). The same is true of the United States. According to a 1975 Gallup Poll survey, about the same percentage of Americans fell into each of the extremes of the spectrum: About 21 percent thought that abortion should be legal under all circumstances, and 22 percent argued that abortion should be illegal under all circumstances. The remaining 54 percent said abortion should be legal under certain circumstances (Gallup 2003, 204). At the same time, there were strong social forces that worked for liberalization, especially the vibrant women's movement toward the end of the 1960s, which radicalized and took to the streets their fight for the right to have legal abortions. On November 29, 1970, Jane Brody (1970) wrote in *The New York Times*:

> A dramatic liberalization of public attitudes and practices regarding abortions appears to be sweeping the country, even in a number of states that still have restrictive abortion laws. (. . .) The new view on abortions reflects the combined action of many social forces, among them a growing concern with overpopulation, increasing demands for women's rights and roles outside the home, rising welfare rolls and illegitimacy rates, growing numbers of child abuse and child neglect cases and a general easing of sexual proscriptions. (p. 52)

When it comes to portraying the mood of the country at that time, it is also noteworthy that 1971 was the year in which John Rawls published his seminal work *A Theory of Justice*. In it, he articulates a version of liberalism that to some extent reflects the spirit of the time but that also sets the stage for subsequent thinking on how to assure equal liberty for all in a pluralist society in which a consensus on values is impossible. He develops a theory of justice as fairness, disputing the utilitarian claim that a political community should always pursue the strategy that seeks to maximize a certain unit of value, be it utility or happiness. This, according to Rawls, fails to take seriously the separateness of persons. He thus rejects the idea that persons may be used in that way for the greater good of the whole. Instead, he insists that persons must be taken seriously as ends in themselves. He maintains that it is the purpose of government to ensure this by refraining from making value judgments that preempt certain individuals from choosing their own good in their own way. As a procedural matter, government should therefore remain neutral on all questions concerning issues that rational people could and would disagree on. It is precisely this kind of bracketing of value choices that, in 1973, the Supreme Court attempted in its decisive case on abortion, *Roe v. Wade.*

"Roe" was an unmarried pregnant woman living in Texas who did not want to continue her pregnancy. Since the Texas statute on abortion permitted the termination of pregnancy only to save the life of the woman and her life was not threatened, she brought a class action challenging the constitutionality of the state criminal statute. When the case reached the Supreme Court, the Court decided the issue in Roe's favor. It did this by circumventing the contentious question of when life begins and by instead taking recourse to the right to privacy. Although this "right" is technically speaking not included in the Constitution, it has nevertheless been inferred from the substantive liberties protected by the due process clause of the Fourteenth Amendment (*Griswold v. Connecticut* 1965). As the Supreme Court stated in a later abortion case: "It is a promise of the Constitution that there is a realm of personal liberty which the government may not enter" (*Planned Parenthood of Southeastern Pennsylvania v. Casey* 1992, 847).

According to *Roe*, because a woman has the right to determine what happens with her body, she may decide to have an abortion up until the point at which the fetus could survive outside the woman's womb, that is, the point of so-called viability. In a closely calculated trimester ruling, viability is assumed to be the state of affairs commencing with the third trimester. As of that point, the state begins to have both an "important and legitimate interest in preserving and protecting the health of the pregnant woman" and, at the same time, an "important and legitimate interest in protecting the potentiality of human life" (*Roe* 1973, 162). During the second trimester, the state may restrict abortions only for the purpose of protecting the health of pregnant women. In the first trimester, the state has no claim to prevent women from terminating their pregnancies.[1]

Although the *Roe* court argued that "the word 'person,' as used in the Fourteenth Amendment, does not include the unborn" (*Roe* 1973, 158), it did not want to determine when life begins: "When those trained in the respective disciplines of medicine, philosophy, and theology are unable to arrive at any consensus, the judiciary, at this point of development of man's knowledge, is not in a position to speculate as to the answer" (*Roe* 1973, 159). This reasoning stands in marked difference to the way the *Byrn* court thought about determining the moral value of embryos. In this sense, *Roe* is a more modest and therefore elegant solution. It does, however, make a similarly clear statement regarding the moral value of embryos as did the court in *Byrn*: that destroying the embryo is not the same as killing a born person. Therefore, as many critics of the decision have been quick to point out, the liberal bracketing solution came at a much higher cost to those who believe that the embryo is a person from the moment of conception than to those who do not believe that the embryo must be protected in the same way born persons must be (Sandel 1982, 21).[2]

Roe never ceased to be highly controversial among Americans. Individual states have continually attempted to undermine[3] or put restrictions on the ruling. Efforts to achieve further restrictions have frequently succeeded,[4] so that several states have added various qualifications to a woman's right to have an abortion, such as requiring minors to notify their parents, compelling women to undergo counseling, and/or demanding that they wait twenty-four hours before having an abortion, as well as severely limiting the permissibility of or even proscribing late-term abortions.[5] However, thus far at least, *Roe* has survived.

Unlike the abortion decisions in Germany, *Roe* itself provided no guidelines for thinking about the moral status of the early embryo. The question is to what extent it commits its proponents (or pro-choice advocates in general) to deny that any embryos should be protected from the moment of conception, or, to put it differently, whether holding that some embryos should be protected from the moment of conception, as the PDP does, would necessarily subvert one's defense of a woman's right to self-determination. To answer this, I look at the case of embryo protection outside of the abortion context.

2. Tort Law: Prenatal Injury Cases

In prenatal injury cases, children (or someone on their behalf) can sue for injuries incurred while in the womb. This poses a potential problem for pro-choice advocates. If they are going to maintain that fetuses are not entities with rights and interests, then it is unclear how fetuses can be injured in any legally relevant sense, at least prior to viability. In other words, to accept prenatal injury cases, pro-choice advocates must acknowledge that unborn children are entities that can be harmed at any gestational age.

Not until fairly recently was it recognized that the embryo is not just part of the female organism. In the early years of the twentieth century, it was generally held that the fetus did not count as a separate entity even right before birth. Take the historical turn-of-the-century case of Ada A. Allaire. On February 2, 1896, she was hurt while riding an elevator in the hospital she was supposed to give birth in a few days later. As a result of her serious injuries, her child, born four days after the accident, suffered severe deformities. Four years later, the Illinois Supreme Court rejected the suit on behalf of the child against the hospital for the injuries he sustained as a fetus, because it argued that until birth the fetus is "part" of the woman carrying it. The court worried that if "the action can be maintained, it necessarily follows that an infant may maintain an action against his own mother for injuries occasioned by the negligence of the mother while pregnant with it. We are of the opinion that the action will not lie" (*Allaire v. St. Luke's Hospital* 1900, 16).[6]

What is noteworthy about this case is the dissent to the court's opinion by Justice Carroll Boggs. He noted that medical science had proven that fetuses toward the end of pregnancy can live separately from the mother, even if she died. Furthermore, he reminded his contemporaries that there were various instances in the common law that granted a fetus personhood starting as early as conception (e.g., in the case of inheritance laws). In addition, Boggs pointed out that the common law provided that if one should unlawfully beat a pregnant woman and thereby kill the fetus in the womb, that crime would be punished as homicide or manslaughter. Moreover, if the child was born alive and then later died as the result of the injuries inflicted during the beating on the embryo from which the child emerged, the perpetrator would be charged with murder (the "born alive rule"). The common law considered life to begin at quickening (i.e., when the "infant is able to stir in the mother's womb"). Given these facts, Boggs came to the conclusion that "it is but natural justice that such an infant, if born alive, should be allowed to maintain an action in the courts for injuries so wrongly committed upon its person while still in the womb of the mother" (*Allaire* 1900, 23).

But it was not until 1946 that the theory of the fetus being merely part of the mother was overruled. In *Bonbrest v. Kotz* (1946), the District Court for the District of Columbia decided that a viable fetus born alive could claim injuries incurred while in the womb. Other cases followed, and a new "theory" of the fetus took hold that recognized the fetus as a separate entity. In the 1960 case *Smith v. Brennan*, the New Jersey Supreme Court held that children could sue for injuries negligently inflicted on them prior to birth. On July 25, 1956, while the infant plaintiff Sean Smith was still in the womb, his mother was involved in a car accident. He was born on October 8, 1956, with deformed legs and feet, most likely as a result of this accident. The court held the following:

> The semantic argument whether an unborn child is a 'person in being' seems to us beside the point. There is no question that conception sets in motion biological processes which if undisturbed will produce what every one will concede to be a person in being. If in the meanwhile those processes can be disrupted resulting in the harm to the child when born, it is immaterial whether before birth the child is considered a person in being. And regardless of analogies to other areas of the law, justice requires that the principle be recognized that a child has a legal right to begin life with a sound mind and body. (*Smith* 1960, 364)

The court understood that it matters to persons what happened to the embryos they emerged from, regardless of what we think of the moral value of embryos quite generally. The justices also mention that it is irrelevant when the injury to the embryo occurred (i.e., whether the embryo was viable at that moment or not). Their reasons for pointing this out, however, are primarily practical concerns regarding the difficulty of determining viability.

> We see no reason for denying recovery for a prenatal injury because it occurred before the infant was capable of separate existence. In the first place, age is not the sole measure of viability, and there is no real way of determining in a borderline case whether or not a fetus was viable at the time of the injury, unless it is immediately born. Therefore, the viability rule is impossible of practical application. (*Smith* 1960, 367)

By this time, the court had arrived at an understanding of the fetus as being intimately connected to the child born from it, either because of the continuous development between them or because of their numerical identity (or both). But how can harm to a person who was not yet a person when the harm occurred be legally redressed? In other words, is this "new" understanding not in direct conflict with *Roe's* holding that the fetus is not a person? Bonnie Steinbock (2011) persuasively argues that there is no conflict in principle for pro-choice advocates to accept prenatal injury cases. This is because it is not the damage to the fetus that is compensated for but the harm that the born child must suffer as a result of injuries that occurred when she was not yet a person: "What matters is that there now exists a harmed individual whose suffering is the result of another's negligence, and who thus deserves to be compensated" (p. 125).

When pro-choice advocates think about the increased potential of harm and injury future persons are subject to when the embryos they develop out of are exposed to genetic testing and/or manipulation, their argument could be very similar. Therefore, just as pro-choice advocates could sign off on prenatal injury claims without coming into conflict with their holding in *Roe*, they could and should sign off on protecting embryos that are intended for birth during ART procedures, PGD, or genetic manipulation. In the case of prenatal injury claims Steinbock argues that children sue in their position as children who have to bear the consequences of harms previously inflicted—regardless of when these harms occurred. Thus, children could sue for damages suffered while they were still embryos consisting of eight cells in a petri dish.

What Steinbock probably would disapprove of is a case in which these very early embryos were appointed guardians who could sue on their behalf, regardless of whether children were ever born from these embryos. This is an important point: The reason embryos are protected in some cases—that is, the reason why harm to embryos can be wrong—is not because the embryos themselves, as embryos, have moral standing of any particular sort. Rather, it is because the persons these embryos will come to be have moral standing. The embryos from which they develop should therefore be treated in anticipation of this standing.

One might think that tort cases are not particularly persuasive proof of the claim that pro-choice advocates should have no difficulty agreeing in principle that at least some embryos need to be protected because not so much is at stake: Tort cases "merely" deal with monetary compensation for the survivors of injuries or of a loss. But a basic commitment to holding that some embryos should be protected while others should not can also be illustrated with criminal law cases.

3. Criminal Law and the Fetus

Attributing any kind of moral status, never mind personhood, to the fetus in criminal law is more of a statement than anything decided in tort law. This, is partly because it involves punishment. Moreover, criminal offenses arguably are of greater social significance, as they indicate those actions that society conceives of as especially threatening to its normative order and therefore condemns. In the following I review two kinds of cases: first, cases in which actions of third parties lead to the injury or death of a fetus (a) and second, cases in which actions of pregnant women endanger the health or life of their fetus (b). Both instances show that there is no difficulty in principle for pro-choice advocates to endorse the protection of fetuses that develop into persons from being injured. This holds also for cases in which the woman herself threatens the health of the fetus she ends up giving birth to.

(a) **Fetal Injury or Death by Third Party.** Many states have developed means to punish crimes that result in injury or death of a fetus by a third party.[7] In some states, legislation has "merely" increased the penalties for crimes against pregnant women.[8] In a number of cases, however, the legislature specifically includes the fetus in its homicide or manslaughter laws.[9] Of the thirty-five states that have fetal homicide laws, more than half include the earliest stages of gestation or at least do not rule these stages out (by not further specifying unborn life). Of those that do not include the earliest stages of a fetus's life, several punish crimes against "quick" fetuses,[10] while others penalize crimes against viable fetuses.[11]

The question is whether the fact that some states declare the fetus a person when it comes to its criminal statutes undermines the basic holding in *Roe*. Ronald Dworkin (1992) does not think so. The reason fetal manslaughter laws are legitimate in Dworkin's estimation is because no one should have the right to harm or destroy (anything for that matter) with impunity.

> There is no doubt that a state can protect the life of a fetus in a variety of ways. A state can make it murder for a third party intentionally to kill a fetus, as Illinois has done, for example, or "feticide" for anyone willfully to kill a quickened fetus by an injury that would be murder if it resulted in the death of the mother, as Georgia has. These laws violate no constitutional rights, because no one has a constitutional right to injure with impunity. (p. 400)

Dworkin argues that, from a pro-choice perspective, declaring the fetus a person in this way—that is, as an entity the killing of which is punishable as manslaughter—is unproblematic as long as this language and law do not infringe on "real people's" rights (i.e., women's right to determine what happens to their bodies). However, it is likely to matter to the person who kills a pregnant woman whether he or she will be charged for one or two offenses. Moreover, as an empirical matter, if all states are allowed to create a set of cases that make the treatment of embryos as persons into precedents, a new reality may be created. This may be a reality in which people have grown used to thinking of embryos as persons and thus change their attitudes about abortion. With this risk in mind, some conclude that crimes against the fetus should always be treated as part of the crime against the mother (Steinbock 2011, 132f.).

This concern highlights a principal dilemma of pro-choice advocates in the United States. On the one hand, they understand that "as a matter of biological fact, the separate existence of the fetus throughout pregnancy must be conceded. It is not a mere body part" (Steinbock 2011, 129). They might even agree that, from a moral point of view, the embryo has some value on its own, certainly once it becomes a sentient or viable human being. But politically, it is endemically difficult for them to express this view without endangering a woman's right to choose to have an abortion.[12]

The concern that precedents might be established on the state level for thinking of the fetus as an independent entity was amplified when, on April 1,

2004, President Bush made it a separate crime to harm the fetus—regardless of its gestational age—during the commission of a federal criminal offense against a woman in the so-called Unborn Victims of Violence Act. It establishes that harm done to the fetus should be treated in exactly the same way as the harm done to the mother, regardless of whether the person harming the fetus was aware that the woman was pregnant or had any intention of harming the fetus.[13] One argument for the passing of the measure was that most states already had fetal homicide, fetal manslaughter, or feticide laws. Therefore, having such language incorporated in federal legislation could be presented as a merely logical extension and necessary addition to the legal framework (Holzapfel 2002, 449). President Bush invoked a moral vision of communal outreach as the reason for why the act was necessary. "The moral concern of humanity extends to those unborn children who are harmed or killed in crimes against their mothers. And now, the protection of federal law extends to those children, as well. With this action, we widen the circle of compassion and inclusion in our society, and we reaffirm that the United States of America is building a culture of life." (Bush 2004, 498)

Thus, the fear may be warranted that treating the death of a fetus as a separate crime will habituate people into thinking that killing fetuses is like killing persons. This, however, is a primarily strategic consideration. The real question is whether it is persuasive to think that the killing of a fetus ought to be treated as an independent offense. To answer this, we need to ask what makes it wrong to kill the fetus of a woman who was planning to give birth to it. There are two possible responses.

First, the embryo is denied its opportunity to be carried to term. This might be taken to imply that killing the fetus should indeed be treated as a separate crime. In chapter 1 I argued that third parties have a duty to value the creation of persons. This would make it wrong for a doctor, a scientist, or even a parent to destroy an embryo if there is a woman willing to be pregnant with it. The case might appear to present itself differently when a third party commits a crime against a woman and thereby kills her embryo. This is because here the embryo is already in the womb of a woman who wants to give birth to it and may be much more advanced in its development than an embryo in a petri dish. The further embryos have advanced and the more women have emotionally and physically invested in their existence, the worse a crime that kills the embryo may be considered to be—for the pregnant woman. From the embryo's perspective, however, the situation is not so different in the two cases. Embryos do not have a right to be born; their creation should merely not be obstructed if there are women willing to be pregnant with them. Thus, although the duty to value the creation of persons may have been violated, embryos will not be wronged in an offense against their mothers that kills them. Moreover, a further complication in some of the criminal cases is that persons can only have violated a duty to honor the creation of persons if they knew or could have known that they were denying an embryo the opportunity to continue its existence through their actions. This would fail to capture all those attacks against pregnant women in which the attacker was not and could not have been aware of the pregnancy. Thus, whatever may be wrong about denying a fetus the opportunity to continue its existence does not amount to constituting a separate felony.

But as already briefly mentioned, there is a second aspect that may render the killing of a fetus that a woman intends to carry to term wrong. This is that the woman suffers a serious loss. Not only did she (presumably) have to endure injuries to her own body, she has also lost the child she was expecting.[14] She has given her physical assistance to continue the life of what she hoped would be her future child and is likely to have much more than her body invested in this process. No one has a right to take something as personal and as important as this away from her with impunity. Thus, there are good reasons to take into account the woman's additional, serious loss when it comes to sentencing the offender.

These considerations show that whatever additional punishment may be warranted in cases in which a criminal offense against the woman leads to the death of her fetus, it should be primarily grounded in the woman's loss and not in that of a separate life. Nothing in this formulation is problematic for pro-choice advocates, as they do not have anything at stake in denying that something of great importance is lost for women who intend to carry their fetus to term if the latter is killed. The really difficult cases arise when, in non-abortion contexts, it is the pregnant woman herself who poses a threat to the well-being of her fetus.

(b) **Woman v. Fetus.** Even for those who believe that a third party should not be allowed to infringe on a woman's reproductive choice by harming her embryo, it is not immediately clear what the verdict should be on women who harm the fetus they intend to carry to term. Traditionally, the issues raised in this situation concern whether and to what extent the state can force a woman to "respect" the life and health of her unborn child. The central question is whether the state can enforce a mother's duty to care for her fetus in the negative sense of asking her not to commit acts that would either endanger the health of her fetus or threaten her fetus's life. Both endangering the health and threatening the life of her fetus are potential consequences of (ab)using crack cocaine, for instance. A separate set of issues involves questions about whether a mother may refuse to consent to surgery either to avert danger to her fetus's health or to save its life.

Consider the case of twenty-three-year-old Regina McKnight. She was the first woman to be convicted of homicide by a state Supreme Court because her baby was stillborn due to her having smoked crack cocaine while pregnant (*State v. McKnight* 2003). She was initially given a twenty-year sentence that was later suspended to twelve years in prison with no chance of parole.[15] The court had decided to expand the definition of "child" in their child abuse statute to apply to a viable fetus. *Whitner v. State* (1997) had previously held that the word "child" as it is used in its abuse and homicide statute included the viable fetus. But mothers who take drugs do not have to kill their fetuses to be prosecuted. Several women have been charged with a criminal offense whose children were born, in many cases apparently healthy (Paltrow 1992).

Feminists have been adamant in rejecting this kind of judicial (or in other cases legislative) activism for its hypocrisy. Some suspect, as does Dorothy Roberts (1991), that "the prosecution of drug-addicted mothers is part of an alarming trend towards greater state intervention into the lives of pregnant women under the rationale of protecting the fetus from harm" (p. 1421). Roberts points out that women who are poor and of color are most susceptible to government intrusions because they are "the least likely to obtain adequate prenatal care, the most vulnerable to government monitoring, and the least able to conform to the white, middle-class standard of motherhood" (p. 1422).

Moreover, many claim that if states are really so interested in the life of the fetus, they should be helping and supporting pregnant women as opposed to threatening them with prison. Janet Gallagher (1995), for instance, scolds that "giving fetuses rights and lawyers, while failing to provide accessible prenatal care and drug treatment on demand for the women who carry them, is mere posturing—a paradigm of social bad faith" (p. 361). Lynn Christopher, director of the women's program at the Mountain Manor Treatment Center at Emmitsburg, Maryland, herself a recovering addict, is quoted as saying: "People think that women who use drugs while they are pregnant are evil. They forget that addiction is a disease. You would never show that lack of compassion for someone who has cancer or another disease" (Norris 1991, A1). One of the chief concerns about this, according to Howard Simon, is that "the practical effect of this kind of prosecution is to drive pregnant women from prenatal care. That is a horrible consequence" (Wilkerson 1991, A15).

From the standpoint of the PDP, as women are always entitled to terminate their pregnancies, cases such as that of Regina McKnight should certainly not provide the basis for a criminal charge. Fetuses are not persons, and as long as a fetus does not develop into a person, there is no person to whom the fate of any particular fetus matters from a first-personal perspective. The issue presents itself differently in cases in which the mother's use of crack cocaine (or some other drug) injures a fetus that ends up being born. When pro-choice advocates and feminists oppose claims to take criminal action against these women, the question is whether this means that they also reject the PDP or, in other words, the claim that embryos that develop into persons need to be protected from the moment of conception. To answer this I take a moment to explore various interpretations of what pro-choice advocates and feminists may propose when they oppose legal measures to protect fetuses from their mothers' behavior. They may be making one of four claims (separately or in combination), only the fourth of which is in conflict with the PDP.

First, they may merely be remarking that if women were helped as opposed to being criminally charged, harm to future persons could be more successfully avoided. This is obviously in sync with the PDP, as the ultimate aim of this kind of objection to the prosecution of pregnant women is to protect both pregnant women and the embryos they intend to carry to term. They just want to accomplish this more effectively.

Second, they may (also) be contending that the state simply has no mandate for punishing women in the name of future persons. Here there is also no reason to think that people making this claim do not believe that there is a moral obligation not to harm future persons. They could, for instance, think that women, who, for whatever reason, violate their duty to protect embryos they intend to carry to term, should be subject to moral blame but are not legitimate targets of legal action. However, given that being subject to moral blame is itself a form of (not so benign) punishment, some might find the third interpretation more attractive.

The third reading is that pro-choice advocates and feminists might be arguing that women are entitled to harm the embryo they are carrying under extreme and for them unavoidable circumstances (e.g., a severe drug addiction) because without their assistance this embryo would neither exist nor be able to continue its existence. Such a claim would also fail to undermine the basic premise of the PDP. The latter states only that it is, in principle, wrong to harm embryos that develop into persons. Arguably, a serious drug addiction is an unavoidable harm that is to be treated akin to the presence of a congenital disease. Although John A. Robertson (1994) would probably not include drug addiction in the category of unavoidable harm, he offers a helpful explanation for why women can damage their children in situations that are inescapable "because there is no way that the child can be conceived or be born and not be damaged" (p. 176).

The reason Robertson would probably not include drug addiction in his category of unavoidable harm is that the drug addiction may damage an otherwise healthy embryo whereas a congenital disease will, from the start, produce an embryo with the disease. But given that there is no way for the otherwise healthy embryo to stay healthy given the drug addiction of its mother, the cases end up being more similar than not. This would be different only in those instances in which pregnant women truly have a choice about whether to take drugs or not, as they presumably have in cases in which they casually (ab)use tobacco and alcohol, for instance. Then, indeed, they would, according to the PDP, have a moral obligation to prevent harm to their unborn children if they intend to give birth to them. Although it remains true that their embryos could not exist, develop, or be born without them, once women have decided to create a second person, they have to treat their embryo in anticipation of their future child.

This brings me to the fourth possible claim pro-choice advocates and feminists could be making in opposition to legal sanctions against pregnant women who threaten the health of their fetuses. They may be saying that women can do with their bodies as they please, at all times and regardless of what effects their behavior might have on their future children. This would clearly go against the grain of the PDP. The latter requires women (who are in a position to do so) to take some responsibility for their decision to carry their embryo to term, especially given that they can change their minds up until the moment that their child is, in fact, separate from them.

Although some pro-choice advocates and feminists may hold this last position, my point here is to show that it is not inevitable that they do. Just because one is generally against criminally sanctioning women who threaten the health of their offspring does not mean that one is necessarily against a duty to protect future persons from harm. In other words, there is nothing in principle preventing pro-choice advocates and feminists from endorsing the PDP as long as two conditions obtain. First, the responsibility to protect embryos that will be born may not be attached to a state mandate to force women to comply or to punish them for not doing so. Second, it is important that women who are held responsible for protecting embryos they intend to give birth to are not held responsible for the wrong things (for not abruptly ending a drug addiction, for instance) and are supported by society in their efforts to do the right things (by being given free and widely available access to prenatal care facilities and drug-treatment programs, for instance). The PDP can easily accommodate both conditions. There is nothing about this principle that would automatically authorize the state to enforce the protection of embryos that develop into persons. One needs additional arguments for transforming moral claims into legal ones. Moreover, as I argued earlier, women cannot be held responsible for unavoidable conditions. The second part of the last condition (i.e., that society has an obligation to help) needs to be argued for separately. I do so in the final chapter of this book (chapter 6, section 3).

Besides drug abuse, there are various other cases that invoke the state's interest in preserving the life of the fetus, even against the mother's explicit wishes.[16] Pro-choice advocates and feminists tend to oppose most of these as well, especially when the fetus concerned is previable.[17] April Cherry (2004), for instance, believes that *Roe* and its progeny went much too far with their pronouncements that the state had a compelling interest in the life of viable fetuses. This, according to Cherry, has given individual states an opportunity to misapply *Roe's* central contention and use it to oppress women in all areas besides abortion. "Both state and federal courts allow treatment of pregnant women when such treatment is believed to be in the best interest of the fetus. The use of *Roe* in this context severely restricts the decisional and physical privacy of individual women, and works to severely limit the citizenship of women as a social group" (p. 724).

Cherry is certainly right to point out that women should not accept a "state interest" overriding their right to self-determination, especially when it comes to their decision to refuse a treatment that would save the life of their fetus. According to the view proposed here, women cannot be obliged to give birth to a living child. They may thus choose a course of action that will result in the death of their fetus.

Consider, for better illustration, the case of *Pemberton v. Tallahassee Memorial Regional Medical Center, Inc.* (1999). Here, a woman who had decided to labor at home with a midwife was forced to travel to a hospital to have a cesarean section. The reason was that laboring at home carried a 4 to 6 percent risk of killing the fetus. At this point, it was not the woman's intention to kill her fetus. She wanted to have this child. It might have thus been imprudent for her to take this extra risk. But if the danger was really the death of the child, the PDP explicitly allows a woman to refrain from giving birth. In the extreme and counter to what actually was the case, her standpoint could be interpreted as saying that she either gives birth the way she wants to or not at all. According to the PDP, this would be entirely legitimate. The situation would be different if the child's health were seriously put at risk if she refused surgery. In this case, and if she continued to want to have this child, she might indeed be morally obliged to undergo certain medical procedures (at this point she may have to decide what she wants less, the surgery or the child). As mentioned previously, we would need additional arguments to make this moral claim into one that is legally enforceable. This is true especially given that the "force" that would have to be applied here would involve coercing women into sometimes extremely invasive procedures that would violate their physical integrity.

In sum, there is no reason why pro-choice advocates (and feminists, for that matter) should not be able to agree that a commitment to protecting persons entails a further commitment to protecting the embryos they develop from. This position does not undermine their ability to remain dedicated to protecting women's right to self-determination. Women are always left to decide whether they want to continue their pregnancies or not. The only thing they would be held responsible for is their decision to carry their fetuses to term. In those cases, they have a moral obligation to protect their future children from harm (if, that is, they have the choice of avoiding such harm). As mentioned earlier, in the final chapter of this book I argue that society, in turn, has a moral obligation to support them in fulfilling this obligation (chapter 6, section 3).

The next question concerns whether those who support technologies that require the destruction of early embryos in vitro (such as assisted reproduction and stem cell research) could adopt a principle such as the PDP. At first it might seem far less likely that proponents of such technologies would agree that some embryos ought to be protected than those committed to the protection of women's interests would. While the position of pro-choice advocates does not depend on any particular view of the embryo (although, as I have tried to show, for political purposes a particular view is often assumed—namely that embryos, especially rather early ones, do not have moral value), supporters of technologies that destroy early embryos seem to be forced to deny that early embryos are anything but a clump of cells. But in what follows I show that there is nothing to prevent supporters of technologies that involve the destruction of embryos from endorsing the PDP, or, in other words, the view that embryos that develop into persons ought to be protected from the moment of conception.

4. Assisted Reproductive Technologies and Stem Cell Research

The first American baby conceived with the help of ARTs was born on December 28, 1981, at the General Hospital in Norfolk, Virginia. Every year since, the number of fertility clinics and the number of ART cycles performed has risen steadily. In 2008 there were 436 clinics (out of a total of 475) that reported 46,326 live births (deliveries of one or more living infants) from ART cycles started that year and 61,426 babies born from ART cycles performed that year.[18]

Today, one of the first ethical issues to be mentioned in connection with ARTs is that during fertilization cycles, more embryos are created than can be implanted. This leads to a situation in which many embryos end up either being frozen or discarded. When reproductive technologies were first introduced, the waste of leftover embryos was not generally perceived to be morally troubling. The focus was on the life that was created and not on the thousands of embryos that would be created and destroyed because they were not needed. IVF was widely taken to mark an increase in reproductive choice. Infertility was listed as a disease by the Center for Disease Control and Prevention, and IVF (or any ART, for that matter) was considered the cure.

Thus, before stem cell research retroactively brought to the public's attention the problem that leftover embryos were created and destroyed in the course of most fertility procedures, the original ethical concerns arose in connection with the possibility of freezing leftover embryos. *The New England Journal of Medicine* drew attention to these issues in 1985 with an article titled "Frozen Embryos: Policy Issues" (Grobstein et al. 1985). The authors believed that two ethical problems were likely to emerge once the practice of freezing embryos became established. The first had to do with the increased risk to the embryo from being frozen and then thawed. The second concerned divorcing the embryo from the reproductive context. The authors described how this separation gives the embryo unprecedented autonomy from the woman's body and opens up several nonfamiliar options, such as producing a pregnancy in a woman not biologically related to the embryo and discarding or using embryos for various research purposes. These concerns made Grobstein et al. plead for rethinking the moral value of embryos in vitro.

If anything, current biomedical technologies have aggravated these issues even further. Just consider the possibility of therapeutic cloning, where stem cells are harvested from an embryo and then implanted into an enucleated egg cell so that the original embryo is cloned. From the perspective of the PDP, this would be neither problematic nor warrant much rethinking, were it not for the fact that some of these embryos might be born, in which case it starts to matter what happened to them in the petri dish or in the freezer. But embryos that end up being born are the concern of the second part of this book. For now, the important question is whether someone supporting ARTs as they are currently practiced in the United States (i.e., involving the creation of leftover embryos that remain indefinitely frozen, are donated for research purposes, or are discarded) could support a principle such as the PDP. The problem could be that persons who believe that embryos can be created in excess and then destroyed might have a hard time justifying why some embryos ought to be protected from the moment of conception.

I claim that holding the view that embryos can be frozen, used for research purposes, and discarded is perfectly compatible with thinking that embryos that are implanted into a woman's uterus should be protected from the moment of their conception. I illustrate how these two views can peacefully coexist by considering the case of stem cell research, beginning with a brief overview of the political controversy that has arisen from it.

Just as in Germany, U.S. stem cell policy was a highly contested political issue in 2001. This was the initial year of George W. Bush's presidency. In his first address to the nation on August 9 of that year, he warned that "we have arrived at that brave new world that seemed so distant in 1932, when Aldous Huxley wrote about human beings created in test tubes in what he called a 'hatchery'" (Bush 2001, 185). Bush pleaded for caution in light of the uncertainty and grave dangers he saw connected with stem cell research. He addressed the moral dilemma of having to weigh the ends of science against the value of unborn life.

At the same time, Bush (2001) recognized the therapeutic promises of stem cell research and praised the nation's "long and proud record of leading the world toward advances in science and medicine that improve human life" (p. 184). He then announced a compromise position, one that allowed restricted federal funding for early embryonic stem cell research, limited to the over sixty already existing early embryonic stem cell lines. In this way, he thought he could avoid ethical concerns by permitting American scientists "to explore the promise and potential of stem cell research without crossing a fundamental moral line by providing taxpayer funding that would sanction or encourage further destruction of human embryos that have at least the potential for life" (p. 186).

His stance turned out to be problematic for all concerned. From the perspective of pro-life advocates, it applied a (moral) double-standard: Whereas federally funded researchers can work on the existing stem cell lines, they are not allowed to derive new ones. The basis for this could therefore not be a rejection, in principle, of the destruction of unborn human life, because that would have required the condemnation of *any* measure that has its origin in violating embryos. Therefore, if the president had considered stem cell research fundamentally wrong, then he would have had to advocate criminalizing private research involving the destruction of embryos, as Germany has, for instance.

The Bush position was criticized even more harshly by those in favor of stem cell research. They accused him of being insincere about wanting to further biomedical research. Most scientists argued that everyone, including Bush, knew or should have known that the five dozen already existing stem cell lines would be far from enough for federally funded scientists to do research on. Defenders of Bush's position were quick to point out that these critics seemed to forget the existence of the Dickey-Wicker Amendment, a law that, since 1996, has been passed annually by Congress forbidding the use of federal funds to destroy embryos.[19] Thus, Bush's defenders argued that instead of actively hampering research, what Bush really did was to open the door a little to allow at least some stem cell research to be conducted with federal funds.

On August 9, 2009, President Obama tried to embrace stem cell research more boldly. With an executive order overriding the previous one by Bush, Obama declared that public funds could be used on stem cells that were obtained from leftover embryos without specifying a deadline before which the embryos had to be destroyed. Although public funds could not be used to destroy the embryos themselves, this still gave federally funded research much greater access to many more usable stem cell lines.

But in August 2010, a federal district judge issued an injunction against the further use of leftover embryos (*Sherley et al. v. Sebelius et al.*). The argument was that the executive order President Obama had given the year before ran afoul of the Dickey-Wicker Amendment. Defenders of Obama's executive order argued that it allowed only the use of stem cells from embryos that had been independently destroyed. They maintained that the research they were supporting was separable from the destruction of embryos. The judge did not agree: "ESC [embryonic stem cell] research is clearly research in which an embryo is destroyed. To conduct ESC research, ESCs must be derived from an embryo. The process of deriving ESCs from an embryo results in the destruction of the embryo. Thus, ESC research necessarily depends upon the destruction of a human embryo" (*Sherley* 2010, 12).

We can thus see that the same forces (for and against embryo destruction) are at work in the United States as in Germany—it is just that the legal-political backgrounds and the historical and cultural contexts are different. In the United States, the debate is not about whether stem cell research should be permitted at all. Rather, it is "merely" about whether it should receive federal funding. The interesting question here is to what extent the position in support of stem cell research is compatible with the PDP.

The problem is this: On the one hand, it appears to be less controversial to be in favor of stem cell research than to be in favor of abortion, because stem cell research involves the destruction of embryos that are merely a few days old. They are certainly at a much earlier stage of development than the embryos that women abort. On the other hand, and as I have said before, the reasons for which embryos are destroyed in the context of stem cell research are much less compelling than respecting women's right to self-determination. In the context of stem cell research, embryos compete with the interests of scientists to deepen their understanding of early embryonic development (and the genetic basis of various diseases) as well as with the interests of (potential) patients to have cures developed for a number of fatal illnesses. Once someone has agreed that embryos can be destroyed for these purposes, it may seem difficult to argue that there are any instances in which embryos need to be protected.

However, stem cell research supporters are likely to hold one of two views, both of which could support the PDP. First, they might believe that embryos have no moral value and that it therefore does not matter what is done to them. But just because stem cell research supporters think that embryos have no value does not mean that they think that it is okay to harm embryos that will be born. Many things lacking value in and of themselves must be treated with care in certain contexts. Consider the case of a brick. Although it generally does not matter how we treat bricks, we might have to treat particular bricks with care if they end up being used for building a sacred temple, for instance.

Second, supporters of stem cell research may suppose that embryos have some value but that this value is always outweighed by the interests scientists (and patients) have in destroying these embryos. It is unclear what it means to say that embryos have "some" value if that ends up having very few consequences—if any. However, advocates of this position could, just as proponents of the first position, think that embryos that develop into persons should be protected because these persons have moral standing. Therefore, both positions, one of which stem cell supporters are likely to hold, can encompass the thought that while some embryos (those that develop into persons) ought to be protected from the moment of conception, other embryos (those that do not develop into persons) can be used and destroyed.

I would go even further than that and claim that supporters of stem cell research could also go along with supposing that, in situations in which there are women who are willing to carry embryos to term, these embryos should not be denied their chance to develop into persons. Although this position does not follow from the PDP I maintained that it is a plausible implication of our commitment to persons. Valuing the creation of persons, as I have called it, would prevent a scientist from using embryos for research purposes that have women wanting to have them implanted. In cases where there are no women willing to be pregnant with particular embryos (and to exclude that, I suggested offering embryos up for adoption for a certain amount of time), these embryos that have no chance of developing into persons can be used for research purposes or discarded.

Thus, there is nothing in principle barring supporters of stem cell research from endorsing the PDP. The reason it is important that they do so becomes more apparent in the second part of this book, where the focus is no longer on whether it is permissible to destroy embryos (which is unproblematic according to the PDP as long as there are no women wanting to carry them to term) but on whether it is permissible to interfere with the development of embryos that will be born (which, as it will turn out, *is* problematic according to the PDP).

5. Conclusion

The main aim of this chapter was to show that there is no reason for pro-choice advocates or stem cell supporters in the United States not to endorse the PDP. Unlike the case in Germany, the reason they should adopt the PDP is not so much to make their position more consistent and more persuasive across a variety of issues. Rather, it is to address a blind spot they may be prone to because of their predominant commitment to women or to stem cell research. The fear of undermining women's right to abortion or of state prosecution of pregnant women who behave in ways that endanger the health of their offspring leads many pro-choice advocates and feminists to be suspicious of claims for the protection of embryos, especially early ones. The fear of losing further sources of funding may lead stem cell research supporters to be more adamant than they have to be about insisting that embryos are merely clumps of cells and that none of them need to be treated as if this was different. But both positions run the danger of creating a situation in which a vital and especially vulnerable group of persons is left unprotected, namely persons of the future, to whom what happened to the embryos from which they develop matters. Thus, even pro-choice advocates ardently committed to protecting women's right to self-determination and staunch defenders of stem cell research should adopt the PDP to be able to argue for the protection of those (early) embryos that will be born.

As already mentioned, our duties to protect early embryos become especially important in light of new reprogenetic technologies that aim at genetically selecting or manipulating them so that persons with particular properties are born. This is the subject of the second part of this book.

SELECTION AND MANIPULATION

In the first part of this book, I argued that there is an obligation to protect embryos that will be born. This is because it matters to persons, whose interests we are committed to protecting, what happened to the embryos from which they developed. Given that the new technologies expose embryos that will develop into persons not only to greater risk of harm but also to being genetically manipulated, this "protection" owed to future people needs to be specified. Thus, in the second part of this book the central question is whether we owe future persons more than not actively harming them. Do we, for instance, have an obligation to make genetic changes and if yes, of what kind?

A number of scholars endorse a wide range of possible genetic alterations that parents can or ought to perform on their future children in the name of liberal values such as freedom, equality, and progress (human and/or technological). Some so-called liberal eugenicists think, for instance, that within certain limits parental discretion should include changing the genome of their offspring. Others embrace the idea of enhancing the human species and think parents should do their part when considering the genetic endowment they can give to their children. Again others consider some genetic changes mandatory in the name of social justice. They believe that parents owe their children the provision of an equal starting position in life.

I claim that these approaches do not adequately respect the equal and separate importance of future persons. If they did, they would have to take into account that future persons have a legitimate claim to be valued as the persons they come to be without others having genetically interfered with them. I contend that interventions must be exclusively grounded in respect for future persons' independence. Interventions that go beyond this support a system of asymmetrical power assertion, that is, a system of domination, between the generations.[1]

When I speak of domination, I am referring to a situation in which one party is able to impose her will on another: first, without having to track the avowed or avowable interests of the latter and, second, without the latter being able to challenge decisions so reached. An asymmetrical power relationship of this kind makes every act of those in the more powerful position regarding those who are dependent on them arbitrary, even if the former are always generous and kind toward the latter. The paradigmatic case is that of benevolent masters and their slaves. Even if the masters were so benevolent that they paid heed to every one of their slaves' whims and treated them like their equals on all occasions—and even if none of this was likely to ever change—this would still constitute an instance of domination. This is because the relationship between masters and slaves is structured asymmetrically so that there is always the possibility of the masters changing their minds without the slaves being able to do anything about it. This should worry liberals: Because all persons have equal moral status, such asymmetries cannot be justified in principle. This is so even if such relationships never result in actual violations of anyone's interests. In that sense, those concerned with domination are not so much interested in "merely" defending persons' liberty rights. Rather, they are interested in social and political structures that make it possible for everyone to defend themselves against the imposition of other people's wills. Thus, the social, political, and sometimes economic status of persons should be such that individuals are in a position, if not to actively choose the relationships they want to be a part of, then at least not to be forced to remain subject to relationships or schemes of social cooperation that they would prefer not to be.[2]

Before it is possible to apply the familiar case of political domination to the realm of intergenerational relationships, however, it is important to take into account that although all persons have equal moral status, there are, of course, some interpersonal relationships in which asymmetries are inevitable. Among those are relationships between caregivers and their dependents, between parents and their children, and between the generations more generally. Confronted with relationships of this kind, those worried about domination in the familiar sense have two ways of responding.

First, they could be motivated to fundamentally rethink their basic premise (i.e., that wherever there is asymmetry between persons, there is reason to worry about arbitrariness and domination) and modify it to holding that only those situations are objectionable in which asymmetries are actually taken advantage of by the more powerful party.[3] But this position would take the punch line out of this particular conception of freedom. Its primary strength lies in pointing out situations in which, although no actual liberty infringements are occurring, the equal status of persons is undermined by the mere possibility of one party acting without having to take the affected party's interest into account and without the latter being able to contest decisions so made. This is problematic even if those in the more powerful position are firmly committed to not taking advantage of their superior position.

Second, they could defend their basic premise but qualify it to accommodate asymmetries that are inevitable and thus do not, in the first instance, reflect disrespect for the equal status of persons. To do this, however, it would have to be shown that inevitable asymmetries are indeed innocuous in this way. Consider, for instance, the relationship between the generations. By procreating now rather than later or not at all, those currently living inevitably determine who is born and who is not. That certainly constitutes an asymmetrical situation. Future persons cannot be asked to consent to their being brought into existence. But this situation does not express disrespect for the equal status of future persons. Moreover, it does not even truly empower the procreators, because they cannot choose who is born and who is not (Hanser 1990, 61). They can merely make it the case that someone is born. In some ways, the existence of particular individuals merely "happens" to both parties concerned, those who bring it about and those who receive their lives through it.

The situation presents itself a little differently when it comes to raising children. Here parents have a number of ways in which they can choose to influence their offspring's lives. Some of this is, of course, also inevitable. As the example of feral children shows, human beings need to be cared for and influenced to develop even such basic skills as human walking and talking. But we often expect parents to do much more than merely ensure that their children have a basic set of human skills. The question is, how much more. Parenting is thus a potentially much more troubling situation from the perspective of intergenerational asymmetry than procreation, because even if parents can generally be trusted to be benevolent "masters," they have ample opportunity not to be.

There are, of course, ways to protect children from situations in which parents overstep their boundaries, both through "soft" and "hard" measures. By "soft" I mean the significant amount of social pressure exerted on parents to conform to parenting "norms." These norms vary widely across different times and places, but today in nearly all modern liberal societies, for instance, many consider parenting measures that involve extreme drilling of children or narrowing down their range of opportunities (by neglecting them, for instance) to be unacceptable. "Hard" measures, by contrast, mean actual state interventions, where children are taken away from violent or otherwise abusive parents. Thus, there are various ways in which parents can be forced to track the interests of their children. In other words, there are ways to prevent parents from imposing too much of their own wills on their children and to make them further their children's critical capacities so that they will develop into adults who can question and, if necessary, object to their parents' decisions of how to raise them. Children should be able to complain, for instance, about having being taught piano as opposed to having been sent to ballet classes, and, what is more, they should be able to switch from piano to ballet classes if that is what they would rather do and have a talent for doing.

This having been said, parents can be forced to track their children's interests only if there is a way for them to ascertain such interests. Although this cannot be perfectly achieved, because very young children, for instance, will either not have particular interests or may not be able to express them, both socialization and education are prolonged processes during which parents are able to get to know their children and learn their preferences, skills, and talents. Moreover, what further mitigates the problem of being only imperfectly able to track children's interests is that both socialization and education involve a variety of different persons, so that the power of the parents is somewhat "diluted" over time and mixed with a variety of other sources of influence. This makes it easier for children to eventually mature and be able to independently evaluate and reject some of the choices their parents made regarding their upbringing.

Thus, we might indeed want to change the premise that all situations of asymmetrical relationships are automatically suspect into a more qualified one that exempts asymmetries under two conditions. First, the asymmetry may not reflect a power structure that is disrespectful of the equal status of persons (which inevitable asymmetries usually do not); and second, those in the asymmetrical power position must be forced to (i) track the interests of those affected (to a reasonable extent) and (ii) provide the latter with the means necessary to contest their choices.

I argue that, judged by these criteria, those forms of genetic manipulation frequently defended by liberal eugenicists fail the second condition on both counts. They do not adequately track future persons' interests, nor do they sufficiently consider what is required for future persons to reject their parents' choices. The closest liberal eugenicists come to realizing what I call the right of future persons not to be dominated, or, formulated more positively, future persons' right to independence, is when they restrict parental entitlements to change their child's genetic structure by invoking a child's "right to an open future." Here they concede that genetic manipulation may not be used to limit a child's range of options. But in contrast to how liberal eugenicists understand a child's right to an open future, I claim that children's futures can be sufficiently "open" only if the world they are born into accepts them for who they come to be—without other people having interfered with their genetic make-up to insert their own evaluative preferences. In other words, parents must respect their children as the genuine "others" the natural lottery allows them to be. This is what I call future persons' right to natural independence.

This having been said, children's futures can be sufficiently open only if they have at least the basic mental and physical capacities required for leading a minimally independent life—a life, that is, in which they are not forced to permanently depend on the charitable help of others. The chief problem with being continually forced to rely on the charitable help of others is that it makes persons especially vulnerable to relationships they cannot determine and that they cannot leave (i.e., to situations, again, of domination). I call future persons' entitlement not to be subject to such situations their right to substantial independence.

I therefore argue that children do not only have a right to be independent from their parents' designs (i.e., in their vertical, intergenerational relationships) but also from their contemporaries (i.e., in their horizontal, intragenerational relationships). This might be thought to create a tension. Moreover, one might wonder how the genetic alterations I propose track future persons' interests any better than other sorts of genetic intervention (proposed by liberal eugenicists, for instance) and why they would not also prevent future persons from being able to contest them. All three of these concerns can be addressed together.

I maintain that the only thing parents can know about their future children is that the latter have a right, as (future) persons, to independence. Therefore, as long as parents intervene only to ensure their future children's independence from the charitable help of others, they do the best they can to track future persons' interests. Rather than violating their obligation to respect their children as the independently genetically constituted individuals they enter this world as, they are enabling their children's future independence by ensuring for them the tools necessary to later contest their parents' choices.

This argument unfolds in the next three chapters. To begin, I use the next chapter (chapter 4) to discuss three prominent liberal approaches to the new reprogenetic technologies. I show that they all systematically sell out their commitment to the equal and separate value of (future) persons by embracing genetic manipulation for purposes other than to respect (future) persons' independence. Then, in chapter 5, I present an alternative account proposed by Jürgen Habermas, who rejects the new technologies in the name of the same liberal values that liberal eugenicists invoke in favor of them. I argue that Habermas is too rash in rejecting most uses of new reprogenetic technologies. But I also maintain that it is his basic intuition about the importance of upholding some kind of symmetry in the inevitably asymmetrical relationship between the generations that inspires my own approach. I use the last chapter, chapter 6, to fully develop my own, alternative argument about the importance of respecting and ensuring future persons' natural and substantial independence.

4 THE LIMITS OF REPRODUCTIVE CHOICE AND DISTRIBUTIVE JUSTICE

Many liberals, by whom I mean persons generally committed to the equal liberty and separate importance of each individual and not fundamentally distrustful of human ingenuity, are likely to endorse the possibilities of genetic selection and manipulation. As already mentioned, they have this tendency for a variety of reasons. Some emphasize the reproductive liberties of adults; others maintain that shying away from the ghosts of progress we have called upon us lacks the bravery required for moving ahead and for challenging our conventional values; and still others believe that genetically manipulating future persons provides a uniquely effective way of addressing problems of social justice. I discuss an instance of each of these three approaches and argue that they all make a similar kind of mistake: They fail to realize that genetic manipulation is a particularly intrusive sort of intervention that must be treated with special care so as not to undermine the equal respect we owe to persons, including those of the future.

I begin my argument by engaging with a claim for reproductive liberties by John A. Robertson. His approach illustrates the general problem liberals run into when they focus primarily on the rights of current adults (prospective parents, in this case) and neglect those of future people (section 1). I then consider the arguments of Ronald Dworkin, who maintains that the new technologies propel us into a state of "moral free-fall" (Dworkin 2000, 446). Instead of being troubled by this, however, he proposes that we consider the presence and widespread use of the new technologies as given and reinterpet what our basic commitments to freedom and equality mean when applied to them. This is problematic for several reasons but particularly so because he assumes what should be at issue, namely that we should extensively use the new reprogenetic technologies (section 2). The final approach I discuss is Rawlsian in spirit and as such primarily concerned with questions of social justice. Among its proponents are the authors of *From Chance to Choice* (2000), Allen Buchanan, Dan W. Brock,

Norman Daniels, and Daniel Wikler. A discussion of their arguments reveals how an approach that merely applies principles of social justice to questions about how to influence the genetic properties of individuals is bound to produce instances of intergenerational domination rather than further the goals of social justice (section 3).

Two central assumptions drive the critique of liberal eugenicists in this chapter. The first is that we owe it to persons to have treated the embryos from which they emerged with the same kind of respect for their independence as we owe to the persons themselves. The second is that genetic manipulation constitutes a novel sort of interaction with future persons both in the way it works and with regard to the developmental stage it is applied to. These features aggravate the danger of intergenerational domination, more so at least than many conventional forms of intervention with a child's development such as socialization or education.

1. Championing Procreative Liberties: John A. Robertson

Liberals such as John A. Robertson want to include a fairly broad range of activities within the scope of procreative liberty, that is, the liberty that protects individuals' choice of whether to reproduce or not. To begin with, procreative liberty entails all those activities that are essential to making reproductive decisions. Being able to access and to make use of genetic information about the likelihood of transmitting disease to offspring may, for instance, be central to determining a person's choice of whether to reproduce or not. So too may be the availability of novel technologies such as preimplantation genetic diagnosis (PGD) to select healthy children. "The more closely an application of genetic or reproductive technology serves the basic reproductive project of haploid gene transmission—or its avoidance—and the rearing experiences that usually follow, the more likely it is to fall within a coherent conception of procreative liberty deserving of special protection" (Robertson 2003, 450).

The crucial question is, of course, which practices are directly related to the successful transmission of genes to the next generation and which are not. Robertson argues that the attempt of fertile couples to clone a child, for instance, would not be obviously related to the goal of reproduction. This is because cloning in this case seems merely to express an idiosyncratic preference, as there are other ways for this couple to have a biologically related child. Their situation is thus different from that of a nonfertile same-sex couple with a desire to clone. For them cloning is the only way to arrive at biologically related offspring. They would, on Robertson's account, indeed have a valid claim to engage in reproductive cloning.

When it comes to nonmedical genetic selection and enhancement, Robertson maintains that it is not always obvious that they are related closely enough to reproductive goals as to be protected by procreative liberty. But he provides no grounds for establishing this, given the large amount of discretion he affords individuals to determine their reproductive goals. According to Robertson (2003), they could, for instance, claim that the only condition under which they would consider reproduction is if they could select a child with a perfect pitch (i.e., the ability to identify and recall musical notes from memory).

> Ultimately, the judgment of triviality or importance of the choice rests within a broad spectrum with the couple. If they have a strong enough preference to seek PGD for this purpose [to select a child with the perfect pitch] and that preference rationally relates to reproductive goals that deserve respect, then they have demonstrated its great importance to them. Only in the clearest cases, for example, perhaps creating embryos to picking eye or hair color, might a person's individual assessment of the importance of creating embryos be rejected. (p. 465)

Contrary to what Robertson suggests in this quote, it is not clear how, on his account, prospective parents' wish for selecting a child with a particular eye and hair color could possibly rejected. What would the objection to such a choice be, if, for instance, prospective parents claimed that they will consider reproduction only if they can make sure that their child will be blond and blue-eyed? In that case, the choice of a particular eye and hair color directly relates to these persons' reproductive goal of transmitting (some of) their genes to the next generation. In this case, it seems, Robertson would leave us with no possible objections to these parents' wishes.

Robertson might, of course, be referring to other criteria that could make a particular reproductive choice illegitimate. He might be contending, for instance, that having a preference for a certain eye and hair color is due to mere social prejudice (against people of a certain eye and hair color) and should be rejected for that reason. But Robertson (2003) is adamant that bad private motives cannot rule out a given procreative choice as "allowing private prejudice is characteristic of individual freedom in the private sphere" and "freedom of association permits persons in the private sphere to discriminate as they choose" (p. 462).

A further candidate for rejecting the choice for or against a particular eye or hair color would be that selecting or manipulating such traits fails to show proper respect for, and thus wrongs, the resulting child. But Robertson (2003) has an interesting take on what it would require to wrong children by selecting them because they have (or lack) certain traits or by genetically manipulating them. He argues, for instance, that if parents objected to having a homosexual child and insisted instead on ensuring that their child is born with the genetic code for heterosexuality (if that were ever possible either through selection or manipulation), they would be entitled to employ reprogenetic technologies to this end. This is because they would have "no particular design for the child beyond being healthy and having the sexual orientation chosen. The child would still be free to be his own person in other regards" (p. 467). If this latter requirement, namely that children are free to be their own persons in some regards, is the only one limiting parental choices in the name of children, then it is hard to restrict procreative liberties at all. Every possible intervention can be justified that stops short of changing every single feature that constituted the person before the intervention took place. Changing eye and hair color would certainly leave enough of the original persons intact so that they can be themselves in some respects.

Moreover, when it comes to genetic manipulation, Robertson (2003) thinks that "because alteration in most cases will generally aim at improving the life-prospects of a child, it will be hard to show that the child is harmed as a result. True, the parents might have hopes and expectations for the child based on the engineered trait, but parents could still be loving and respectful of a child whose genes they have altered" (p. 474). The only genetic alterations Robertson rules out are those that would diminish the child's prospects in life (p. 480). In general, he seems to have more qualms about genetic alteration than about selection. He thinks that genetic alteration for nonmedical enhancements are not as obviously or as directly related to legitimate reproductive goals as genetic selection is (p. 478). Earlier in the debate, he had thus narrowed down the scope of reproductive liberties to "protect only actions designed to enable a couple to have normal, healthy offspring whom they intend to rear" (Robertson 1994, 167). In practice, however, this makes no difference, as Robertson still thinks that nontherapeutic genetic enhancement should be protected as part of parental discretion in raising children. "If special tutors and camps, training programs, even the administration of growth hormone to add a few inches to height are within parental rearing discretion, why should genetic interventions to enhance normal offspring traits be any less legitimate?" (p. 167). Thus, although genetic manipulation for nontherapeutic purposes may not be part of adults' procreative liberty, it is part of the entitlements that come with raising a child.[1]

As it arguably makes little difference by what name we refer to the rights of parents to genetically manipulate their offspring (i.e., whether we call it procreative or parental liberty), it is not clear on what basis Robertson distinguishes between selection and enhancement. According to Robertson (2003), all that matters for rendering persons' reproductive choices legitimate is that they seek the goals of reproduction. It seems irrelevant on that standard whether persons who refuse to reproduce unless their child is blue-eyed select their blue-eyed child through PGD or whether they genetically alter the eye color of their child to make it blue. Robertson himself suggests that there would be no difference in this case (p. 479).

But there is an important difference between genetic selection and design, one that might implicitly motivate Robertson's increased skepticism about manipulation but one that his account cannot capture. Let me illustrate this difference with the following example. Imagine two couples, each willing to reproduce only if they have a child with an IQ of exactly 130. The first couple seeks to genetically manipulate their embryo so that the child it comes to be is expected to end up with an IQ of 130. To do this, they have to level their embryo's intelligence down, as it would have "naturally" developed into a child with an IQ of 150. The second couple wants to genetically select an embryo that is likely to mature to be a child with an IQ of 130. They can choose among several embryos, most of which are equipped with IQs around 150. They choose the embryo that promises to develop into a child with an IQ of 130. For Robertson, both couples' choices seem similarly legitimate.[2]

The crucial distinction, however, is that the interaction between parents and children is different in the two cases. When prospective parents select a future person because they have (or lack) a certain trait, they are not genetically interfering with this particular (future) person. They are "merely" choosing one individual over another (which may be objectionable on other counts, such as their unwillingness to accept whatever child would be born to them). In contrast, if they alter the genome of a future person to ensure the existence or absence of particular features, they are genetically interfering with the fully constituted genome of a particular future person. The problem with this is that genetically altering future persons in this way (and for whatever reasons), does not properly respect them for who they would have come to be without another person's intervention.[3] There is (presumably) nothing wrong with an IQ of 150. Changing it to better fit particular parents' prefer-ences, however, suggests that there is. More important, it implies that parents need not accept their children as they would come to be without their inter-vention. Nevertheless, just as we would surely never consider it legitimate to order our neighbors to the plastic surgeon so that their noses are rendered more pleasant to look at when we interact with them, it is not clear why we would consider changing future persons to our liking just because we happen to be in a position in which we can.

Robertson, by having his judgment on new reprogenetic technologies rely entirely on his assessment of whether and to what extent they serve legiti-mate reproductive goals, is oblivious to this distinction between genetic selec-tion and manipulation. Quite generally, his primary focus on spelling out procreative (and parental) liberty leads him to pay little attention to rights persons may have (retrospectively) against their parents' designs. As briefly mentioned before, the closest he gets to acknowledging such rights is that he does not think that parents are entitled to diminish future persons' capacities to a point that embryos that would otherwise develop into healthy and "nor-mal" persons end up beneath the threshold of what would count as healthy and "normal" (Robertson 2003, 480). Apart from this, Robertson does not provide much ground for individuals to hold anything against their parents' reproductive (or parental) rights. As already suggested, however, persons are entitled to substantially more than this. As the case of the 130 IQ shows, it would appear that they have a right not to be made worse off relative to how they could have been without any intervention at the embryo-stage of their development (even if that still leaves them well above a certain minimal threshold of well-being). Or, even beyond that, persons may have a claim that the embryos from which they developed were not changed by other persons, just as the mature adults they will grow into may not be changed by other persons. This claim would apply regardless of whether the change was meant to increase or decrease certain traits. It is this latter kind of entitlement I defend in what follows.

But first let us consider another liberal approach, one that is more attuned than Robertson's to taking future persons' rights seriously, namely that of Ron-ald Dworkin. Dworkin thinks, for instance, that a life, once begun, should suc-ceed rather than fail. Therefore, he argues that pregnant women are obliged to make use of modern reprogenetic technologies to ensure, from the beginning, that the lives of the persons developing from the fetuses they are carrying are successful. Dworkin claims that the new technologies render our conventional moral concepts obsolete. Thus, a woman's right to bodily integrity may no longer have the weight we used to attribute to it. In what follows I show why this is not convincing.

2. Embracing Scientific Advance: Ronald Dworkin

When Dworkin (1996) first considered the moral, social, and political implications of the new reprotechnologies in a lecture titled *Politics, Death and Nature*, he was concerned that the boundaries between what is natural and what is personal (those choices and virtues we are responsible for) may shift, or, in other words, that the balance between who we are and what we do could become disrupted. He did not explicitly speak out against bioengineering but was given pause by the feeling of unease that overcomes most of us when confronted with the new technologies. He explained this uneasiness as an expression of our notion of the sacred. This is an essential notion that honors those aspects of our human nature that we are not responsible for but that are "given." He argued that "it is indispensable to us that some features of ourselves and our situation are just given; are no one's fault; no one's choice; just the luck of the draw; the throw of the dice; what nature did; and what nobody is to blame for" (Dworkin 1996, 215).

Dworkin went on to explain the implications of dispensing with this aspect of our human nature, the given, by means, for instance, of genetic engineering and design. He argued that this is an overwhelming thought, since it is unclear how to expect individuals to make something of their lives if they do not have a background of given conditions that delineate the outer boundaries of their choices. Dworkin compellingly asked how one can even start thinking about "designing" a good life from a blank slate. Moreover, he maintained that it is impossible to imagine how someone could continue to derive pleasure from her achievements (he used a marvelous round of golf as an example) if she knew that they are the product of other people's (as opposed to nature's) design.

> As lawyers know, the distinction between what nature has done and what other people did is at the center of our moral life. All our notions of responsibility hinge on the distinction not between us and our nature, but between us and other people. This, too, can be thrown into jeopardy. Children have enough scope for resentment as it is. Suppose their resentment embraced not just what their parents did or did not give them or do for them, but how they made them. The crucial intergenerational sense of independence would be forfeit. (Dworkin 1996, 216)

In this passage, Dworkin describes his serious concern about the loss of independence between human beings once nature is replaced by human design and, thus, by human responsibility. He is sensitive to the potential conflict that may arise once children learn in what ways their parents interfered with who they came to be.

Nonetheless, and somewhat surprisingly, as Dworkin continued to develop his thoughts, he radically departed from these initial qualms. In his article *Playing God: Genes, Clones and Luck* (Dworkin 2000), which appeared a few years later, Dworkin further elaborates on the shifting of balance between who we are and what we do, those things that are given and those things we are responsible for. But at this point his doubts about the new technologies have vanished. What previously concerned Dworkin about the loss of independence between persons now inspires him to tackle these issues head-on, fully embracing whatever changes may occur.

> There is nothing in itself wrong with the detached ambition to make the lives of future generations of human beings longer and more full of talent and hence achievement. On the contrary, if playing God means struggling to improve our species, bringing into our conscious designs a resolution to improve what God deliberatively or nature blindly has evolved over eons, then the first principle of ethical individualism commands that struggle, and its second principle forbids, in the absence of positive evidence of danger, hobbling the scientists and doctors who volunteer to lead it. (Dworkin 2000, 452)

The two principles of ethical individualism Dworkin invokes in this quote demand both human enhancement and that those at the forefront of reprogenetic research are not impeded in their pursuits. Before discussing these principles in more detail, it is interesting to note how Dworkin arrives at them in the first place. He claims that they emerge as a result of the changing boundaries between who we are and what we do. This will "destabilize much of our conventional morality" (Dworkin 2000, 448). By "conventional morality" Dworkin seems to mean particular applications of the concepts of equality and freedom. Today, for instance, we have a certain conception of what freedom means when invoked in the context of a conflict between a woman's right to bodily integrity and an embryo's claim to have its health protected. If people appeal to a woman's right to bodily integrity, they are pointing out her freedom not to be subject to invasive medical procedures against her will. Dworkin maintains that freedom does not necessarily, but only by convention, translate into this particular right in this specific context. As we will shortly see, he thinks that freedom, when stripped of our conventional understanding, could come to describe the freedom of an embryo to be genetically diagnosed even if the required procedure violates a woman's right to bodily integrity—conventionally understood.

Dworkin (2000) suggests that once common morality has lost its quality as a guide (i.e., once the specific content of claims to freedom and equality is no longer clear), we must fall back on what he calls our (personal) "critical moral background" (p. 448). This consists of each individual's basic moral convictions that Dworkin claims are more fundamental and abstract than those moral principles that guide our everyday choices. He gives an example of how his own critical moral background guides his reasoning on bioethical issues. This is where the two principles of ethical individualism come into play. According to the first principle (sometimes referred to by Dworkin as the "principle of equal importance"), it is important that a life, once begun, should succeed rather than fail. This should be equally true for every human life (p. 448). The second principle (sometimes referred to by Dworkin as the "principle of special responsibility") is that persons bear responsibility for their lives and therefore have a right to make fundamental choices about what, for each person individually, a successful life should look like (p. 449). The first principle demands governmental policies that treat each person as equally valuable; the second demands that individuals are left free to decide how to structure their lives according to their choices and desires.

Thus, let us return to the example regarding the meaning of freedom in a conflict between the interests of a pregnant woman and the embryo she is carrying. If we had the technology to diagnose a serious defect in a fetus, Dworkin's (2000) two principles of ethical individualism would give the embryo the "right" to be diagnosed even against the will of the woman. "The principle of special responsibility would no longer justify allowing a pregnant woman to refuse tests to discover such a defect in an embryo she carries, and the first principle of ethical humanism—an objective concern that any life, once begun, be a successful one—would counsel mandatory testing" (p. 450).

So far in his writing, Dworkin has not regarded the human embryo as a life that has begun *in earnest* (Dworkin 1992, 1994). Therefore, he must be assuming that an embryo attains such a right only in those cases in which a woman actually carries it to term. This would be very similar to the proposal defended in the first part of this book regarding the moral value of embryos, which is that those embryos that a woman ends up giving birth to have claims to assert against her (in the name of the persons they develop into), whereas those embryos that a woman aborts have none.

To make an argument along these lines, however, our conventional moral convictions need not be challenged. They can easily support the view that women have to take special care of the embryos they carry to term. The availability of new kinds of (genetic) tests only provides further ways for them to do this. What this availability alone does not solve is the question of whether a woman can be required to make use of these additional options. To answer this we should explore whether or to what extent administering such tests would conflict with a woman's right to bodily integrity. Dworkin offers an interesting response: "This flat principle of bodily integrity may, however, be one of those artifacts of conventional morality that seemed well justified before the possibilities suggested by modern genetic medicine were plausibly imagined, but not after" (Dworkin 2000, 450). Dworkin seems to think that we cannot be concerned that a future life, once begun, ought to succeed rather than fail and, at the same time, be committed to upholding a woman's right to bodily integrity. This is not convincing. I have already suggested several ways in which this can be achieved (see chapters 1, and 3). If we respect a woman's right to decide whether or not she wants to carry her embryo to term, we can also ask her to treat the embryo she gives birth to in anticipation of the person it will develop into. Morally speaking, this might sometimes require testing (or even surgical intervention). This having been said, as the discussion of the feminist critique in chapter 3 (section 3) showed, we should not be too quick to dismiss women's claims against forceful interventions into their bodily integrity (especially by the state). In this regard, Dworkin's critical background ends up being rather uncritical.

Thus, it is unclear why Dworkin thinks that the new technologies propel us into a state of moral free-fall. There is no reason why our existing principles should not equip us well for dealing with the new challenges presented by reprogenetic technologies, especially if we do not just throw them overboard, as Dworkin suggests. The general problem with his argument is that he takes for granted what should be at issue. Instead of asking whether and to what extent we want to make use of the new technologies, he merely assumes that these technologies are here to stay (Dworkin 2000, 448) and that we should change our moral concepts in light of them. What starts out as a diagnosis about why many people have reacted with fear and suspicion to the new technologies, namely because the latter threaten to blur the boundary between chance and choice and thereby cause moral insecurity, quickly turns into a normative prescription. In fact, we all *should* leave our conventional categories aside and fall back on our "critical moral background" to then emerge with new concepts that, without question, embrace the new technologies. This seems to have it the wrong way around.

To illustrate this more concretely: It is, for instance, not clear by what standard Dworkin's first principle of ethical individualism measures what it takes for a life, once begun, to succeed rather than fail. This principle says nothing about what constitutes a successful life. If we read Habermas, for instance (discussed in detail in the following chapter), succeeding in life may just as well lie in rejecting (at least part of) the new technologies. Therefore, the question is why Dworkin presents his first principle of ethical individualism so that it is already skewed toward utilizing the new technologies, suggesting that their use is the only way to allow certain lives to succeed. Dworkin probably means to say that there is an ethical imperative to help where we can. This would mean that, in the case in which a woman intends to carry an embryo to term that may have a certain serious genetic defect, there are reasons for wanting to diagnose and then, if possible, remove the defect. While the option of correcting this defect may not have been available previous to some medical breakthrough, the spirit in which this option is taken advantage of (given the medical breakthrough) is not new. The only thing rendered obsolete is any previously held conviction that this particular genetic defect was incurable.

Thus, Dworkin neither shows that the new technologies thrust us into a state of moral free-fall nor does he provide any compelling reasons for why we should simply skip the question of whether we want to endorse the new technologies in the first place. This having been said, the idea of the new technologies inducing a state of moral free-fall haunts many in the debate. Buchanan et al. (2000), for example, also have several passages that speak of how changing human nature may transform the anthropological basis of morality. Unlike Dworkin, they, however, draw virtually no conclusions from this and merely go on to apply "conventional" concepts of morality to the issues at hand. While this allows them to provide a more compelling argument for endorsing some uses of the new technologies, they go much too far. They lose sight of the basic "conventional" principle that should guide the way, namely respect for separateness of (future) persons.

3. Ensuring Equal Opportunity: Buchanan et al.

In *From Chance to Choice*, Buchanan et al. (2000) explore the implications of a genetically malleable human nature for a concept of justice as developed by John Rawls (1971) in his seminal work *A Theory of Justice*. They argue that the new technologies, by making the natural lottery partly replaceable by human design, have expanded the domain of justice. The authors contend that the new ability to respond directly to natural disadvantages brings with it the responsibility to remove opportunity-limiting conditions not only socially but also genetically.

> If precise and safe control over the distribution of natural assets becomes feasible, then those who believe that justice is concerned with the effects of natural assets on individuals' life prospects will no longer be able to assume that justice requires only that we compensate for bad luck in the natural lottery by intervening in the social lottery, rather than by attacking natural inequalities directly. (Buchanan et al. 2000, 64)

A responsibility to genetically remove opportunity-limiting conditions arises irrespective of whether these conditions count as diseases or not. Thus, the authors claim, we ought to work toward removing all those natural or social features from future persons' lives that end up preventing them from having equal opportunities and from being included as full members in the prevailing social cooperative scheme. We should do this even if that means significantly enhancing a person's traits or talents.

Before going into more detail regarding what kinds of genetic interventions the authors envision, I want to briefly return to the thought that ended the previous section: Buchanan et al. share with Dworkin a concern about the effects of genetic manipulation on our moral system. But while Dworkin chooses, in response, to revise conventional moral concepts, Buchanan et al. decide to largely ignore the threats they anticipate. This is somewhat surprising, given the nature of these risks. Exploring two of these is helpful in various ways. To begin with, it shows an internal inconsistency in Buchanan et al.'s approach. Beyond that, and more important, it highlights the vagueness of such concerns. Finally, it smoothes the path for one of the central arguments by Jürgen Habermas, discussed in the next chapter, who claims that the new technologies threaten to undermine our morality as a whole.

Thus, I use the first of the following three steps of the argument to spell out the ways in which Buchanan et al. worry about the effects of changing human nature on morality (section 3.1.). Then, in the second step, I discuss the limitations Buchanan et al. consider when it comes to parents' freedom to genetically manipulate their children (section 3.2.). In the third step I explain why, despite these limitations, Buchanan et al.'s approach still leads to a situation of intergenerational domination (section 3.3.).

3.1. Genetic Manipulation, Justice, and our Moral System

The first concern Buchanan et al. (2000) have about genetically interfering with human nature regards the limits of justice (when it comes to determining changes in our genetic code). The authors worry, for instance, that "if theorizing about justice begins with a conception of human nature as given, then it is hard to see how it can provide answers to such questions as: Ought we preserve human nature (as we have understood it thus far)? Or, if it is permissible to change 'human nature,' how should we change it?" (p. 88). Here the question is what the authors consider "human nature" to be and what they think it would take to change it. If justice cannot tell us how to change human nature, then it is not clear how the authors think they can pursue a liberal eugenic policy according to the dictates of justice in the first place. They even contend that "in contemplating the disturbing challenges that the possibilities of genetic intervention pose for our traditional ways of thinking about justice, it is tempting to conclude that we are ill equipped to make any form of judgments about what justice requires" (p. 96).[4] They go on to say that this temptation should be resisted and that "some conclusions can be drawn about the requirements of justice in the genetic age" (p. 96). They must think that some genetic changes are safe to make without changing human nature while others are not. Unfortunately, they do not elaborate on this distinction.

The second concern has to do with the motivation to cooperate in a common moral system and the willingness to consider each other as moral equals. The authors maintain that "we can no longer assume that there will be a single successor to what has been regarded as human nature" (Buchanan et al. 2000, 95). Once we have altered our human nature to an extent that we have created several sorts of humans with distinctly different natures (i.e., we have eroded the basis for a shared humanity by artificial genetic diversification), there might be a motivational problem with morality. "The effectiveness of people's motivation to act consistently on universal moral principles may depend significantly on whether they share a sense of common membership in a single moral community" (p. 95). The authors then say that "for all we know, it might turn out that if differences among groups in characteristics other than a common rationality become pronounced enough, they would not treat each other as moral equals" (p. 95). Although the authors are not concerned that the anthropological basis of morality itself, or what they call "common rationality," will change, they do think that a lack of commonality in other areas may erode our willingness to cooperate on equal terms.[5]

Presumably, these differences in characteristics among groups could come about in two different ways. First, they could occur because some (wealthy) people are able to buy themselves different and ultimately better enhancements than others. This may eventually lead to a divide between the rich and the poor not only on the basis of material goods but also in terms of their genetic make-up. At different places in their book, Buchanan et al. have slightly different responses to this threat. At first they say that "if access to such enhancements according to ability to pay exacerbated existing unjust inequities, justice might require either that they be made available to all or that they not be available at all" (p. 98). Later, however, they qualify this claim somewhat. They argue that the strength of our objections to marketing the means of further advantage relates to three factors: first, whether the existing inequalities in income and wealth are just or unjust; second, whether the poorest are denied access to health care (as opposed to the wealthy "merely" being able to purchase more enhancements); and third, whether the enhancements the wealthy can buy bestow truly significant advantages (p. 187). This sounds as if the authors can well imagine a system that would allow the wealthy to buy enhancements that the poor do not have access to. This may indeed eventually lead to different group characteristics and then threaten to undermine the motivation of both groups to cooperate together in one single moral system.

There is yet a second way for such a development to come about. If genetic manipulation became a global practice so that every parent in every society and culture stood obliged to genetically remove their children's opportunity-limiting conditions, over time the genetic constitution of different groups of human beings is also likely to turn out differently. Societies and cultures differ, for example, with respect to the talents and traits they value and which they consider to be opportunity-limiting. Moreover, external factors such as climate and geography require different forms of adaptation to make persons equal competitors in their particular society or culture.

All in all, it is not clear whether Buchanan et al. (i) (mistakenly) think that the changes they propose will not have the effect of eventually creating different groups of humans with distinct characteristics or (ii) want to bite the bullet and argue that even if their proposed changes had this effect, they should be undertaken nevertheless. Either way, it is remarkable how Buchanan et al. can acknowledge these dangers and then proceed to make their suggestions about how to apply the new technologies without further reference to them. In other words, given the troubling consequences it would have if the human motivation to cooperate in a common moral system were undermined, it would seem that the authors should end up with an extremely cautious position, trying hard to avoid a situation in which differences in group characteristics become pronounced. In the discussion that follows, it becomes obvious, however, that these concerns are not on the authors' minds.

3.2. Limiting Parental Powers: Respecting a Child's Right to an Open Future

When assessing what kinds of liberties parents should have in pursuing the "best" for their child, Buchanan et al. (2000) argue that genetic intervention is, in principle at least, not fundamentally different from traditional socialization (this again is somewhat surprising given their concerns about how genetic interventions may alter human nature). Socialization works to change our phenotype by training our muscles and our cognitive abilities. These changes affect how we "are" and "feel" in the world. By contrast, genotypic[6] changes, such as a genetically improved immune system, will just as often go unnoticed with regard to what is essential to our character (p. 161). Thus, as with education and other socializing methods, parents should be encouraged not only to remove opportunity-limiting conditions but also to use genetic interventions to enhance "general purpose means." These are "capabilities that are broadly valuable across a wide array of life plans and opportunities typically pursued in a society like our own" (p. 174).

There are, however, certain restrictions on the parental liberty to use genetic interventions as they wish. First, there is an obligation to make genetic changes in the best interest of the child. Second, parents ought to be discouraged (but probably not legally prohibited other than in extreme cases) from genetically changing their children in idiosyncratic ways. Third, parents should abstain from bestowing on their offspring merely positional advantages (these are advantages with the principal effect of making some better off than others). Fourth, parents have a duty not to "so narrow children's range of opportunities as to violate their right to an open future" (p. 171).[7]

This right to an open future warrants some further attention. According to the authors, the right to an open future chiefly consists in children having a certain number of options, no less than they would have had without the genetic intervention and preferably more. Each genetic change should be limited so that it "leaves the child's critical capacities substantially intact, or better yet helps to develop and improve them" (p. 166). Buchanan et al. claim that this goal is "usually" achieved by giving the child "a broader array of capacities." These should "provide individuals with greater adaptive capacities to correct for the errors and mistakes of their parents" (p. 172). This provision clearly does not limit the quality or quantity of permissible genetic interventions but merely rules out genetic alterations that would reduce the child's initial range of options. In this way, the authors' understanding of a child's right to an open future is somewhat at odds with what they consider to be a person's interest in liberty. Buchanan et al. suggest that a person could, in principle at least, level this interest against being genetically interfered with. But the authors do not think that a very early embryo has such an interest. "If the intervention were early enough in life, it would be implausible to argue that the individual's interest in liberty—in being free from nonconsensual medical treatment—outweighed his or her interest in avoiding significant limitations on opportunity" (p. 78). This is strange. As an embryo is not a person yet and has no interests of its own, the interests that must be attributed to it (by retroactive extension) are those of the future person it develops into. If a person can be expected to have an interest in not being subjected to nonconsensual medical treatment, it is not clear why this person's early embryo would have any other kind of interest.

Moreover, what the authors embrace as a child's right to an open future is not necessarily what Joel Feinberg (1980), the first to spell out this right and to whom the authors explicitly refer, originally intended it to mean. Feinberg argues that part of what it means to be a C-right, namely a right generally possessed by children (as opposed to an A-right, which is generally possessed by adults) is that it obliges us to respect the choices of the adults children will become if—and this is the part of the formulation Buchanan et al. refer to— their "basic options are kept open" *and*—this is the part I want to draw the reader's attention to—their "growth [is] kept 'natural' or unforced" (p. 78). Although Feinberg certainly did not have the possibilities of modern reprogenetics in mind when writing his much-cited text, his words can be interpreted in a narrow and in a wider sense with respect to genetic manipulation: In the narrow sense Buchanan et al. understand it, the right to an open future restricts genetic interventions that would limit a child's range of options. This is narrow because it focuses merely on a claim about the quantity of options. However, a child's right to an open future could also be taken in a wider sense to indicate that beyond there being something good about having more rather than less options available, there is something valuable about the particular range of options a child "naturally" comes to have (i.e., the particular range of options a child comes to have without having been genetically interfered with).

There is some evidence that Feinberg (1980) would interpret a child's right to an open future in this wider sense. For instance, he argues that for a court (he has the Supreme Court in mind) to make a truly neutral decision about what the goal of education should be for a child, it has to determine this goal in such a way that it neither reflects the state's nor the parents' designs. Rather, it should make sure that education equips "the child with the knowledge and skills that will help him choose whichever sort of life best fits his native endowment and matured disposition" (p. 84). Any form of genetic manipulation cannot really count as a child's "native" endowment. Feinberg assumes that "right from the beginning the newborn infant has a kind of rudimentary character consisting of temperamental proclivities and a genetically fixed potential for the acquisition of various talents and skills. The standard sort of loving upbringing (. . .) will be like water added to dehydrated food, filling it out and actualizing the stored-in tendencies" (p. 96). This again portrays children's right to an open future as a right that is relative to children's "native" endowment and as one that grounds children's claims to having this—and not some other, genetically altered—endowment realized.

There is a reason I am pointing this out. If my alternative understanding of a child's right to an open future is correct, then the wide-ranging parental rights and duties to interfere with their child's genetic make-up that Buchanan et al. envision show little respect for the genetic endowment persons are born with. As I argue in what follows, Buchanan et al.'s proposals allow parents to interfere with their offspring without really tracking their interests and without having to acknowledge how difficult it may be for children to contest their parents' genetic choices. It is this latter aspect one would expect liberals to be particularly concerned about.

3.3. The Danger of Intergenerational Domination

Buchanan et al. base their liberal view of parental entitlements on three problematic assumptions. First, they believe that there is no fundamental difference between genetic interventions and social or educational influences (a). Second, they assume that the interests they impute to future children are of an objective kind and therefore legitimize or even mandate parental interventions (b). Third, they posit that there is a workable way to distinguish opportunity-limiting conditions that are due to social prejudices (against women, homosexuals, or persons of color, for instance) from those that are due to "genuine" disabilities (c). There is reason to be skeptical about all three premises.

(a) Socialization and Genetic Manipulation. Like Robertson, Buchanan et al. suggest that sending children to school to further their critical capacities is, in principle, the same as genetically enhancing children's memory or intelligence (if that were possible). Therefore, they think that we can derive justifiable uses of genetic enhancement from looking at the kinds of improvements we consider to be legitimate when it comes to socialization. But there are very important differences between socializing influences on and genetic interferences with a child's development. These differences should prevent us from applying the principles that govern socializing practices to practices involving genetic manipulation.

Socialization begins to influence children's development after they are born. It comes from outside and must be communicated in some verbal or nonverbal way. Moreover, it occurs over years and is a result of a constant struggle and bargaining between social standards imparted through a multiplicity of sources (parents, siblings, nannies, friends, teachers, etc.) and the wants and needs of the children. Children, even as newborns, can "defend" themselves against some of their parents' designs by screaming, kicking, crying, or merely by refusing to cooperate. In this way, educational and socializing schemes rarely work out the way they were designed. A critical factor in their success is always the particular children they are applied to, who may or may not accept the influences they are subjected to.

All of this is different with genetic manipulation. Such an intervention occurs within seconds, is "done," is not communicated to embryos, and does not (and, in fact, cannot) take into consideration anything particular about the persons whose embryos are being genetically altered. At the point of intervention, future persons have no means of "defending" themselves against what is happening to them. Genetic changes are literally "inserted" into embryos, and, once persons are born, there is no way for them to make a distinction between who they would have been had no one interfered and who they are because of other people's designs. I return to this distinction in chapters 5 and 6. For now, it is important to note that genetic intervention and socialization present two different modes of interaction with children and cannot simply be compared.

(b) Knowing What is "Best" for Children. Buchanan et al. assume that parents can make "good" genetic choices for their children, especially if these choices increase their children's range of options in life. This is a vital assumption because it allows Buchanan et al. to claim that it is indeed possible for parents to "track" their children's interests with their genetic interventions, thereby rendering these interventions nonarbitrary. I want to show that this is not as easy as the authors think. My claim does not rely on the trivial observation that, at the moment of intervention (i.e., when embryos are only a few days old), future persons are incapable of having actual interests. While this is certainly true, it would obviously be mistaken to claim that we cannot know anything about their future interests, because these are at least in part the result of factors we can predict, anticipate, or are directly responsible for. Often, however, these factors are problematic. To illustrate, I explore the two kinds of interests we can know something about. The first is subjective and the second objective.

Let me begin with the subjective interests. Presumably, one way to legitimize a certain genetic intervention would be to invoke children's expected approval of it. In this sense, arguing that genetic change X is in the (best) interest of particular children can be understood literally: we are reasonably sure that these children will develop an interest in having this genetic change X. Taken at face value, such a desire could be interpreted as having tremendous normative force, obliging parents to provide such a change. In many cases, we are able to predict what children are likely to favor on the basis of knowing something about both the immediate environment they will grow up in and the larger sociocultural context. Consider, for instance, a case in which parents have a strong preference for good-looking, overachiever-types of children and genetically manipulate theirs to be that way. Then, of course, they could fairly accurately anticipate that their children will come to appreciate being such good-looking overachievers. Or imagine a society that greatly rewards individuals for being superior athletes. Here we would have good reasons to believe that children who are given superior athletic abilities will turn out to be grateful for their parents' choice.

Subjective desires of this kind are easily predicted but also easily produced, as they can be expected to develop in response to the changes parents make. This, in turn, is due to two factors. First, persons usually have a certain healthy bias for liking the way they are. Second, children can be expected to internalize their parents' (or society's) preferences. But that gives the later endorsement of the genetic alterations that were made on account of parents' (or society's) preferences the quality of a self-fulfilling prophecy. It thereby largely undermines the normative force of such an endorsement.[8]

This brings me to the "objective" interests children can be expected to develop. Parental values that influence those of their children are in turn largely shaped by the values and preferences of the society and culture they live in. Consider qualities such as heightened intelligence or exceptional memory, which are generally esteemed in our society. They are therefore frequently portrayed as so-called "all-purpose-means" (Buchanan et al. 2000, 174). These are means that are considered to be useful across a wide array of life plans typically pursued in a society such as our own. They are thus often taken to be valuable in some "objective" sense. In other words, many people would argue that it is intrinsically good to have more of these properties than less. But if "objective" is supposed to indicate anything intrinsically valuable, something that is not again relative to the time and circumstances of a particular person's upbringing, then there is nothing "objective" about an interest in being more intelligent or having a great memory, for instance. This is for three principal reasons.

First, I doubt that, above a certain threshold of intelligence required for maneuvering around freely in everyday life, there is any intrinsic value in having an increased amount of it (I have more to say about this threshold in chapter 6). Surely, up to a point, certain mind exercises might be easier, and persons may be able to enjoy more "sophisticated" pleasures to a greater extent than they otherwise would. But they may also turn out to be more neurotic or less attuned to their emotional lives, ending up less happy than they might have been had their access to the joys of "lower" pleasures not been forestalled. Who is to say what is in someone's interests?

Second, just because a trait is good for a wide variety of life plans typically pursued in a society such as our own does not mean that any particular child will, in fact, end up being engaged in a life plan typically pursued in such a society. Consider the case of a child with an exceptional memory. This feature could be fortunate if she ended up being an academic. Just as likely, however, it could turn into a curse if she ended up being a soldier at war, for whom the ability to forget can be the only means of survival.

Third, even if there were traits that are valuable across all possible life plans typically pursued in a society such as our own (which I obviously doubt), it is not clear why we should assume that what is typically pursued by us is something that will or ought to be pursued by those of the future. Therefore, all these choices, instead of responding to "objective" or "authentic" interests, would do little more than impute to future persons the values and prejudices of the previous generation.

If Buchanan et al.'s so-called all-purpose means are not in the objective interests of future persons, then genetically manipulating future persons so they have more of them is clearly not an expression of having tracked their interests. However, if such interventions are nothing more than expressions of the preferences and prejudices of the previous generation, as I am making them out to be, they are arbitrary with regard to future persons. If this is combined with the assumption—discussed in section (a) above—that, unlike socialization and education, genetic intervention makes it more difficult for future persons to contest their parents' choices, genetic manipulation according to the principles envisioned by Buchanan et al. appears to constitute a form of intergenerational domination. These principles should therefore be rejected.

A further shortcoming of Buchanan et al.'s argument aggravates the problem; they fail to convincingly show why a concern about unequal opportunities should be principally addressed by changing the genome of future persons. Why, in other words, should we not first try to change the social infrastructure to make the world a more accessible place for persons with a variety of genetic dispositions and different levels of ability?

(c) Are all Opportunity-Limiting Conditions Created Equal? When Buchanan et al. license parents to remove opportunity-limiting conditions from their child's life, they run into the problem of having to distinguish different kinds of opportunity-limiting conditions. Our society, for instance, limits opportunities for women, homosexuals, and persons of color. These, however, are not among the opportunity-limiting conditions Buchanan et al. want to remove. The way they try to separate these from other opportunity-limiting conditions is by claiming that some of them are clearly due to prejudice and discrimination whereas others are "genuine" disabilities. This is a hard case to make, because, arguably and as the authors are well aware of, disabilities are often only disabilities if the dominant social cooperative framework makes them so, by, for instance, constructing the world in such a way that those who are deaf, blind, or bound to a wheelchair have severe difficulties partaking in everyday (social) life.

The authors contend that transforming the social environment to be maximally inclusive of all persons with different levels of abilities would be costly and difficult, much more so, they maintain, than it would be to work against prejudice and discrimination. They argue that modifying the dominant cooperative scheme to be maximally inclusive would impose a social cooperative scheme on all that is in the interest only of those who are currently disabled. All "normally" abled persons would be systematically underchallenged and prevented from effectively participating in such a cooperative framework in a fulfilling way (Buchanan et al. 2000, 294). Therefore, the authors propose that, from a moral point of view (i.e., one that takes into account all interests, including those of the "normally" abled), we ought to reject the idea of changing our dominant social cooperative scheme in a way that is maximally inclusive. Rather, we should find a compromise solution between including more people with different abilities and genetically changing some people to be better competitors in the dominant social cooperative scheme.

This argument is not convincing. It is not clear why restructuring our social world to include a wider range of persons with different levels of ability would necessarily prevent some (of the more abled) from effectively participating in the social cooperative scheme in a challenging and fulfilling way. If that were the case then persons in the top 10th percentile of intelligence would suffer tremendously in the world as it is today, as would everybody with talent who is forced to function in an environment in which not everyone is equally talented. Moreover, it is all but clear that it would be less costly to work against prejudice and discrimination than to make the world a more accessible place for persons of different levels of ability. While the former seems to require something as extensive and intrusive as changing the minds of people, the latter requires mostly infrastructural changes; it is certainly the more tangible of the two goals. Therefore, Buchanan et al. offer no compelling argument against a more inclusive social cooperative scheme.

Thus, all three assumptions on which Buchanan et al. rely to make their argument for liberal eugenics turn out to be problematic. To begin with, the authors overestimate the similarity between genetic interventions on embryos and more conventional forms of influencing the development of children. At the same time, they underestimate the problems that stand in the way of knowing what might be "best" for children. Finally, they fail to show why we should use genetic manipulation instead of other, more traditional means to achieve greater inclusion, such as changing the infrastructure, so that disabilities are no longer inherently opportunity-limiting.

4. Conclusion

I have argued that the liberal approaches discussed in this chapter either do not take the equal moral status of future persons seriously enough, or, to the extent they do, they underestimate the challenges posed by the new reprogenetic technologies for our interactions with future persons. With his focus on adults' procreative liberty, Robertson remains oblivious to claims pertaining to the quality of the relationship between the generations. He fails to realize that the central issue is not just about whether future persons end up above a certain threshold of capacities but about how they end up where they do.

Dworkin takes future persons' rights more seriously—too seriously, perhaps, as he wants to throw conventional interpretations of moral norms overboard, including the interpretation of freedom that has hitherto given a woman's right to bodily integrity significant moral weight. Although there is a way to read his approach on the same lines as the suggestions made in the first part of this book (i.e., that women are obliged to treat embryos they eventually give birth to in anticipation of the persons these embryos will develop into), Dworkin's embrace of the new technologies remains largely unmotivated. He gives his readers no reasons to champion these new technologies other than by expressing his support for the ambition to enhance the species. He seems to have it the wrong way around. Were he to claim that respect for persons, including those of the future, mandates certain uses of the new technologies, his proposal would be far more convincing.

Buchanan et al.'s approach has two problems. The first concerns the way the authors frame the issue: On the one hand, they wonder how justice can tell us how to change human nature and worry about what might happen to our motivation to cooperate with each other in a common moral system once there are different groups of humans with distinct genetic characteristics. On the other hand, neither of these concerns has any influence on their suggestions for how genetic manipulation ought to be used. Instead, the authors merely apply principles of social justice, taking no heed of the long-term consequences (on morality) their distributive scheme may have.

The second problem with Buchanan et al.'s approach regards their substantial assumptions, several of which I objected to. I denied, for instance, that socialization and genetic manipulation are similar ways of influencing future persons' development, that parents can know that the possession of traits that are widely considered to be valuable in a society such as our own will be in the "best" interest of their children, and, more generally, that genetic modifications should be a preferred way of arriving at a more inclusive society. I maintained that if Buchanan et al.'s assumptions are mistaken in this way, their proposed way of using the new technologies will facilitate a system of intergenerational domination. Those currently living will impose their will on future persons without tracking their interests and without the latter being able to contest the choices made by the previous generation.

Next we turn our attention to Jürgen Habermas's arguments. He too is concerned with the consequences genetic manipulation may have on our moral system. But unlike Dworkin and Buchanan et al., Habermas rejects most uses of reprogenetic technologies. He argues that the main reason we should refrain from genetically manipulating future persons is because this may introduce a new kind of asymmetry into intergenerational relationships. Such an asymmetry would have detrimental effects on all concerned, undermining persons' ability (or motivation) to regard themselves and others as free and equal members of the moral community.

Habermas's claims offer a helpful corrective to the liberal accounts discussed so far. Unlike his colleagues, he is acutely aware of the significance of symmetrical relationships between persons, including relationships across generations. However, I show that he concentrates too much on the possible psychological effects of asymmetrical relationships, thereby losing from focus the central normative objection to them.

5 TROUBLING INTUITIONS

JÜRGEN HABERMAS AND THE DANGERS OF CHANGING HUMAN NATURE

After having discussed several liberal approaches in favor of applying new reprogenetic technologies in a variety of ways, Jürgen Habermas's perspective is particularly intriguing as he makes the original—and surprising—attempt to develop an argument against many uses of these technologies (including a number of those endorsed by liberal eugenicists) in the name of liberal values such as freedom and equality. Habermas has two kinds of concerns about a liberal approach to new reprogenetic technologies. First, he fears that genetically manipulated individuals may no longer be capable of perceiving themselves as free and equal members of the moral community. If this occurred, Habermas worries that second, our familiar liberal morality—or perhaps even morality as such—may be impossible to maintain. He argues that this is nothing we can want to happen.

Habermas offers exciting arguments, not because they are particularly compelling or even because they work (which I claim they do only in part) but because of the spirit in which they are pursued. Regarding the possible psychological effects of genetic manipulation, he is driven by the intuition that there is something troubling with regard to intergenerational relationships once we start exchanging the natural lottery with human design (i.e., replacing a random act of nature with deliberate human intervention). This worry can be traced back to a concern that underlies much of his work, namely that of reification (Iser 2008, 148). Although I argue that it is not so clear as to what extent reification is something to be especially concerned about in the particular case of genetic manipulation, it is still his basic attentiveness to this danger that makes him uniquely sensitive to what is wrong with one generation genetically manipulating the next. It allows him to see not only that genetic manipulation is different from more traditional forms of socialization (at least in some important respects) but also that future persons ought to be treated in anticipation of the persons they will come to be and that such treatment demands respect for who they end up being without other persons' intervention.

Regarding the possible effects of genetic manipulation on our moral system, Habermas fears that the new technologies threaten to undermine the very principles on which our liberal moral system, perhaps even morality as a whole, rests. I find his specific arguments about morality being threatened unpersuasive. But it must be acknowledged that Habermas, unlike his liberal eugenic colleagues, draws the only viable conclusion from the diagnosis that once we start genetically manipulating future persons, our moral system may be detrimentally affected—namely that we should reject those uses of the new technologies that jeopardize our moral system.

The following discussion of Habermas's argument is divided into four parts. The first provides a brief overview of his concerns about the psychopathological development of genetically manipulated individuals as well as the effects that genetic manipulation may have on those who perform it (section 1). I then critically discuss three aspects in particular to illustrate the ways in which Habermas overemphasizes the psychological effects and thus pays too little attention to the genuinely normative aspects of his critique of genetic manipulation (section 2). The third section explores Habermas's fears about how employing the new technologies may change human nature and, with it, our entire moral system. I show why his claims about the potential threat to morality remain unpersuasive (section 3). In the concluding section, I draw out the attractive features of Habermas's argument for the alternative account I propose in the final chapter (section 4).

1. Habermas's Rejection of Liberal Eugenics

Habermas recoils from the prospect of "liberal" eugenics. He insists that, once we have understood the moral, social, and political implications of the new technologies, our only reasonable reaction can be to abstain from them. He approves of only two ways of using reprogenetic technologies. First, he considers all cases of self-regarding use to be legitimate. This is because individuals who are the authors of their own genetic manipulation assume full responsibility for the procedure and its consequences for their character and development as persons. Habermas (2003) likens such use of genetic manipulation to cosmetic surgery (p. 86).

Second, Habermas approves of certain cases of other-regarding use, which tend to be problematic in principle whenever consent cannot be obtained from the affected person. But even in cases in which the intervention takes place at a stage of human development at which no consent is possible, genetic manipulation is morally permissible whenever future persons' (hypothetical) consent can be reasonably presumed. Habermas contends that future persons' consent can be presumed in this way only for actions that follow a very narrowly understood logic of healing. He therefore thinks that only the prevention of grave harm can be considered to be in their interest. For instance, performing genetic manipulation to save a child's life or to avert a lethal or otherwise serious genetic defect follows the logic of healing and is, according to Habermas (2003), therefore justified (p. 51).

That he considers these various uses of the new technologies to be morally acceptable shows that Habermas (2003, 87) is clearly not essentially against the intervention in, or the manipulation of, the human genome. He also does not have anything (positive or negative) to say about humans transgressing limits set by nature or the natural order. This, from the very start, distinguishes his approach from that of his more conservative colleagues, even those who ultimately have a less restrictive view. Michael Sandel (2004), for instance, invokes respect for the natural order when he endorses only those uses of the new technologies that are in sync with humility toward the "given" world (p. 55; also see Sandel 2007, 27). Although Sandel's criterion of respecting the natural order seems to point to a much more circumscribed view than the one Habermas offers, Sandel ends up considering many more uses of reprogenetic technologies morally permissible, including stem cell research, many uses of PGD, and genetic manipulation for treatment purposes. I return to this comparison later. For now, let us consider Habermas's concrete concerns.

As I briefly mentioned in chapter 1, Habermas worries that allowing stem cell research and PGD may fundamentally change our attitudes toward human life. The same is true of genetic manipulation for enhancement purposes. The latter technology is of particular concern because instead of "merely" destroying human life, it effects changes in the DNA of individuals who will be born (i.e., will be persons). These persons' self-perception as free and equal members of the moral community may be undermined and, with it, the psychological preconditions necessary for upholding our moral order. According to Habermas, persons' self-perception as free and equal members of the moral community can be maintained only as long as they remain subject to the natural lottery. This is for two reasons: first, because only the natural lottery ensures limitations on the influence other people can possibly have on the constitution of a person's identity and second, because only the natural lottery guarantees that individuals can assume full (ethical or personal) responsibility for their lives.

Habermas (2003) attributes great moral importance to having a "natural origin." Until now, he maintains, it has been the accidental character of the natural lottery that provides persons with an independent point of reference, one that lies beyond traditions and the educational contexts of interactions (p. 59). No one can claim authorship over who persons are when they are born. All that happens to them from that point on will happen in reference to that part of their identity that is prior to their entering intersubjective relationships with others. This natural "fate" is what enables persons to differentiate between who they are and what happens to them. This has always been a primary source of freedom. If designed persons no longer have the freedom 'to be' their body but are forced only 'to have' a body, a fundamental precondition of being themselves may be endangered. The differentiation between the objective and the subjective, between the naturally grown and the artificially made, could become muddied. This, in turn, may undermine the (perceived) equality between those who design and those who are designed. "Knowledge of one's own genome being programmed might prove to be disruptive, I suspect, for our assumption that we exist as a body or, so to speak, 'are' our body, and thus may give rise to a novel, curiously asymmetrical type of relationship between persons" (Habermas 2003, 42).

Interestingly, Habermas emphasizes the problem connected to knowing that one was programmed rather than the programming itself. Some may conclude that this makes the solution obvious: Any potential predicament connected to knowing about one's genetic manipulation can be circumvented by simply not telling manipulated children about their having been manipulated. This, some may say, would not be different from how it is for children who are "naturally" conceived and who are also not regularly told about every single fact and detail involved in their conception and upbringing.[1] Here, however, Habermas (2003, 87) quickly points out the irony he sees in trying to add insult to injury by not only genetically manipulating children but then also deceiving them about the origin of their genetic constitution. He thereby implies that children always have a right to know about whether or not they have been genetically manipulated.[2]

The combination of persons knowing of their genetic manipulation and other persons being responsible for manipulating them, however, may have two kinds of psychological effects. First, not only may it (negatively) affect manipulated individuals' self-perception as equal to other members of the moral community but also the ability of persons who undertook the manipulation to view others (including themselves) as equals. Second, it may (negatively) influence the extent to which manipulated persons can continue to see themselves as autonomous authors of their own life story.

Regarding the effect on persons' ability to experience themselves and others as equal members of the moral community, Habermas (2001) describes how two features of "eugenic programming" create a potential problem. First, there may be detrimental consequences involved in designed persons knowing that it is not merely by chance that they cannot make the same kinds of fundamental decisions for their designers as the latter made for them. Both parties "know that it is impossible in principle for them to change their social places" (p. 169; also see Habermas 2003, 65). This knowledge may make symmetrical relationships impossible by leading manipulated individuals to "self-devaluate" their moral standing vis-à-vis others. This, in turn, may affect a "subjective qualification essential for assuming the status of a full member of the moral community" (Habermas 2003, p. 81). Second, from the perspective of those who design, genetic manipulation both expresses and furthers a problematic attitude toward the equal moral status of future persons and toward the equal moral status of persons more generally.

Regarding the psychological effect on persons' self-perceived autonomy, Habermas (2003) is concerned that genetic design takes place prior to, and outside of, the sphere of communicative interaction. This makes it far more difficult for genetically manipulated individuals to critically respond to their genetic programming should they object to the genetic choices made by their parents. "From the adolescent's perspective, an instrumental determination (...) does not permit the adolescent looking back on the prenatal intervention to engage in a *revisionary* learning process. *Being at odds with* the genetically fixed intention of a third person is hopeless" (p. 62; emphasis in original). Manipulated individuals may therefore end up unable to take full (ethical or personal) responsibility for their lives or to assume sole authorship over them. These claims warrant some further exploration.

2. Irreversibility, Responsibility, and Appropriate Attitudes

The first of three principal problems Habermas identifies about new modes of genetic alteration is their irreversibility. This, he thinks, may have negative effects on manipulated individuals' self-perception as equal and as free (a). The second concern is the potential dislocation of responsibility genetic manipulation may bring about. This may have detrimental effects on genetically altered persons' self-perception as autonomous authors of their lives (b). From the perspective of those who genetically manipulate others, the chief challenge is, third, the troubling attitude that is thereby expressed and encouraged vis-à-vis those they design. Such an attitude may undermine the equal respect due to persons more generally (c). All three issues point to important concerns regarding the quality of intergenerational relationships. But Habermas thinks that genetic manipulation is only truly problematic if it presents itself as such to the manipulated persons or, in the case of those who design, if there is the danger that a questionable attitude is being attached to or encouraged by their actions. Pace Habermas, I argue that genetic manipulation is problematic from a normative point of view, regardless of the psychological effects it may have on particular individuals or the attitudes that may or may not be expressed or encouraged on account of purposefully interfering with the genetic make-up of others.

(a) Irreversibility. Habermas mentions the problem of irreversibility as part of what leads to the pathological element of asymmetrical relationships between those who design and those who are designed in two different contexts. The first arises in connection with Habermas's concern that those who design and those who are designed can never change social places with each other. Unlike the relationship between parents and children where no genetic manipulation is involved, Habermas seems to think that genetic design is a highly particular act that cannot be repeated. By contrast, he appears to believe that when parents create their children under "normal" circumstances, the asymmetry can be neutralized once these children grow up, face their parents as their equals, and in turn become parents to their own children. Arguably, of course, designed children will also grow up and face their parents as their equals, and they could always themselves turn into designers of their own children. Thus, it is not clear why Habermas thinks that genetic manipulation per se would inevitably "freeze" social roles any more indefinitely than they already are (or not, as the case may be). Therefore, the irreversibility of social places constitutes no particularly plausible reason for objecting to genetic manipulation.

But there is a second, more pertinent way in which irreversibility causes Habermas to worry. He is concerned about the prospect of babies being born with social norms and values irreversibly imprinted into their genomes (i.e., so that they cannot later be "cured" or changed). Rebellion, or cure of the neurosis that may result from an unsuccessful rebellion, is thus impossible. According to Habermas (2003), the entire (i.e., not just the pathological) process of socialization is reversible because it can be reawakened, forced to speak and subjected to answers. This kind of freedom "through retroactive communication" is what makes socialization morally acceptable. As this possibility is foreclosed with genetic manipulation, he considers this technology to be objectionable.[3]

> The genetic program is a mute and, in a sense, unanswerable fact; for unlike persons born naturally, someone who is at odds with genetically fixed intentions is barred from developing, in the course of a reflectively appropriated and deliberately continued life history, an attitude toward her talents (and handicaps) which implies a revised self-understanding and allows for a *productive* response to the initial situation. (p. 62; emphasis in original)

Interestingly, as long as designed individuals happen to agree with their parents' genetic choices Habermas sees little problem (p. 61). Only if designed persons object to their design will they be unable to ever claim undivided authorship over their lives (p. 63). In the latter case, their problem would be that they are unable to talk back at the traits they hate since they are "mute," (i.e., never internalized through some form of communicative discourse but always already irreversibly internal). But if the particular mode of interaction that genetic manipulation constitutes is problematic, that is, it being a mute and unanswerable fact, then it ought not to matter whether genetically manipulated persons happen to agree with their manipulation or not. As I argued before (in chapter 4), it is quite likely that manipulated individuals will come to appreciate who they were born as. So the real problem with irreversibility when it comes to genetic alterations is that it makes the choices of the designers so much harder to contest. It does not matter whether genetically manipulated persons actually try to contest them or not. Thus, the irreversibility of genetic manipulation would have to be highly problematic in all situations and not just in some, as Habermas implies.

(b) Responsibility. A further aspect that follows from the irreversibility of genetic changes is a partial but substantial relocation and, ultimately, dislocation of responsibility. It strikes Habermas as problematic that parents who interfere with their child's genetic endowment acquire a kind of responsibility for the life of their future child that they cannot possibly live up to. The difficulty with responsibility thus arises on two fronts: first, when it comes to parents making choices about what would be in the "best" interest of their children and second, when it comes to children being able to take over (ethical) responsibility for traits their parents chose for them.

With regard to parents' choices, Habermas is skeptical about their possession of the prognostic knowledge to make decisions about the "good" of their child. Thus, even those interventions that appear—at first sight—to be uncontroversial, such as increasing intelligence or ensuring good health, are not necessarily in the child's "best" interest. Both can be beneficial but can also become burdens—depending on the particular life context within which they occur.

> In many situations [outstanding intelligence] is a predictable advantage. But how will the "head start" of high intelligence play itself out in a competitive society—for example, in the character formation of the highly talented person? (. . .) Not even the highly general good of bodily health maintains one and the same value within the contexts of different life histories. Parents can't even know whether a mild physical handicap might not prove in the end to be an advantage for their child. (Habermas 2003, 85)

One solution to this conundrum could, of course, be to relieve individual parents of the responsibility and to ask the public to standardize eugenic practices according to the rules of democratic decision-making. Habermas (2003, 66) quickly rejects this option because he believes that it would be impossible to regulate positive eugenics by democratic consensus. This consensus would either be too strong or too weak: "Too strong, because a *binding* commitment to collective goals going beyond the prevention of evils agreed upon would be an unconstitutional intervention in the private autonomy of citizens; too weak, because the mere *permission* to make use of eugenic procedures would not be able to relieve parents of their moral responsibility for their highly personal choice of eugenic goals" (p. 66; emphasis in original). For Habermas, there is thus no way out of the "responsibility problem" other than to leave things the way they are now, where future persons are subject to the natural and not a social lottery. As already argued in the previous chapter, it is indeed highly questionable whether parents can ever make decisions about what is "best" for their children. I therefore completely agree with Habermas on this point.

This takes us directly to the second front at which problems with responsibility arise, namely with regard to manipulated individuals assuming sole authorship over their lives. When Habermas worries about genetically manipulated persons not being able to assume such authorship or responsibility, he could (mistakenly) be taken to refer to moral responsibility. Such a claim would certainly not be maintainable. If genetically manipulated individuals were absolved from moral responsibility, then our entire criminal system would need to be recalibrated. Consider, for instance, the case of an office worker who claims he knocked down his colleague with a hockey stick in an act of rage and loss of judgment caused by the kinds of sugars and trans-fats contained in the cookies he consumed at the morning meeting. Compare this to another office worker who commits the exact same crime but claims that her parents are the ones to blame because they gave her a gene that, as a side effect, made her body react to sugar consumption (same source and amount as above) with uncontrollable rage and loss of judgment. Although the causal connection between sugar consumption and its physical consequences may limit agency in both cases, the source of the culprit gene does not. It is a matter of bad luck for both office workers and perhaps of terribly bad judgment in the case of the parents who did not know or accepted the risk of making a particular genetic change with this side effect. No matter how angry someone may be at the parents' choice, however, the fact of the matter remains the same. It is futile to blame them for something they might have been responsible for creating but are not responsible for wielding. Thus, no matter where certain traits originate from, at the end of the day the person living with them will have to take moral responsibility for exercising them. In extreme cases, in which parents, for instance, deliberately make it the case that their child will react aggressively in certain situations, they may be held responsible in addition to their child having to account for his or her actions.

For Habermas the real problem arises with regard to ethical or personal responsibility. He maintains that genetically manipulated persons might not feel "at home" in their bodies and may therefore be unable to claim "authorship" over their lives. So even if parents could make good guesses about what might be "best" for their children, it is anything but clear that children could make their parents' choices their own in the same way they could do this with a "natural" endowment (in the sense of not chosen by other people).

One might object that Habermas takes the influence of genes too seriously and underestimates the effects of socialization. But he probably has in mind something along the following lines. Imagine two sets of parents, both desiring their children to be ballet dancers. The first set chooses to achieve its goal the "traditional" way and starts sending its children to ballet classes from a very early age. The second set of parents chooses to try it the "advanced" way and genetically manipulates its children to have a petit frame and a high level of flexibility. It also sends its children to ballet classes from a very early age. Suppose further that both sets of parents have children of the same age, that the children end up being in the same ballet classes together, and that it so happens that they are all equally good at what they do. Habermas thinks that there is a profound difference between these cases. First, the genetically manipulated children may feel that whatever success they have as ballet dancers is due more to their parents' doing than their own. Second, once the genetically manipulated children discover that they would prefer to do something else, they will have difficulty coming to terms with how their parents made them. They might think that had it not been for their parents' choices, they could have ended up tall and strong so that they could have performed better at basketball (which they might prefer over ballet). Should, by contrast, any of the nonmanipulated children choose to do something else, they are much more likely to come to terms with their—perhaps ill-suited—physique, which was not designed according to someone's plan but just turned out that way. In other words, they could never have had a different body from the one they were born with and cannot hold others responsible for the features they may come to dislike.[4]

Here again, the trouble with Habermas's account is that he thinks that problems of this kind (i.e., regarding authorship and responsibility) materialize only if genetically manipulated children come to disagree with their parents' choices. But as argued before, it cannot matter whether genetically manipulated persons happen to agree with how they were designed. They are indeed quite likely to. It is worse (for them), of course, if they do not, as they then have to tangibly feel that their parents overstepped their boundaries. What matters here is not so much how genetically manipulated individuals (happen to) feel about their manipulation but that the manipulation itself is wrong because, in Habermas's own terms, it commodifies future persons (i.e., does not treat them with the appropriate amount of respect).

(c) **Appropriate Attitudes.** To Habermas, the attitude with which a doctor creates and destroys an embryo or with which parents "choose" an embryo during PGD is crucial in the same way that the attitude with which parents genetically interfere with their future offspring is significant. The problem begins once these attitudes are reifying, which, Habermas contends, they are likely to be in most cases in which parents make use of modern reprogenetic technologies for purposes that do not strictly follow the logic of healing. Having such troubling attitudes will affect not only persons' views of the embryos and future persons they manipulate but also the way they value human life quite generally and other members of the moral community, including themselves.

Before I discuss some ramifications of the problem of reifying attitudes, let me briefly mention one possible misconception about Habermas's argument in this context. This may arise because the appropriate attitude envisioned by Habermas will, in many instances, require respect for the way the natural lottery rolls the dice. This could lead to the impression that his claim is not fundamentally different from that made by his more conservative colleagues when they invoke the moral value of the natural order to point out the limits of permissible human action.

Sandel (2004), for instance, calls for accepting "life as a gift." As humans, he claims, we ought to respect the natural order and not seek perfection from a "Promethean aspiration to remake nature, including human nature, to serve our purposes and satisfy our desires" (p. 54; see also Sandel 2007, 26). Sandel (2004) maintains that such "drive to mastery misses, and may even destroy, (. . .) an appreciation of the gifted character of human powers and achievements" (p. 54; see also Sandel 2007, 27). Thus, instead of being concerned about the appropriate attitude one person should have toward another (future) person, Sandel is thinking of the proper attitude humans ought to display toward the natural order. When he speaks of life as a gift, he wants to emphasize the humble and appreciative attitude persons should display when receiving this gift. According to Sandel, it would be in bad taste not to be grateful for re-ceiving the life we are given or, even worse, aspiring to "(ex)change" parts of it. Nature and the natural lottery play a very different role in Habermas's argu-ment. What makes the natural lottery preferable to human design is that the latter introduces a power asymmetry into human relationships whereas the former does not. The problematic attitudes Habermas is concerned about are not toward nature or "the given" but toward other persons.

This brings me back to Habermas's argument and a discussion of what he means when he rejects genetic manipulation performed for the wrong rea-sons. Arguably, the parents envisioned by Buchanan et al. (2000), for instance, with their far-ranging entitlements to alter the genome of their offspring, are presumed to be well intentioned and not, in the first instance, to be seeking mastery over their children. However, the danger Habermas sees in such (ap-parently) innocuous actions is not only that the actions themselves express a disrespectful attitude but that they will eventually lead to genuinely problem-atic ways of thinking that provoke parents into believing that they can and perhaps even ought to "make" their children according to the image of their perfect dream child. The mistake they would then have fallen prey to is that they would no longer see future persons (and with them, persons more generally) as their equals.

Attitudes of this kind are certainly of serious concern. But the difficulty with focusing so exclusively on persons' attitudes and intentions is that they are hard to predict and monitor. Rather than concentrating primarily on the attitudes and intentions of those who design, it might be easier to attend to the actions themselves—in other words, to look at the genetic interventions in question and see whether they express respect for the future persons on whom they are supposed to be performed. What I am suggesting is a very subtle rearrangement of the argument Habermas offers. I am claiming that even if it could be shown that parents' genetically manipulating their children has no effect on parents' attitudes toward their children (or toward other members of the moral community more generally), certain forms of genetic manipulation will still be wrong. This is because future persons are entitled to the same respect for the way they are (without other persons having interfered with them) as the (actual) adults they will develop into.

In sum, I have argued that Habermas is generally too concerned with the psychological effects genetic manipulation may have on those who design and those who are designed. I have insisted instead that we should focus on the interventions themselves and ask whether they display a sufficient degree of respect for future persons. Before I discuss what it takes to display a sufficient degree of respect for future persons in more detail in the next chapter, however, there is yet another dimension to Habermas's rejection of many uses of the new technologies. It, too, requires further exploration. He argues that we ought to be concerned about individuals who are no longer able to perceive themselves and others as free and equal members of the moral community because such pathological perceptions may undermine the basis of our (egalitarian universalist) morality.

3. The Anthropological Foundations of Morality

When Habermas thinks about the effects changing human nature may have on morality, he comes up with a far more viable solution to the problem than his liberal eugenic colleagues. Instead of declaring conventional moral concepts obsolete, as does Dworkin (2000), or of acknowledging but then ignoring the potential dangers, as do Buchanan et al. (2000), Habermas makes a compelling case for why possible threats to our morality should persuade us not to risk bringing them about. This having been said, just because Habermas draws a viable conclusion from a given set of premises does not mean that the premises themselves are correct. That they are is indeed rather doubtful. To begin with, Habermas's claims remain vague. He seems to maintain, for instance, that what can properly be called "morality" can only exist within a community of individuals who view each other as free and equal. This would imply that only contemporary Western liberal society in its ideal and uncorrupted form can truly be said to constitute a system that can legitimately be called "moral." But when Habermas speaks of the dangers to our moral system, one is under the impression that he does not "merely" seek to imply that our particular morality is endangered by the new technologies. It frequently sounds as if he believes that morality as a whole is on the line.

Habermas (2003) maintains that "what is at stake (. . .) is the ethical self-understanding of the species, which is crucial for whether or not we may go on to see ourselves as beings committed to moral judgment and action. Where we lack compelling *moral* reasons, we have to let ourselves be guided by the signposts set up by the *ethics* of the species" (p. 71; emphasis in original). Habermas claims that our fundamental ethical self-understanding, our "species-ethos," is what makes our moral community possible in the first place. Our species-ethos is responsible for whether and to what extent we are willing, as a species, to function together in and as a moral community. Constitutive of this basic willingness is the recognition that persons are free and equal. This would seem to imply that the only anthropological feature that is necessary for this willingness to materialize is the presence and functioning of whatever faculty we need to recognize the freedom and equality of persons.

However, instead of focusing on the presence and functioning of this faculty, Habermas concentrates on the importance of interpersonal relationships being symmetrical. Once interpersonal relationships have become asymmetrical in the way Habermas claims they will due to the new technologies, he thinks that humans might lose their ability to recognize each other as equal moral agents. This could mean that they have completely lost their ability to see each other as equal moral agents. Alternatively, this could imply that they will merely be making a "mistake." This mistake could then be pointed out to them in the same way that such mistakes can be (and often are) pointed out to persons who, due to their race or gender, for instance, feel superior (or inferior) to others.

Habermas seems to argue the former. Instead of maintaining that those engaged in asymmetrical relationships are "simply" making a mistake, Habermas (2003) asserts that they are venturing down a path where their self-understanding makes it impossible for them to be moved by moral arguments. As the previous quote shows, he claims that "what is at stake (. . .) is (. . .) whether or not we *may* go on to see ourselves as beings committed to moral judgment and action" (p. 71; emphasis added). He pleads with his readers not to move in this direction. For him, appreciating human beings as of equal moral importance is not a question about right and wrong but about an ethical choice of the species as such. He contends that the ethical self-understanding we have of ourselves as members of the species and the moral system thereby enabled are worth protecting because, without them, life would be insufferable.

> Without the emotions roused by moral sentiments like obligation and guilt, reproach and forgiveness, without the liberating effect of moral respect, without the happiness felt through solidarity and without the depressing effect of moral failure, without the "friendliness" of a civilized way of dealing with conflict and opposition, we feel, or so we still think today, that the universe inhabited by men would be unbearable. (p. 73)

Habermas invokes the ethical self-understanding of the species because he believes that we need reasons for morally engaging with each other that cannot themselves be moral.[5] In the following I show, however, that there is no cause for Habermas to step outside morality to develop an argument against certain uses of the new technologies. The reason Habermas (to my mind mistakenly) thinks there is such a cause has to do with the way he imagines a world in which people no longer perceive themselves as moral agents. Early on in his participation in the bioethical debate, Habermas himself likened the situation of the new kinds of individuals to that of slaves (Habermas 2001, 164). He has since distanced himself from such a claim (Habermas 2003, 78). But the metaphor of a "slave morality" made it easier to understand where his primary concern lay, namely with the asymmetry between those who design and those who are designed. Moreover, the notion of the slave (rather than that of a genetically manipulated person) evokes a tangible picture of individuals being denied essential human entitlements by others. However, it also suggests the image of persons who have not ventured down a path of no return but whom we expect to be able to free themselves from the chains of slavery.

We may come even closer to the real concern if we look at a still earlier pronouncement Habermas made quite independently of current bioethical challenges. In a response to Karl-Otto Apel's (1976) argument for an ineluctable basic principle of morality, Habermas (1994) graphically described how we might imagine future people who no longer desire to be part of a moral system, namely as zombies.

> This demonstration of the factual inescapability of substantive normative presuppositions of a practice internally interwoven with our sociocultural form of life is indeed conditional on the constancy of this

life-form. We cannot exclude a priori the possibility of its undergoing changes. But that remains an empty possibility since—science fiction scenarios that transform human beings into zombies aside—we cannot even imagine a fundamental alteration of our form of life. (p. 83)

This shows how quickly things can change: What was yesterday's science fiction (thinking that it was unlikely and unreasonable to suppose that human nature could fundamentally be altered) has turned into a real possibility. Moreover, this quote illustrates that before the new reprotechnologies were on the horizon, Habermas thought that only once humans turned into zombies would something so fundamental have changed that our perspective on morality (as a necessary implication of our human form of life) could conceivably be transformed. Unless, however, the deficiently autonomous and unequal children of the designer generation *are* zombies, it seems as if the prerequisites for morality are significantly more vulnerable according to the current picture Habermas paints. Here, the future of morality hangs on something as fragile as nonpathological self-conceptions. I am not convinced by this recent move.

As mentioned before and as his images of zombies and slaves show with even greater force, Habermas is worried about autonomy and equality not only from the perspective of the manipulated individual. He is also concerned about whether others will be able to continue to respect genetically manipulated individuals as free and equal participants in the moral community. That said, it is not clear how genetically manipulated individuals' view of their place in the moral community and the moral community's view of them interact, nor is it obvious how either view relates to anthropological "facts." Three scenarios are possible to imagine.

First, one could be concerned about a situation in which individuals continue to have all capacities needed for them to assume that they are autonomous actors, equal to all others, but others refuse to let them see themselves this way, either because these others get it wrong or because they have bad intentions. This case is probably that of societies whose normative system is not based on a belief that every person should be treated as free and equal. In racist or sexist societies, for instance, the vast majority of people might believe that, due to their "superior" race or gender, they are "better" or more valuable than others. Buchanan et al. (2000) probably have such a scenario in mind when they worry that changing human nature so that we end up with different human natures may undermine our motivation to engage in a common moral system. Although a lack of motivation is a grave concern, none of this changes anything about the fact that inhabitants in these worlds make mistakes when they consider some superior to others. After all, these are mistakes they can, in principle at least, become (or be made) aware of even if the reigning value system might make it very hard for them.

Second, although it may no longer be true of certain individuals that they have all capacities needed for them to assume that they are autonomous actors, equal to all others, their social surroundings could still be able to construct a narrative that allows them to continue treating these individuals as if these capacities were still present. This could occur if the latter were genetically manipulated to an extent that changed the anthropological "facts" on which their freedom and equality were grounded (if that indeed were possible) but where the social surrounding could still pretend it was otherwise—in the same way, perhaps, that some people choose to treat their pets as if they were persons.

Third, suppose again that genetically manipulated individuals lose the capacities required for their participation in the moral community as free and equal members. Suppose further that their surroundings cannot (or do not want to) pretend as if it were different and instead treat them according to their diminished autonomy and equality. These manipulated individuals would grow up with the accurate self-perception of being unequal and nonautonomous members of the moral community.

Habermas oscillates between envisioning the first and the third scenario. On the one hand, he thinks that the changes occur predominantly in the minds of persons and as a result of asymmetrical relationships, that is, are mainly cultural. This would suggest that being genetically manipulated will not actually change anything about persons and their nature (such as turning them into zombies) that would make it impossible for them to perceive themselves as free and equal members of the moral community or for others to regard them as morally equal. If genetically manipulated persons nevertheless were to view themselves as unequal or were to be treated as such by others this would be due to a certain (mistaken) interpretation of these persons' moral status. On the other hand, Habermas implies that the mere use of genetic manipulation in certain ways (to enhance athletic ability, for instance) might irreversibly undermine humans' ability to recognize each other as moral equals—in very much the same way as it would be lost if persons were to become zombies or have their capacity for moral agency otherwise destroyed. It is not clear which of the two alternatives he means to invoke.

If asymmetrical relationships inevitably and incurably made it impossible for people to recognize the equal worth of persons, then we could not explain how those subject to slavery all their lives can eventually rise against their "masters" and claim their right to equal treatment. Even if their social conditions made it very hard for them to gain this insight (partly because their own preferences may have adapted to the situation), we would not be surprised if it turns out that they have the resources the first scenario offers, namely to understand that their unequal treatment has no foundation and that they, as persons, are of equal moral worth to those who oppress them. Likewise, if Habermas's third scenario were correct, we should not be worried about the irreversibly detrimental effects of being subject to asymmetric relationships. Rather, we should be troubled by the prospect of genetic manipulation being used so that individuals lose their capacity for moral agency. I am assuming that this is not a goal many people would intentionally aspire to or accept as a foreseeable side-effect of other kinds of pursuit. Habermas is certainly not implying otherwise. Short of actually having lost the capacity for moral agency, however, there is no world in which individuals capable of moral agency can legitimately treat each other as if they were of different moral standing. Depending on the worlds we envision, persons' (culturally shaped) inclination to treat each other as moral equals may, of course, come in different degrees. We can still, however, morally blame persons who fail to treat others with the appropriate amount of respect and we can do this for reasons that do not require us to leave the realm of morality to be found.

Thus, Habermas's concern with asymmetrical relationships should give him a straightforward, moral claim against certain uses of genetic manipulation. This claim is that people who use reprogenetic technologies on future persons for purposes other than to avert a fatal or otherwise terrible disease fail to display the appropriate amount of respect toward them. Implied hereby is also that unless we use genetic manipulation to transform ourselves into zombies, no one will have disregarded a species-ethical signpost and rendered themselves or others incapable of responding to moral reasons.

I have argued that compared to Dworkin (2000) and Buchanan et al. (2000), Habermas provides the only compelling response if we assume that changing human nature constitutes a threat to our moral system. If there was such a threat, we would certainly have more reasons to oppose the new technologies than to endorse them whole-heartedly (Dworkin 2000) or to ignore the threat altogether (Buchanan et al. 2000). This having been said, none of the authors make a credible case for the dangers they suspect for morality.

Dworkin thinks that our conventional moral concepts become blurred once the boundary between chance and choice has been rendered indistinct. I maintained that there is no reason not to apply our conventional moral concepts; they do not cease to provide guidelines. In other words, there is no cause for not respecting a woman's bodily integrity just because there are new ways of making sure that the life of her embryo succeeds rather than fails. Buchanan et al. worry that once human nature changes in different directions, there will no longer be common ground for participating in a moral community. This concern is formulated ambivalently. I argued that it probably should not be taken to indicate that once there are different kinds of humans they will no longer be able to participate in a moral community. Rather, the author's worry is best understood as referring to the human motivation to continue cooperating with each other. In response to Habermas, I claimed that our moral system need not be undermined just because some technologies may render social relationships asymmetrical. This is true at least as long as these technologies do not destroy the human capacity for moral agency or whatever else may be required for recognizing persons as free and equal. If this capacity remains intact, so does the human ability to detect mistakes in the treatment of others (despite the social conditions that may render this extremely difficult in any given case).

I do not want to make light of the dangers the authors identify. The motivation to cooperate with each other on equal moral terms may indeed be undermined if some persons were to consider themselves superior to others due to their own genetic composition or due to having been in a position to manipulate others. This would be a serious concern and one that should council us to caution. It would not be desirable to morally regress to a stage in which many have lost sight of the egalitarian universalist principles that rightly govern relationships among persons.

4. Conclusion

For Habermas it matters how the intervention in a person's nature takes place and that what hitherto was an arbitrary[6] process turns into an attributable action. Habermas's basic intuition is compelling that there is something troublesome when one generation substantially interferes with the genetic structure of the next. This is potentially true of every way in which one generation can influence the development of the next but perhaps particularly so with the new technologies. Even without believing in genetic determinism, it makes intuitive sense to follow Habermas in his differentiation between socialization (that takes place after birth) and genetic alterations (that are programmed into a child just after conception). Whereas the former influences the development of an already genetically constituted individual, the latter create one. Genetic manipulation thus constitutes a new form of interaction between the generations.

However, I doubted that certain uses of the new technologies are problematic because they produce the psychological pathologies that Habermas portrays. I suggested instead that it would be more persuasive if he made straightforward normative claims about the ways in which certain forms of genetic intervention fail to express the appropriate degree of respect for (future) persons. With regard to Habermas's concerns that using the new technologies may erode the anthropological foundations of morality I was skeptical because it remains unclear how this would occur.

With this in mind, in the next chapter I discuss my own, alternative approach. It spells out what the appropriate kind of respect for (future) persons amounts to when it comes to utilizing the new reprogenetic technologies.

6 FUTURE PERSONS AND THEIR INDEPENDENCE

As might have become clear by now, I consider there to be something deeply ironic about so-called liberal eugenic pursuits that propose enhancements for the purpose of making life "better" for future generations. The irony lies in the fact that liberals have classically desired to be free from their neighbor's and government's intrusions, especially when it comes to the more intimate spheres of people's lives. Now, suddenly, with the arrival of the new reprogenetic technologies, many of them advocate that presently living persons have the right to perform remarkably intrusive interventions into the genomes of future individuals. This means taking the genetic fate out of the hands of a neutral arbitrator (i.e., nature) and laying it into the hands of people.

The question is not who of the two—nature or human beings—does a better job or has the right to do it. Nature obviously has some serious shortcomings, including that she is arbitrary in her judgment and, sometimes, for no good reason at all, overly stingy with her gifts. But the discussions in the previous two chapters show that there is something extremely problematic if one generation genetically interferes with the next. It is not clear why different rules should apply to personal relationships just because they are between persons of different generations and not between contemporaries. Thus, it is unclear why, if we consider it wrong to subject persons to the arbitrary rule of their contemporaries, we should agree to the subjection of future persons to the arbitrary rule of their ancestors.

In this chapter I continue and complete the argument that has been developing over the course of this book, namely that we owe it to persons not to take advantage of our asymmetric power position over the embryos from which they emerge. Rather, we must respect their independence from us and try to limit their vulnerability to being subject to asymmetrical relationships with their contemporaries. Thus far, I have suggested that the danger of parents interfering with their future child's genetic make-up is that certain genetic interferences will translate into illegitimate forms of a new kind of social domination. I say "new" because the way this would work is not literal (i.e., in the way that two grown-ups would conspire together to create their own slave-child). Instead, future generations' genetic structure would be determined by the particular ideas and values of previous ones. This may not enslave anyone in the future or necessarily make them worse off. In fact, by some standards (those provided by Buchanan et al. [2000], for instance), they might be judged to be better off. But just as we believe that respect for persons means respect for who they are and not, primarily, for who we think they should be, it is not clear why respecting future persons for who they will turn out to be would translate into anything different. The only reason this is not as obvious as it might seem is because of the way new persons come into this world: unfinished and helpless, so that those presently living have the asymmetrical power to determine their existence, their identities, and the circumstances under which they will be born and develop.

Until now, and mostly in opposition to liberal eugenicists, I have argued that persons have a right to their "native" endowment. In other words, we owe it to persons that the embryos from which they emerge are only interfered with to the extent that it would be appropriate for other people to interfere with the persons themselves (without their consent). I maintained that part of the reason for this is that genetic manipulation is unlike other, more familiar and generally accepted forms of interference with persons' development. This difference, I contended, is aggravated by virtue of our knowing very little about what might "objectively" be best for future persons. I have not said much, however, about the standard of independence I am proposing as an alternative (liberal) approach to the employment of new reprogenetic technologies. I thus use this chapter to complete the argument, proceeding in four steps.

To clarify my position and to show at what point my assumptions diverge from those I am arguing against, I begin by describing the asymmetry between the generations and the problems this gives rise to when it comes to formulating intergenerational obligations. Starting with a brief discussion of the Non-Identity Problem, I point to a mistake in solving it that can lead to embracing the kinds of interventions liberal eugenicists such as Buchanan et al. propose (section 1). I then turn to my own, corrective account to explain the central idea underlying the two aspects of independence we must respect and try to achieve when it comes to future persons. After explaining both natural and substantial independence as well as the central idea connecting the two, I discuss the implications of the principle of independence I am proposing for the treatment of and attitude toward disability as well as for our views regarding the importance of relationships of dependence. Moreover, I spell out what I take independence to mean vis-à-vis autonomy, what the relative advantage of my approach is over the one liberal eugenicists offer and what a concept of independence means for the anthropological foundations of our (conventional) morality (section 2). I go on to say something about the "we" in "what we owe to future persons." The question is whether this refers to anyone specifically (i.e., individual parents). My answer to this is negative. It is society as a whole that must provide the material means to ensure that future persons are not wronged (section 3). I end the chapter and this book with a brief review of all major arguments and some concluding remarks (section 4).

1. Precarious Intergenerational Relationships

A traditional problem with establishing intergenerational obligations is that we cannot harm future persons before they exist (i.e., before conception), at least to the extent harming implies making particular persons worse off than they would otherwise have been. This has come to be known as the Non-Identity Problem. But even once future persons exist (i.e., after having been conceived), it may not make sense to say that, from a first-person perspective, they were made worse off than they could have been had their early embryonic development gone differently from how it actually did. This is referred to as the Identity Problem (section 1.1.). One way to circumvent these problems is by identifying obligations that arise quite generally between persons or within certain types of relationship between persons, regardless of who in particular happens to be part of these relationships (i.e., whether or not they already exist). Thus, in order to determine what we owe to future persons we need to adequately describe our relationship with them. Here, I show, is frequently where the mistake is made that leads some to embrace a very permissive view regarding the kinds of genetic changes they allow parents to undertake on their future children (section 1.2.).

1.1. The Non-Identity Problem

There is a principal difficulty in arriving at obligations toward future persons: No particular person of the future will be able to blame those who brought her into existence for anything they did related to her conception, because had they acted otherwise, a completely different person would have been born. For a better illustration of this so-called Non-Identity Problem, consider a famous example by Derek Parfit (1973, 111). He imagines the case of a woman who has a temporary medical condition. She knows that if she conceives a child now the child is likely to develop a disability, whereas if she waits three months and allows the disease to pass, her child will probably be healthy. The question is whether the woman will harm her child if she decides to conceive now. Parfit denies this by pointing out that an entirely different child would have been born had she waited three months.

The Non-Identity Problem shows that in cases in which the question is whether to have a child now or later, the choice is between having two different children rather than a choice between having the same child with different properties. In other words, whatever the woman decides, from the perspective of the born child the only alternative would have been nonexistence.[1] Put this way, it would appear that future persons cannot be harmed by any of the actions that led to their conception and that therefore, the woman with the temporary medical condition cannot harm her child by conceiving now.

This having been said, depending on the severity of the disability and our notions of what kind of life we should provide for future persons, we might have different intuitions about what the woman should do, regardless of whether she could be said to have harmed any particular child. This is because we may think that the woman has certain obligations toward her future child, no matter who ends up assuming this role. Let me mention three different kinds of obligations that come to mind. To begin with, we might think that she has an obligation to (a) maximize the well-being of future persons. This would make it wrong for the woman to bring into existence the child whose well-being is likely to be below that of the other. Alternatively, if we do not want to judge by mere comparison, we may hold that she has an obligation to bring into existence children above a particular threshold of well-being. There are two possible kinds of threshold. On the one hand, we might think that the woman should (b) not bring into existence a child below the threshold of what it would take to lead a life worth living. On the other hand, we might think that the woman should (c) not bring into existence a child below the threshold of what we consider to be a problematic existence if (but only if) she has the opportunity to prevent this from occurring. Here, "problematic" needs to be further defined according to some standard that, however, does not—as in (b)—refer to the idea of a life not worth living. Let me say more about each of these options.

Parfit (1984) chooses the first kind of obligation (a) when he refers to Principle Q: "*The Same Number Quality Claim or Q: if in either of two outcomes the same number of people would ever live, it would be worse if those who live* are worse off, or have a lower quality of life, than those who would have lived" (p. 360). The problem with (a)—or Q, for that matter—is that it fails to take seriously the separate importance of persons. It does not spell out our duties to persons but asks us to maximize well-being (which is produced through them). Moreover, if we change the example just a little, it leads to a counterintuitive result. If, for instance, the question was whether to bring into existence a child with a great life or another child with an even greater life, Q would make it wrong to give birth to the child with the great life. The wrong in question would not be a wrong to the particular child but a violation of our duty to maximize well-being quite generally.

The reason (b) is not persuasive is, first, because it is problematic to assume that anyone is in a position to determine which particular lives are worth living and which are not (even if I agree that there are some conditions that may make it hard to justify bringing persons into existence, e.g., states of excruciating, permanent pain that lead to a very early death). Taking such a standard as a threshold would make it wrong to bring children into this world if their lives would be below that threshold, even if there is no alternative (i.e., there is no way of bringing other children into this world above the threshold or of moving the children below the threshold above it). In other words, it describes a state of affairs that should always be avoided. Then, however—and this constitutes the second problem— we have to set the threshold so low that very few conditions fall beneath it. For instance, without knowing more about the disability that may be caused by the woman's temporary condition in Parfit's example, it is likely that, even if it was serious, it would not fall below the threshold of a life not worth living. But we might think that we owe more to future persons than merely to prevent their being born in such dismal conditions. We may think, for instance, that if a woman has the choice of bringing her child into the world in a problematic situation (that needs to be further defined but that is far from making a life not worth living) and bringing another child into this world in a nonproblematic situation, she may have an obligation to bring into existence the latter child.

If this is the case, we are left with (c). This is an attractive solution as it prevents us from even considering the case of the child with a great life (compared to the child with the even greater life) as problematic, on the one hand, but it also does not force us to set the threshold so low as to capture only cases in which we think that lives below it are not worth living. Rather, for (c), the choice is between a life that is problematic and one that is not problematic. This distinction is enabled by a threshold that is set so that we would wrong our future child if we did not take advantage of the possibility of bringing about the nonproblematic situation. In contrast, if we had no choice but to give birth to a child below the threshold, we would not necessarily commit any wrong (as our child is still likely to have a life worth living). This shows that (c) does not primarily ask about the good- or badness of certain end-states in themselves (although they are taken into account). Rather, (c) is concerned with the obligations that arise for potential parents with regard to their future children—whoever may end up filling that place—in light of choices that have an impact on the latter's well-being and beyond what is required for preventing a life not worth living.

In the remainder of this chapter I spell out these obligations in terms of future persons' claim to independence. Before I begin, however, there is a question regarding the relevance of non-identity cases (and their solutions) for the issues of primary concern in this book, namely, genetic selection and manipulation. One might think that the Non-Identity Problem applies only in preconception cases. But preimplantation genetic diagnosis (PGD), which involves postconception genetic selection, confronts prospective parents with choices that are very similar to that of the woman with the temporary medical condition. The principal difference is that prospective parents using PGD decide between a child with a disability or without a disability or with great life prospects or even greater life prospects by choosing from a number of already existing embryos.[2] Just as in classical non-identity cases, persons who develop from embryos thus selected could never complain that they were harmed by having been chosen over others. I suggested earlier (chapter 1) that this is the reason why it would not be wrong to select an embryo with an IQ of 130 instead of one with an IQ of 160 during PGD, whereas it would not be similarly permissible to diminish an embryo's IQ from 160 to 130 (as one would clearly be taking something away from this embryo that rightfully belongs to the person developing from it). But just like in classical non-identity cases, this does not mean that prospective parents can do nothing wrong when they select embryos. Here again, it matters whether the genetic condition parents want to (de)select lies above or below the threshold (of what I spell out as independence) and what the other possibilities are.

This shows that there is at least one sort of postconception case that the Non-Identity Problem has something to say about. What remains true, of course, is that it has nothing to say about choices that affect one and the same individual through one's actions[3]—and these are the primary concern when we think about what parents might owe to their children by means of genetic manipulation, for treatment or for enhancement purposes. However, David Velleman (2008) has argued that a version of the Non-Identity Problem also applies to the various possible identities of a single person. In what he calls the Identity Problem, he maintains that one can have no first-person interest in one's possible selves as opposed to one's past and future selves. This means, for instance, that there is no way for Oedipus to rationally and from a first-person perspective connect to the person he could have been had his life turned out differently (i.e., had his feet not been pierced by a spear and bound together by a father who feared for his life more than for his son's well-being). By the same token, this implies that children cannot blame parents for things they did or failed to do to them, because a person cannot care about who she could have been had things gone differently. So, whereas Parfit argues that we cannot care about those other people who would have been born instead of us, Velleman (2008) maintains that we cannot rationally have a first-person concern for our other possible selves.

> The adequacy of a child's initial provision is not relative to what could have been provided for that selfsame child. The child will not be in a position to identify his interests with those of the better-or-worse-provisioned children he might have been. From the child's perspective, the better or worse starts he could have had in life will not be a matter of self-interest, because his self-concern will extend only to his actual present and possible future selves, not children inhabiting possible histories that will already have diverged from reality. (p. 253)

Velleman's argument could be taken to suggest that members of this generation have virtually no responsibilities with regard to what kinds of genetic manipulations they undertake on their future child, because whatever they do to their embryo will irrevocably be part of the life story of the person the embryo develops into.

This clearly seems to be mistaken. Consider the case of parents who are so fond of young children that they genetically manipulate their offspring, who would otherwise develop "normally," so that they will never mature beyond the mental and physical abilities of three-year-olds. Once the necessary genetic interventions have occurred, there is no way for these children to continue to be self-interested in the persons they could have been had their parents not interfered. Does that mean that there is nothing the parents can be blamed for?

I do not think so. There would be something wrong about parents genetically manipulating their children in this way. Here, just as with the Non-Identity Problem in the context of PGD (or preconception cases more generally), the wrongness of the parents' action has nothing to do with whether the children can be self-interested in their merely possible selves. Rather, in chapter 1 I already identified the possible wrong in question, namely that these prospective parents are taking something away from their (future) children that legitimately belongs to them. In other words, the action itself is wrong because it fails to express the appropriate amount of respect for (future) persons.

But this case may be too obvious. What about postconception cases in which the question is not one of diminishment but one of enhancement? One might think that just because parents may not take anything away from their future children's genetic endowment does not mean that they cannot add to it. Thus far, I have suggested that adding to it would be wrong and disrespectful to future persons except in all those cases in which it is necessary to provide them with the capacities for leading an independent life. To develop this account more fully, I must show how to arrive at this central obligation of respecting future persons' independence. This obligation emerges from an adequate description of the particular relationship that holds between prospective parents and their future children when the decision of whether or not to interfere with the latter's genetic endowment is to be made. Coming by such a description, however, can be tricky. The idea that prospective parents are entitled to perform wide-ranging genetic interventions on their offspring, for instance, stems from a mistaken portrayal of the relationship that pertains in the relevant situation.

1.2. Determining the Nature of Intergenerational Relationships

To see how the description of the pertinent relationship can go wrong, consider Rahul Kumar's (2003) contractualist approach. In an attempt to get around the Non-Identity Problem, he maintains that regardless of whether children already exist and whether they are left worse off than they might have been, parents can be said to have wronged them by committing acts that are in and of themselves morally wrong (Kumar 2003, 108). Kumar contends that whether an act is morally wrong hinges on whether it expresses respect for persons. More specifically, and within the realm of actions that express respect for persons, it depends on the terms of the relationship between the persons in question.

Kumar conceives of persons as "types" who stand in certain "types" of relationships to each other, such as drivers and pedestrians or parents and children. Kumar describes the type of person who is responsible for a child as a caretaker and the type of person a child (always) is as a dependent. Dependents have certain legitimate expectations of their caretakers, and caretakers, in turn, have certain obligations toward dependents, regardless of who this dependent will turn out to be. Kumar (2003) claims "that the particular psycho-physical identity of the person in question, at the point in time at which compliance with the duty is required, may still be an indeterminate matter turns out to be of no consequence, as the other retains her standing as a certain type to whom certain duties are owed regardless of what her token identity turns out to be" (p. 113). By focusing on responsibilities between types of persons, Kumar shows that there can be obligations between us and whoever will turn out to live in the future. The problem with this approach begins, however, as soon as we ask how to identify and characterize the relevant relationships. Getting this right is crucial for determining what kinds of obligations result from these relationships.

Kumar assumes that the relevant relationship is best described as one between caretakers and their dependents. In what follows, I argue that this description remains too abstract to yield any meaningful results. Moreover, I maintain that the relevant intergenerational relationships at issue here are parent–child and adult–embryo (or: prospective parent-future child) relationships, which are not only distinct from each other but also different from caretaker–dependent relationships in important regards.

Among the obligations Kumar thinks he can derive from a general description of caretaker–dependent relationships are, on the one hand, respect for children's right to have their capacity for rational self-governance realized and, on the other hand, a host of entitlements children have on account of a principle Kumar borrows from Buchanan et al. (2000), Principle M: "Those individuals responsible for a child's, or other dependent person's, welfare are morally required not to let her suffer a serious harm or disability or a serious loss of happiness or good, that they could have prevented without imposing substantial burdens or costs or loss of benefits on themselves or others" (Kumar 2003, 112).

Even if it were possible (and later I argue that it is not) to directly apply the principles that generally govern caretaker–dependent relationships to that between parents and their children as well as to that between adults (prospective parents) and the embryos entrusted to their care (future children), we would not learn much from the principles Kumar presents. This is because they leave open the vital question regarding the extent to which caretakers ought to ensure a child's welfare or her capacity for rational self-governance. It is also unclear what it would mean for a child not to suffer a "serious loss of happiness or good." For parents to be obliged or entitled to do this could mean anything from caring for their children when they are sick, to enhancing their children's intelligence and memory, to making sure that their capacity for rational self-governance is optimally realized, their welfare is maximized, and their happiness and good are guaranteed. All of these goals could also, of course, conflict in any given case. We are left with no way to weigh them against each other. As mentioned earlier, Kumar merely adopts Principle M from Buchanan et al., who partly allow but also partly oblige parents to genetically interfere with their embryos quite liberally for treatment but also for enhancement purposes if they can thereby remove opportunity-limiting conditions from their children's lives (chapter 4).

However, the main problem with simply taking an underspecified principle such as M, which allows various interpretations, including that of Buchanan et al., is that it is not only devoid of critical normative content but also blind to the power asymmetry between generations. Kumar erroneously assumes that the relationship between caretakers and their dependents is in all relevant aspects similar to the relationship between parents and their children as well as to that between adults (prospective parents) and the embryos for whose care they are responsible (future children). All three relationships are, however, distinct from each other in important ways. First, analogizing caretaker–dependent relationships with those between parents and their children captures only one aspect of care, namely that which arises from a child's needs. It does not address the kind of care required for helping children flourish and mature into independent adults (a). Second, likening caretaker-dependent with adult-embryo relationships fails to take into account that, at the moment when adults (prospective parents) are thinking of interfering with their embryo's development (i.e., altering their future offspring's genetic make-up), they are engaged in a very different kind of interaction with their future child than when parents are trying to actively shape their born (already genetically constituted) child's future (b). Third, treating parent–child relationships as if they were the same as adult–embryo relationships ignores that the mode of interaction is quite different in both cases. As discussed in some detail in chapters 4 and 5, genetic manipulation is unlike other forms of socialization that we approvingly subject children to from the moment of their birth (c).

(a) Describing the relationship between parents and their children as one between caretakers and their dependents captures only one—albeit important—aspect of this relationship. Children do not always require their parents' care. Sooner or later they mature and grow up. Part of the joy of being a parent lies in watching children develop into independent adults who are eventually able to provide for themselves and reciprocate the support, love, and attention bestowed on them during their childhood. This means that the relationship between parent and child is geared not only at taking care of needs but at ensuring the child's future development and establishing a relationship with the separate person she will turn into. Thus, the obligations that arise in parent–child relationships go far beyond what is required in straightforward caretaker–dependent relationships.

(b) An easy way to see what distinguishes relationships between caretakers and dependents from that between adults (prospective parents) and the embryos they care for (future children) is by considering a typical case of the former—for instance that of a doctor and her patients. Here, the role of the doctor can be described as that of a caretaker in part because her patients' identities and interests developed separately from the doctor's interventions. The doctor merely stands in the service of already constituted persons whose need of help did not arise due to anything the doctor did. If, by contrast, the latter was at fault for causing the need for help in the patients, the doctor's response to these needs would not be properly characterized as caretaking. Rather, it would constitute some form of amends or compensation.

In some ways, parents (actual or prospective) are always responsible for a child's needs, at least insofar as they are responsible for bringing this child into existence. This having been said, actual parents who did not interfere with their child's genetic constitution will have to respond to needs that arose independently of their particular actions (as opposed to the basic action of calling their child into existence). By contrast, at the time at which adults (prospective parents) consider changing their embryo's genetic make-up, their future child's identity and interests substantially depend on their decisions. There is no "care" in the normal sense of the term involved, as prospective parents are not responding to any needs that can be attributed to their future child (as these needs are up for grabs in these instances).

Even if one was to reject this analysis, however, and insisted instead that nothing distinguishes the relationship between (actual) parents and their (born) children from that between adults (prospective parents) and the embryos in their care (future children), it is not clear that prospective parents should be entitled to alter their child's genetic composition in the same way parents may be at liberty to influence their child's development through socialization. As we saw in chapter 5, replacing the natural lottery with a social one may come at a high price. Persons must be subject to the natural lottery for their personal history to have a socially uninfluenced starting point (Habermas 2003, 59). This is highly valuable from the perspective of nondomination.

It assures that there is no arbitrary interference with future persons' lives, that is, no deliberate intervention that fails to track children's interests and prevents them from later being able to separate out who they are from the choices other people made for them. As argued already in the introductory paragraphs to the second part of this book, even if a person's parents mated by design or for eugenic purposes, without additional interference and manipulation, it is still a matter of chance as to who ends up being conceived (Hanser 1990, 61).

At this point the critical reader may want to object that we make irreversible choices for children all the time without being in a better position to track their interests; thus, what is so particularly worrisome about genetically manipulating children while they are still embryos? This brings me back to the differences concerning the mode of intervention, discussed at some length in chapters 4 and 5.

(c) Although there are significant differences between the relationship of parents and their born children and that between adults (prospective parents) and the embryos in their care (future children), there are presumably similarities when it comes to the (prospective) parents' concern for the well-being and future development of their offspring (or embryo) into an independent adult. If both cases are similar in this way, however, why not just apply what we consider legitimate actions for parents with regard to their children's socialization to the case of genetic intervention? In other words, if we think it legitimate for parents to send their children to school to further their critical capacities as part of their fiduciary interest in ensuring their children's development into independent adults, could we not also think it legitimate for parents to genetically enhance their children's memory or intelligence (if that were possible) to the same end? As argued in chapters 4 and 5, the reason we cannot is because genetic manipulation is quite different from socialization. While children stand little chance of rebelling against their parents' genetic choices, they will more successfully (and more likely) be able to object to their parents' decisions about how to socialize them.

In sum, the alleged parallels between caretaker–dependent, parent–child, and adult–embryo relationships do not hold up in crucial respects. We cannot derive a full set of obligations from caretaker–dependent relationships for the other two, least so for adult–embryo relationships. Moreover, we also have to be aware that the ways in which parents interact with children is different from the ways in which adults interact with the embryos in their care when they seek to genetically manipulate them. Liberals fail to realize these distinctions when they advocate that those presently living are entitled to perform wide-ranging alterations in their children's genetic endowment. They do not understand that, at the moment at which adults think of interfering with their future child's genetic make-up, they should not, in the first instance, act as their future child's caretakers or as nurturers who, through constant interaction with their (born) child, help the latter mature. Instead, they should act as individuals who are welcoming new persons into existence, whose independence and separate importance needs to be respected *before* acts of nurturing and caretaking can legitimately commence.

Thus, an alternative account is needed that appreciates the particular nature of our relationship to future persons and that protects them from domination by (the) previous generation(s).

2. The Importance of Independence

Respect for persons, including those of the future, demands caring about their independence. But what exactly does that mean? I have claimed that one major mistake of Buchanan et al.'s (2000) approach is that they construe a child's right to an open future too narrowly. They take it to limit parental genetic interventions only with regard to a certain quantity of options that must remain available to those who are genetically interfered with. I argued instead for a wide understanding, that is, for one that values children's genetic endowment before any intervention has occurred. It is therefore far more cautious about parental liberties to interfere. In that sense, I interpreted a child's right to an open future as relative to that child's "natural" (i.e., noninterfered-with) genetic constitution and not relative to a certain number of options the standard of "openness" may require at any given time. This means that before parents start thinking about genetically interfering with their children's development, they should respect their children exactly the way they enter this world.

This view is neither idiosyncratic nor new. John Locke (1690, XV, § 173), for instance, famously claims that parental power should be limited in terms of both its scope and the time that it lasts. He argues that parental power does not include command over children's property, by which he means the property individuals have in their own person and in their goods (XV, §173). To the extent we understand future persons' genetic constitution as belonging to the actual persons they develop into (as argued in chapter 1), parental rights would not extend into that realm, at least not in principle. Moreover, and more important, Locke limits parental powers in its temporal dimension. He insists that parental power "must be far from an absolute or perpetual Jurisdiction, from which a Man may withdraw himself, having Licence from Divine Authority to *leave Father and Mother and cleave to his Wife*" (Locke 1690, VI, § 65;

emphasis in original). Thus far, I have maintained that genetic changes, unlike socialization practices, make it far more difficult for children to completely sever the ties to their parents. From the perspective of limiting parental powers temporally, then, bringing such changes about would be a clear instance of parents overstepping their boundaries.

The claim that no person should, in principle at least, be entitled to interfere with another person's genetic structure is meant to protect future persons' independence from the genetic imprinting by members of the previous generation, just as contemporaries are protected from each other's interventions. But the problem with not interfering with future persons' genetic endowment at all and under any circumstances is that this might lead to the birth of children who will predictably never develop the necessary physical and mental capacities to lead an "independent" life—a life, that is, in which persons are not forced to permanently depend on the charitable help of others and be subject to relationships they cannot choose (to leave). Locke also saw this problem: "If, through defects that may happen out of the ordinary course of Nature, any one comes not to such a degree of Reason, wherein he might be supposed capable of knowing the Law, and so living within the Rules of it, he is *never capable of being a Free Man*, he is never let loose to the disposure of his own Will (. . .) but is continued under the Tuition and Government of others" (VI, § 60; emphasis in original).

If one insists, as I do, that there be no domination between generations, one has good reasons to similarly limit the vulnerabilities to being dominated by one's contemporaries. Otherwise, the independence in the former realm would come at the price of dependence in the latter. Thus, genetic interventions that promise to secure a minimal level of independence vis-à-vis a person's contemporaries should be part of what we owe to future persons.

This proposal causes a tension between the requirement not to intervene in the genetic endowment of future persons and the requirement to intervene in it—both in the name of independence. It might even appear as if two conflictual notions of independence are at work. In what follows I address this tension, beginning with an explanation of what I am referring to as "independence."

2.1. Natural and Substantial Independence

The starting assumption of this book is that we have a certain normative commitment to the category of individuals who are "persons." Even those who do not accept the way I specify who counts as a person (chapter 1, section 1), would probably agree that the normative commitment to persons consists of respecting their independence. This includes respect for their separate moral importance as well as respect for who they are and choose to be. Translated into obligations to future persons, this means that we should first respect what I have called their "natural independence," the independence they have by virtue of being subject to the natural lottery. However, when we say we respect the independence of persons, we mostly assume that the persons we are referring to can be independent in another sense of the term. This is what I call "substantial independence." This means that they are able to provide for themselves and move about freely, without having to permanently depend on the charitable help of others. If persons are not independent in this way, we often consider it necessary to assist them in their pursuits of being more independent. We do not, for instance, think there is a need to help people with diseases or impairments only if they are suffering under acute pain. Being short of sight or hard of hearing are not inevitably painful conditions. But without being corrected in some form they impede a person's ability to participate in daily life without other persons' assistance. Thus, even if a condition is not painful, we recognize the significance of enabling individuals to arrange their lives as independently as possible.

For those invested in the idea that we should avoid situations in which some are dependent on the arbitrary will of others, it is important that people have the means to choose their dependencies and are not merely subjected to them. It is thus vital that people are, to some reasonable degree, independent both from their parents as well as from their contemporaries. This means that future persons' right to independence obliges those that come before them, including their parents, in two complementary ways: first, to respect the way their offspring enters this world without genetic interference and second, to ensure that if, for example, a genetic defect were to predictably render it impossible for the future person to develop into a mentally and physically independent individual, this defect is remedied up to the threshold above which a minimally independent life becomes possible.

By "mentally and physically independent person" I mean someone who can rebel against her upbringing (or endorse it for her own reasons) and who can physically pick up her belongings, leave home, live her own life, and provide for herself. This is presumably also what Locke means when he quotes the bible about man having license from divine authority to leave mother and father and cleave to his wife (Locke 1690, VI, § 65, quoted above). The particular lives thereby pursued need not be of any particular quality; they just need to be lives individuals themselves endorse and in which they can go about their daily chores without necessarily having to depend on others (any more, that is, than most people have to depend on others to produce, ship, and sell the food they want to buy, for instance).

This shows how the two seemingly conflictual interpretations of independence stem from one common idea, namely to make people independent both in their vertical relationships across generations as well as in their horizontal relationships with their contemporaries. This having been said, the critical reader will notice that this may still leave some practical tensions unresolved. It might seem that any genetic intervention necessary to ensure substantial independence will violate a person's right to natural independence. This tension can be alleviated only in part. While natural independence is supposed to function as a limiting condition to possible parental designs, substantial independence is a threshold conception. Thus, until this threshold is reached, any intervention in the name of substantial independence does not undermine independence in a wrongful way (although it does, of course, interfere with a person's natural independence). In that instance, both notions are weighed against each other and substantial independence trumps natural independence.

A concern with ensuring substantial independence is that, just like any other genetic intervention, it is not contestable. Therefore, one of the conditions ensuring that (asymmetrical) relationships are not dominating remains unfulfilled. But as persons need substantial independence to be able to turn against their designer's choices in the first place, it would be strange for individuals to resent being able to do this. Arguably, if they did object to having been manipulated in this way, they would be making a mistake. They would be rejecting the very precondition of their being able to object.

Note that, according to this proposal, there is no argument for using genetic manipulation to heighten offspring's level of independence, if that were possible. As a threshold conception, there is no excuse for doing more than necessary. Some people may think that if some minimal amount of substantial independence is important and necessary then being even more independent is desirable and certainly can do no harm. However, it is not clear what it would mean to be "more" independent. Many will surely think that the higher the IQ of persons, the greater their athletic abilities and the better their general health, the more independent they are going to be from other people and the freer to pursue their goals. These features are certainly much esteemed and both socially and economically rewarded. But above a certain threshold of independence, persons cannot be made "more" independent. While it is important from the standpoint of independence that persons are minimally free to move about at will and choose the life they want to live and the relationships they want to be part of, it is not important that they can do all of this "even better" (whatever that may stand for).

Let me briefly sum up the arguments in response to the concern that natural and substantial independence stand in irresolvable tension to each other. I hope to have put this worry to rest by showing that both interpretations of independence emerge from the same basic idea, namely to avoid situations of domination or increased vulnerability to such situations both intergenerationally and among contemporaries. It thus limits the use of reprogenetic technology to those instances in which the independence of future persons needs to be minimally secured. It therefore ends up being far more restrictive than the liberal eugenic accounts discussed earlier but more permissive in allowing the use of genetic manipulation than Habermas's approach.

Before I go on to consider five possible objections to my proposal, I want to spell out what my suggestions imply for the case mentioned at the outset of this chapter, namely that of the woman with the temporary medical condition. As I said before, she faces a parallel moral problem to the one with which parents are confronted when they select embryos through PGD.

What is right or wrong for this woman to do (or for parents to choose during PGD) will depend on how severe the disability is that her child would be born with and what she can do about it. If her child would be capable of leading a substantially independent life despite the disability, the woman would do no wrong by conceiving her child in the presence of her temporary medical condition. If the disability the child would be born with is one that makes an independent life impossible, then the woman could permissibly conceive if there was a way to genetically alter her child after conception to move it above the threshold of what is required for a substantially independent life. In the latter case, the woman would stand obliged to perform the necessary genetic alteration.[4] If no such genetic alteration is available, the woman could be asked to wait for her disease to pass, unless, of course, it was known that all of her children would end up below the threshold (but still with a life worth living). In that case, she could conceive the child now. In other words, she has an obligation to bring into this world a child above the threshold of what is required for a substantially independent life only if (i) that is an option for her and (ii) her child's life below the threshold will, in all likelihood, still be worth living. In cases in which adults select their children through PGD and can choose only between embryos that will most likely not develop into (substantially) independent persons, we cannot expect them to "wait," that is, to go through the (for the woman) arduous process of creating embryos in vitro again. They therefore can permissibly pick one of the embryos currently available to them without wronging their future child (as long, that is, as this child's genetic endowment does not also lie below the threshold of what is required for a life worth living).

Thus, substantial independence functions as a threshold concept that makes it wrong to conceive children below it only if parents could choose to bring into existence another child above the threshold, or if the children they conceive will not only end up below the threshold of what makes a substantially independent life possible but also below the threshold of what constitutes a life worth living. Above the threshold of substantial independence, parents are obliged to respect the way their children come into existence, that is, their natural independence. Parents can therefore not permissibly do anything to enhance or to diminish their children's traits, regardless of whether their children would end up above the threshold or below due to their interventions. In this way, the standard of independence I am offering involves a threshold to demarcate certain obligations but is not primarily concerned with bringing about particular states of affairs. Rather, it tries to ensure the symmetry of interpersonal relationships so that (future) persons are adequately respected.

For further clarification of my views, I address several questions and possible objections to them in the following sections. Some may be gravely concerned by my suggestions so far; others may be puzzled; and some may be both. For instance, there is a legitimate concern about what a plea for independence says about disability and the value of a life with a disability (section 2.2.). Another worry may be that I am vastly overstating the importance of independence in interpersonal relationships, thereby missing the significance and value of various forms of interpersonal dependency (section 2.3.). Moreover, one possible source of confusion may lie in my very use of the term "independence." Thus, something further needs to be said about how the notion of independence as I am defending it differs from notions of autonomy that are more frequently invoked when it comes to spelling out children's right to an open future (section 2.4.). Several readers may furthermore doubt that the normative idea of independence is any less likely to be shaped by the preferences and fashions of particular societies than the criteria are that liberal eugenicists employ (section 2.5.). Finally, some might ask to what extent the proposal offered here manages to circumvent the problem that has come up repeatedly in the discussions of Buchanan et al., Dworkin, and Habermas, namely of how to deal with the possibility that allowing some genetic changes might detrimentally affect our moral system (section 2.6.).

2.2. Independence and Disability

One concern about the notion of independence defended here is that it may be thought to pass a negative judgment on people with disabilities. There are several forms this concern can take of which I will mention four: First, one might be under the impression that independence is something only persons without disabilities can achieve and that therefore, a decision to emphasize the importance of independence automatically categorizes disabilities as "problematic" conditions. But there is no necessary connection between the notion of independence suggested here and disability. The independence I am primarily concerned with is not so much focused on anyone's level of ability (above a certain minimal threshold) but more on the quality of inter- and intragenerational relationships. Moreover, even substantial independence does not rule out disabilities or value them less. People with different levels of ability merely have to be put into a position of being independent—whatever that takes. As Adrienne Asch (2002, 134) has pointed out, the question regarding which variations in human development turn out to be enabling or disabling depends largely on how society chooses to organize itself.

Take the case of someone bound to a wheelchair. If our world was structured so that there were enough ramps for wheelchairs everywhere, then using one would no longer be an impediment to living an independent life on one's own terms. As mentioned before, given the importance of natural independence, it would always be preferable to change social arrangements to enable individuals to be more independent rather than to manipulate their genome. This having been said, there are two factors to bear in mind. First, depending on the disability, it will not always be possible to change social arrangements to accommodate it. Second, there is a downside to relying on technical and other kinds of infrastructural aiding devices for achieving independence: They need to be designed, produced, maintained, and sometimes operated by other persons. In that way, some of these devices may increase rather than decrease dependence on other persons. Thus, in both cases, we may have reasons to consider making use of new reprogenetic possibilities.

Second, my suggestion that liberals in particular have good reasons to be committed to the notion of independence could be taken to imply that there is a consensus regarding the aim of a liberal polity, namely "to produce and nurture people who are capable of physical and mental independence."[5] All I mean to argue, however, is that a liberal polity concerned with protecting the individual from arbitrary interference by others should be sensitive to situations that make individuals particularly vulnerable to such intrusions. Again, an interference is "arbitrary" when (i) it is subject only to the will of the person interfering, (ii) this person is not forced to track the interests of those affected by the interference (or, in the case of embryos, cannot adequately track them beyond a certain point), and (iii) the latter have no way to veto or challenge the interference. People who have to depend on the charitable help of others are particularly vulnerable to these kinds of interferences, because they may neither be able to be involved in deciding the terms of the relationships they are forced to be part of nor be able to leave them. Therefore, we must make sure that future persons have the mental and physical capacities required for participating in symmetrical relationships so that their risk of being taken advantage of is minimized. Of course, it will be hard for people to agree exactly on what constitutes an independent life—both with regard to the philosophical criteria as well as with regard to which cases are included. However, I would already consider it a great accomplishment if I could persuade readers that it is the preconditions for an independent life that we owe to future people.

Third, some may be concerned that the approach defended here implies that persons who remain dependent on the charitable help of others even after our best efforts, are lesser members of a liberal society.[6] This is certainly not what the pursuit of independence, especially substantial independence, aims to achieve. Quite to the contrary, it seeks to ensure that persons are (made) as invulnerable as possible to infringements on their physical and mental integrity by other persons. There will always be a considerable number of people who cannot live independently, even with technological help, such as young children, persons of old age (sometimes), and people with certain illnesses or disabilities. Thus, where technical instruments are not sufficient to achieve independence, the duty to ensure persons' substantial independence requires institutional arrangements to guarantee these persons' protection from abuse. This is the same as in all other cases in which we want to avoid domination. Moreover, just because we take care to avoid certain kinds of scenarios certainly does not imply that we think less of those who end up suffering under them nevertheless (similarly, we might want to do everything possible to prevent torture without thinking less of people who find themselves in situations in which they are particularly vulnerable to being tortured or actually end up being tortured).

The final question is whether it would be correct to conclude from my views that embryos that are likely not to develop into persons with the mental and physical capacities necessary for an independent life ought to be deselected after PGD or aborted. With regard to PGD, we should—if possible—choose an embryo that promises to develop into an independent person. But prospective parents could, of course, choose an embryo that is likely not to develop into an independent person if there was a way to genetically alter this embryo after selection to provide it with the necessary capacities. This having been said, given the importance of natural independence, it might be better to bring about situations where one would not have to genetically intervene, if one had the choice. In other words, selecting the independent embryo may be preferable because, from the perspective of the future person, genetic selection is always less problematic than manipulation.

If, counter to what I just suggested, it was not possible to select an embryo that promises to develop into an independent person, potential parents would not be committing a wrong by choosing one of the available embryos. As I have mentioned before, unlike the woman with the temporary medical condition who is thinking about when to conceive, persons selecting their embryos through PGD cannot be expected to "wait" and repeat the (for the women) taxing process of an in vitro fertilization to create another set of embryos to be screened.

With respect to the question of whether embryos should be aborted that are not and cannot be, for some reason, endowed with the capacities necessary for developing into independent persons, the answer is "no." This is because pregnant women who are thinking about whether they have an obligation to abort under these circumstances are in a situation in which they are faced with a choice they cannot be asked to make. Unlike the woman with the temporary medical condition in the preconception case, they cannot just bring about the life of another person by merely waiting to become pregnant another time. They are already pregnant and would have to undergo the physically intrusive and psychologically traumatic experience of having an abortion. Thus, as long as their children are likely to have lives worth living, these women would not wrong their children by bringing them into existence despite the fact that they may not end up developing into independent adults.

In sum, I have argued that there is no necessary connection between disability and lack of independence. Moreover, I have claimed that the obligation to try to decrease the probability that future persons will be vulnerable to relationships of domination does not imply that persons who are vulnerable to such relationships have less moral worth or that they will have lives not worth living.

2.3. Independence Versus the Significance of Dependence

Some will surely think that this proposal is making too much of independence as a virtue of interpersonal relationships. They might contend that "everyone is dependent on some others for at least some stages of life and few if any human beings are ever completely self-sufficient at any stage of life. Being dependent on others for at least some times or some aspects of survival is the common lot of all human beings. There is nothing to scorn in dependency" (Friedman 2008, 255). All of this, of course, is true. But that does not change the importance of trying to make it possible for individuals to choose the various dependencies they want to be part of. Being dependent on other persons for their love and support is an essential and inevitable feature of our lives. However, it is important that the different parties involved in relationships marked by various degrees of dependence are active, voluntary participants and not merely subjected to these relationships. "Voluntary" here does not mean to imply that anyone would choose to be a child, ill, or very old and in need of help. It simply indicates that persons who require assistance should be free, in principle at least, to choose the relationships they want to enter into and that promise to provide the support and help they need in a way that is respectful. This means that children, the elderly, and the sick, should have ways to leave abusive families or caretaking facilities. For future persons, it means that we have an obligation to try to ensure that they are mentally and physically equipped to make certain choices about their lives and be aware of various options available to them at different times. They will still be dependent on other people in the same way we all are. They will just not have particular dependencies imposed on them without being able to do anything about it.

2.4. Independence Versus Autonomy

Some readers will wonder to what extent the notion of independence I am invoking is different from that of autonomy. The distinction might be slight but points to an important variation in emphasis. Both autonomy and independence are concerned with self-determination. But whereas autonomy is primarily concerned with self-determination insofar as it guards persons against being slaves to their own unreflected desires, independence is concerned with self-determination insofar as it protects persons against being dominated by others.

I take even a very weak version of autonomy to imply at least some distance from one's first-order desires, that is, some form of reflection on one's inclinations and impulses so that one can claim authorship over them. Suppose I were to follow a certain first-order desire (to go to Paris) that I have failed to reflect on and of which it is highly likely, that—if I did reflect on it—I would choose to do something else (since I do not have the money to go, going will thwart some other, more important goals of mine, or I have some prior moral obligations where I am). As long as no one is forcing me to go to Paris and I am doing this solely from my own first-order desire, I am making this choice independently. What is unclear, however, is whether I am making this choice autonomously, since I failed to reflect on and endorse this first-order desire in a way that would allow me to call my trip to Paris fully self-governed. At this point one might object that this is a highly artificial distinction. The same factors that make the person who goes to Paris follow her first-order desire and unable to fully endorse her decision will dispose her to being manipulated by the wills of other people. To the extent this is true, for my theory of independence much will depend on peoples' ability to reflect on their motives and aims, thereby practicing self-governance in some stronger sense of the term. However, the importance of such self-determination is grounded first and foremost in a concern that individuals must not be manipulated by the wishes and desires of others and not primarily in a concern with individuals "mastering" their impulses.

The difference between independence and autonomy is more apparent when it comes to physical capacities. Persons with severe physical handicaps could certainly be autonomous in both a weak and a strong sense. But it is very likely that they will have to depend substantially on the charitable help of others. This, again, makes them more vulnerable to someone taking advantage of this asymmetrical situation.

2.5. Independence as a (Relatively) Independent Notion

At this point some readers might wonder to what extent independence fares any better than the suggestions made by Buchanan et al. when it comes to imposing particular values and prejudices of the previous generation on future persons. As I argued at some length in chapter 4, Buchanan et al.'s approach is very dependent on particular trends and fashions. I maintained that allowing parents to genetically alter all those traits and features that may, at any given time, reduce their children's opportunities in life permits parents to genetically imprint their offspring with a panoply of values that happen to be en vogue. I already mentioned that today a high IQ and athletic aptitude would make the top of the lists of many. Moreover, by making everyone better competitors in one particular reward system, Buchanan et al.'s proposal can be expected to encourage a transformation of this system sooner rather than later. It is likely to change, for instance, as a result of rewarding similar traits at a much higher level (i.e., where what was hitherto considered "normal" eventually counts as below average). Buchanan et al. (2000) are quite aware of this possibility and contend that "it is conceivable that genetic enhancements of normal human functioning, if sufficiently valuable and widespread, might lead us to revise upward our conception of normal species functioning, with the result that where we draw the line between health and disease, and hence between enhancement and treatment, would correspondingly change" (p. 98).

One might now suspect that independence is subject to the same concerns—that it may vary with time and place and that a successful attempt at making more people substantially independent will itself change our understanding of independence faster than we know it. As the discussion on disability showed, what counts as an independent life will, of course, differ from place to place and from time to time. But the fluctuation will not be nearly as pronounced as it is with Buchanan et al.'s principle. The reason is that we can generally tell whether persons are able to live minimally independent lives by looking at whether they can take care of and provide for themselves (this may, of course, require different skills in different places, but usually a very basic set of mental and physical capacities will enable people to provide for themselves wherever they are).[7] By comparison, the features that limit opportunities Buchanan et al. want to eliminate differ greatly across cultures and places and even more so across time (with the exception perhaps of clear cases of severe disease or disability). While reading capacities, advanced rhetorical abilities, and social skills might be widely valuable in a society like our own, hunters and gatherers are likely to reward an entirely different set of traits. We therefore cannot even be sure that those traits that function as general purpose means in our society would be of much use in others.

Moreover, respecting and ensuring independence is far less likely to change our notion of what is required to be independent than removing opportunity-limiting conditions is prone to alter our notion of what limits opportunities. Natural independence, for instance, changes nothing about our conception of independence. Ensuring substantial independence is more troubling in this regard as it does mandate certain genetic interventions. However, it too is limited to ensuring independence only up to a certain threshold. Having more persons just above the threshold of what is required to lead an independent life is not likely to move upward our notion of what independence requires.

Thus, although what counts as being independent might be subject to some changes depending on time and place, these modifications will be far less influenced by differences in the dominant reward system and are far less likely to accelerate the transformation from one reward system to another than Buchanan et al.'s model is. This brings me directly to the next concern, namely to what extent my proposal about independence generates the same types of fears regarding the effects of changing human nature on morality as do some of the other proposals discussed in this book, such as those of Dworkin, Buchanan et al., and Habermas.

2.6. Independence and the Future of Morality

Dworkin, Buchanan et al., and Habermas share a feeling of unease about how engaging in genetic manipulation may change the anthropological foundations of our morality, either contemporary egalitarian universalist morality as we know it today or, as Habermas sometimes also seems to suggest, morality as a whole. I argued that these concerns all remain much too vague to gain proper traction. Dworkin is concerned that blurring the boundary between chance and choice will cause a kind of moral insecurity that requires us to challenge our conventional moral concepts and to fall back on our own "critical moral background." I claimed that this is either a trivial observation (in the sense of saying nothing more than that, with the advance of new technologies, we have to apply our moral concepts to unfamiliar issues and situations) or not plausible (in the sense of giving us no reason for throwing some conventional moral concepts overboard and endorsing others). As my account of independence shows, "conventional" moral concepts are quite capable of reining in the new technologies.

Buchanan et al. in turn are worried that once we change human nature, the characteristics of humans may eventually differ so much that they are no longer motivated to cooperate with each other in a common moral system. This is a serious concern and thus makes it all the more surprising that when Buchanan et al. spell out their approach to the new reprogenetic technologies, they take no further notice of it. In contrast, the genetic changes I am advocating are so limited that they do not run the risk of changing human nature. This is a significant advantage given the kinds of dangers Buchanan et al. mention regarding increased genetic diversity among humans.

Habermas offered the most serious concern by maintaining that once parents start genetically manipulating their children, they will undermine the latter's capacity to perceive themselves as autonomous and equal members of the moral community. The results of this are asymmetrical relationships of a sort that may, in turn, undermine our capacity or basic willingness, as a species, to cooperate with each other in a moral system at all. The chief concern, however, remains somewhat vague. First, it is not always clear whether Habermas refers to a particular moral system being undermined (an egalitarian universalist one) or morality as a whole. Second, Habermas leaves his readers to guess whether genetic manipulation will undermine our capacity for moral cooperation or (merely) our motivation to cooperate. Moreover, the arguments Habermas offers about the problem of establishing asymmetrical relationships between persons give him enough material to make a straightforward moral claim against various applications of the new technologies, namely that it is wrong to subject future persons to genetic modifications they cannot be expected to consent to. It is therefore not immediately obvious why he chooses to make an argument from outside morality (by invoking our species ethos) so that he is left having to plead for the preservation of our moral system (or morality as a whole). Using genetic alterations in the name of independence circumvents these problems. To begin with, independence offers a normative standard by which to criticize certain uses of the new technologies from within morality. Moreover, as mentioned before, genetic alterations produced in the name of independence are so restricted that they are not likely to affect either our egalitarian universalist moral system or morality as a whole.

Before concluding the argument, I briefly turn to the question of who the "we" refers to when I speak of "what we owe to future persons." In other words, who exactly owes it to future persons both to respect their natural independence and to make them less vulnerable to being victims of asymmetrical relationships by ensuring their substantial independence?

3. Who is Responsible? Exculpating Parents

In response to the question of who owes something to future persons and why, several scholars have come up with a definite answer. Velleman (2008), for instance, begins by arguing that "being begotten is not, as many believe, the original birthday present" (p. 246). He maintains that "to be born as a human being is to be handed a job of work, with a promise of great rewards for success, a threat of great harm for refusal and a risk of similar harm for failure" (p. 250). From this observation Velleman concludes that biological parents, by causing a child to exist, automatically shoulder the full responsibility for assisting their child in dealing with both the unique opportunity and the grueling task of having to succeed in life. In particular he maintains that biological parents have an obligation to help their child "to acquire the capacities whose exercise will enable it to flourish and whose lack would cause it to suffer" (p. 251).

Seana Shiffrin (1999) goes even further than this. She argues that by intentionally procreating, parents make themselves responsible not only to "assist" their child but are accountable for anything that might go wrong. This is true even if the child is not made worse off by anything the parents do and even if parents do nothing (wrong) to produce their child's frustrations.[8] Children should be able to hold their parents liable for their hardships because, according to Shiffrin, procreation "is not a morally straightforward activity, but one that ineliminably involves serious moral hazards" (p. 136). What may seem like an exceptional opportunity and adventure is also an overwhelming challenge:

> By being caused to exist as persons, children are forced to assume moral agency, to face various demanding and sometimes wrenching moral questions, and to discharge taxing moral duties. They must endure the fairly substantial amount of pain, suffering, difficulty, significant disappointment, distress and significant loss that occur within a typical life. They must face and undergo the fear and harm of death. Finally they must bear the results of imposed risk that their lives may go terribly wrong in a variety of ways. (p. 137)

Velleman and Shiffrin make two clear pronouncements. First, they maintain that those who procreate are the ones who are responsible for their children's hardships. Second, by describing the predicament of being born in the way the authors do, they explain what kinds of obligations emerge from the relationship between those who procreate and the children they beget, committing the former to a great deal of support and assistance to ensure the well-being of the latter. Neither of them considers the possibilities of genetic manipulation. Although it remains unclear what they would have to say about the extent to which parents should make use of new reprogenetic technologies to make life "easier" for their child, one can see how their reasoning could be taken to support liberal eugenic proposals.

However, the point I want to discuss here is the first claim, namely that regarding procreative responsibility. Even if one grants Velleman's and Shiffrin's contentions about life being a predicament, this predicament arguably goes two ways, affecting not only the children thereby produced but also those who procreate. Thus, in the following I argue that while those responsible for bringing future persons into this world are certainly among those who must protect future persons' natural independence, it is not clear that they are the ones primarily in charge of ensuring their offspring's substantial independence (which might, in any given case, come at some cost). Rather, society as a whole has to provide whatever is required to this end. The reason for this lies in the role that individual reproduction plays in many societies where having children is only partly an unencumbered private choice.

Consider the following analogy to the case of childbearing: Suppose a governmental agency had good reasons to seize people's property. To seize the property, government requires agents to knock on people's doors and collect it. Only certain people qualify for the job. There is a preference for men between the ages of twenty and forty. Of these eligible men, it is regularly the case that many voluntarily apply to become agents. They do this for different reasons: some because they attach a certain value to the job; others because they feel that it is expected of them. No one knows exactly what to look forward to, although it is generally intimated that these jobs are expressions of manliness and among the best things that can happen (to a man) in life. Surely, we do not think they, as agents, are responsible for seizing the property, and those whose property is being taken do not blame their loss on the particular agent who happens to knock on their door. Those affected understand that the agent, by taking on his job, did not intend to affect their lives in particular. What these agents are certainly responsible for is executing their job well. But there is no obvious way to accomplish this: Should agents write letters announcing their visit and, if yes, how many? Should they knock several times, smile and be friendly, or use violence in any cases? Most of these questions are settled by some governmental policy and only to a very small degree are a matter of personal style. However, regardless of the policy, agents are required to adhere to it to some reasonable degree if they do not want to be reprimanded or, in particularly severe cases, even lose their job.

In many respects, childbearing is similar. Individuals sign up to become parents, frequently out of their own volition. Then they take part in a process that is much larger than them, which they did not author and from which they profit only as a side effect: Just as the agents do not receive the benefit of the property they are seizing but only the salary they are paid for doing their job, parents may enjoy having children, but many of the benefits of reproduction are reaped by the human collective(s) they help propagate (family, society, the species as a whole). Moreover, just as no agent is responsible for the property-seizing policy and the effects this has on those deprived of their belongings, no one in particular is responsible for the fact that birth occurs the way it does and may indeed be the ambivalent kind of blessing both Velleman and Shiffrin make it out to be.[9] Birth, in this sense, merely "happens" to people, most literally to those it brings about but also—to some extent at least—to those who bring it about. Even if people decide to participate in this process (reproduction), the workings of which they can do nothing about, they do not always know exactly what to expect. Pregnancies and the feelings attached to them are often unpredictable, as is the experience of actually having a child. Finally, just as the agents' performance in the analogy is judged by governmental standards, it is mostly society that defines the rules of what is required to be a good parent.

Readers are surely tempted to think that some (maybe even all) of these suggestions are preposterous. The proposition most likely to attract objection is probably the one about parents not being wholly responsible even if they intentionally initiate the existence of a new person. One might ask: How can those who intentionally procreate (or intend to have a child in vitro) and freely agree to be the ones to raise their child not be held fully responsible for their reproductive choice if it is true that anyone can decide not to become a parent (especially in cases of assisted reproduction)?

Many people argue that passing up an opportunity to have a child is not a moral wrong. We generally do not blame people for deciding not to have children. This, however, cannot be entirely true. If everyone passed up this opportunity, societies would be faced with major problems regarding their self-perpetuation. Perhaps people might say it would not be a moral wrong, just imprudent for the survival of societies or, if the unwillingness were widespread, the species. But then, what is our individual responsibility to further the survival of societies and the species? Some may think that due consideration for the importance of human life requires us to ensure that our race does not become extinct (e.g., Velleman 2008, 254). This would make it obligatory that a sufficient number of people choose to be parents. I am not sure that such an obligation exists. So far, however, societies have generally been able to trust that a sufficient number of people will decide to create families (with the exception of modern industrialized societies perhaps) so that a little free-riding can go unnoticed. But this may be largely because of a combination of biological and social pressures that facilitate such a choice. One can generally be sure that if biology does not "persuade" us, social pressure will: It is not accidental that infertility is treated as a disease. In many cultures, infertility makes women feel less feminine and men less masculine.

Therefore, at least in societies and cultures that encourage certain stereotypes about the family and fertility, there are good reasons to think that society has a substantial obligation to support individuals who choose to reproduce.[10] Such obligations would have to include a variety of emotional and material measures to assist parents in fulfilling the duties we think they have by choosing to beget and/or to raise a child. Thus, it is we, as a society, not individual parents, who must come up with the full amount necessary for ensuring future persons' substantial independence.

The claim that children largely benefit society is, of course, also highly controversial. Many believe that children constitute a distinct enrichment for parents and that having children fulfills a deep human interest. Harry Brighouse and Adam Swift (2006, 2009), for instance, argue that being a parent is a unique source of human flourishing. They agree that this may not be so for everyone in all circumstances, but they generally believe that parents feel this way. This is because of the beauty and singularity of the parent-child relationship, which the authors praise for its unique asymmetry and lack of reciprocity. In this relationship, children are wholly dependent on their parents for their well-being. It offers virtually no exit options and is characterized by an unparalleled quality of intimacy: The child's love for the parent is spontaneous, unconditional, and beyond the child's rational control. Brighouse and Swift assert that "parents have an interest in being in a relationship of this sort. They have a non-fiduciary interest in playing this fiduciary role. The role enables them to exercise and develop capacities the development and exercise of which are for many (. . .) crucial to their living fully flourishing lives" (Brighouse and Swift 2006, 95).

Interestingly, it seems as if most of the unique qualities offered by parent–child relationships as described by Brighouse and Swift could be readily fulfilled by acquiring a pet. To avoid such a conclusion, the authors need to show that, beyond individuals experiencing their parenthood as uniquely enriching to their lives, there is something inherently valuable in a parent–child relationship that cannot be replaced by anything else. Robertson (2003), for instance, maintains that "quite simply, reproduction is an experience full of meaning and importance for the identity of an individual and her physical and social flourishing because it produces a new individual from her haploid chromosomes" (p. 450). Some may want to add to this that individuals sometimes have an interest in reproducing because they think that it will ensure their immortality. Having children is often perceived as a way to live on in the world, be remembered, and carry one's blueprint through the generations.[11] This, however, is a beautiful illusion at most. Just as having children is not a necessary condition for leading a flourishing life, children do not guarantee that their parents will be remembered. Sometimes, children may just prefer not to (although they might not be able to forget their own parents, they could make it the case that their children have no recollection of their grandparents); also, there are many things besides having children one could do to remain in people's thoughts after one has passed on.

However, even if we were to concede that reproduction offers a distinct benefit for individuals, it cannot be denied that society has a vital interest in it as well. Although individuals may have important subjective experiences to gain by bringing other individuals into existence, societies and the species as a whole need children to continue and flourish. Therefore, as emphasized before in the chapter on Germany (chapter 2), if and when women bring new persons into this world, they should be thanked for their "reproductive services" to whatever human collective they thereby help to perpetuate.

In essence, I propose a reevaluation of the role of parents: They are not those who are responsible for care-giving by default, only by choice. Those who are willing to take on this project should be entitled to as much help and aid of society as they might need in fulfilling the daunting task that lies ahead of them. This is especially important because, by agreeing to raise children, as fulfilling as this may be, parents accept a substantial number of burdens, all things considered. They have to consent to meeting the needs of unfinished, helpless but nevertheless separate individuals for many years and then to letting go of them. Letting go might be one of the hardest tasks, but its importance reaffirms what I have been emphasizing throughout, namely that parents have to respect their children's independence.

4. Conclusion

This chapter finalizes the argument that began in the first part of this book. In chapter 1 I claimed that it follows from our normative commitment to persons that we honor their backward-oriented interest that the embryo from which they developed was not harmed. In other words, we have to treat embryos from which persons develop with anticipatory respect for their later personhood. I call this the Personhood Dependent Principle. I argued that because there is thus far no way for persons to be born without women enduring substantial and particularly intrusive kinds of burdens for a significant amount of time, women are the ones on whose actions it depends which embryos develop into persons and which do not. In response to the epistemic concern about how to know beforehand which embryos end up being persons, I suggested a Principle of Precaution, according to which we should treat all embryos as if they were going to be persons until it has been made the case that they cannot mature any further. Regarding embryos in petri dishes (whose fate is still undetermined) I maintained that a certain appreciation for the creation of persons requires that they should not be denied a chance to develop further if there are women who would like to carry them to term. In chapters 2 and 3 I showed how, in light of new biomedical technologies that increasingly expose the early human embryo to public view and access, this way of construing our obligations to the unborn offers an attractive position both for countries with strong prior commitments to protecting all embryos, such as Germany, and for countries in which the question of the moral value of the embryo has largely remained bracketed, such as the United States.

I continued the discussion of what we owe to future persons in the second part of the book, this time focusing on the possibilities of genetically manipulating embryos that will be born. I began with an exploration of liberal eugenic approaches in chapter 4, concentrating in particular on arguments for using the new technologies in the name of liberal values such as reproductive freedom, progress, and social justice. I argued that it is puzzling that liberals, usually so keen on protecting individuals, especially their intimate sphere, from other persons' interventions, would so willingly embrace many of the uses of new reprogenetic technologies while largely neglecting future persons' claims to being free from such designs.

Chapter 5 showed that, unlike his liberal colleagues, Habermas realizes the dangers with regard to the quality of intergenerational relationships once genetic manipulation is widely used. He persuasively makes the case that persons have a right to remain free from genetic interventions to which their consent cannot be presumed. I rejected those parts of Habermas's argument that too intimately tie his criticism to the possibly detrimental psychological effects the employment of new reprogenetic technologies may have for all parties involved. I maintained instead that the criticism should be based on straightforward normative claims about whether or not genetic manipulation expresses the appropriate degree of respect for (future) persons.

This led me to my final arguments in this chapter. I contended that respect for persons, including those of the future, means to ensure their independence, both from members of the previous generation and from their contemporaries. This, I declared, translates into two different duties. First, to facilitate intergenerational independence, it is important that, as long as future persons are genetically endowed so that it is likely that they will mature into adults who can lead minimally independent lives, they should be accepted the way they come into existence without anyone genetically interfering with them. Second, to the extent future persons are not genetically endowed so that it is probable that they will mature into adults who can lead minimally independent lives, some genetic alterations may be required in order to limit their vulnerability to being subjected to asymmetrical relationships with their peers.

Before this book about beginnings comes to an end, let me briefly return to Tristram, with whose laments my argument was introduced. Is he right to complain about his parents' behavior during the intercourse that led to his creation? Probably not. Although it matters what happened to the embryo from which Tristram emerged, it is, as mentioned before, rather unlikely that Tristram's worries have much substance (i.e., that he—his character, mind, and body—were detrimentally affected by the animal spirits not having properly escorted his father's sperm to his mother's ovum). But even if we laugh at Tristram Shandy's grievances in this particular instance, the new reprogenetic technologies may very well lead to other Tristrams who will have reason to complain because their genomes will have been illegitimately interfered with. My theory of unborn life seeks to provide a way of thinking about these Tristrams that helps us to prevent such violations of their independence from occurring.

NOTES

INTRODUCTION

1. As of 2007, there is a new way of deriving human embryonic stem cells that does not require destroying viable embryos: Adult stem cells can be reprogrammed so that they behave virtually like embryonic stem cells. However, notwithstanding the similarities, so-called "induced pluripotent stem cells" (iPSCs) still behave somewhat differently from embryonic stem cells and, to date, remain riddled with viruses frequently used for their reprogramming. As it is therefore not clear to what extent they can replace embryonic stem cells, the need to address the ethical problems involved in having to destroy embryos for research purposes remains.

2. The term "reprogenetics" was originally coined by Lee Silver (1997) in his book *Remaking Eden.* "What has yet to catch the attention of the public at large (. . .) is the incredible power that emerges when current technologies in reproductive technology and genetics are brought together in the form of *reprogenetics*" (p. 9; emphasis in original).

CHAPTER 1

1. There is not even consensus regarding the more fundamental issue of whether questions pertaining to the embryo's moral worth are essentially ethical or moral, where "ethical" refers to questions about the good life that should be left to each individual to decide and "moral" refers to questions of right and wrong that are universally binding.

2. I generally avoid referring to the embryo's moral value as its "status," as I am not sure much is gained by calling it "status." I take "status" to refer to a place in a hierarchy of values that, presumably, is fixed by a common standard. As persons are frequently considered to have a particular moral status, it is difficult to see which other entities can be in the same hierarchy with them. If the moral status of persons is determined by features persons share with other animals, one might speak of higher and lower moral status and assign other sorts of moral values to entities that do not share the features bestowing moral status (Kamm 1992, 2005). This is sometimes confusing. Although it may be clear how entities

of higher moral status can be weighed against entities of lower moral status, it is not always obvious how to weigh entities with lower moral status against entities that have significant moral value (especially if the source of their moral value lies in their meaning for entities with higher moral status). Frances Kamm (2005, 285), for instance, argues that all beings for whose sake we can act have moral status. This includes persons and animals. All other entities have moral value, such as the Grand Canyon. But she also thinks that, in any given case, we may have more reason to protect the Grand Canyon than a bird, if, let us assume, many people greatly enjoyed the Grand Canyon while no one cared much about the bird. In that case, the interest the bird has in preserving its own life would be outweighed by the value that many people attach to the Grand Canyon. Only if the situation was different and the same number of people cared about the bird as about the Grand Canyon would we have reason to save the bird (Kamm 2005, 286). This is because the bird's interest in its own survival (an interest the Grand Canyon does not have) would tip the balance in the bird's favor. This shows that moral status may not amount to much in cases in which the moral status holders are not persons. Moreover, any system that attributes moral status to beings besides persons usually attributes additional moral privileges to persons to make sure that their moral status always trumps that of other moral status holders. Kamm (2005, 287), for instance, argues that while both persons and animals have moral status, persons are also rights-holders. In any case, for the purposes of this book I consider persons to have moral status by virtue of their capacity for moral agency. Every individual capable of moral agency is a person and thus has moral status. According to this way of using the concepts, "person" and "moral status holder" are identical. Given that they are interchangeable, I choose to speak of "person" rather than of having "moral status." This way, I hope to avoid the impression that I consider there to be higher and lower forms of moral status. When it comes to entities besides persons I attribute to them different degrees of moral value that can, in principle at least, be compared with one another. For a more general discussion of why moral debates would be greatly enhanced if talk of moral status were abandoned, see Benjamin Sachs (2011).

3. Dieter Birnbacher (2006, 53–74), for instance, maintains that much confusion could be avoided in bioethical debates if people stopped referring to the vague concept of "person." But to the extent the term *person* is taken to identify individuals to which we have certain, clearly discernible normative commitments, it is a helpful concept to use. As soon as we think about who is a person and why, the issue becomes less clear. However, for the argument presented here, the indeterminacy of this latter question is only of secondary concern. What matters primarily is that the normative category of persons exists and that some (human) beings belong to it.

4. The term "person" can, of course, be used in a variety of different ways that do not have any normative implications. If I read a sign in an elevator telling me

how many persons it holds, the word "person" is a mere enumeration and thereby used in clearly non-normative terms. For an account of various ways in which the term "person" can be used, see Quante (2007, 1–4).

5. Depending on when one believes personhood begins and in virtue of which particular features, personhood-related entitlements will vary: There will be a number of entitlements persons have at some stages of their lives that they do not have at others (the right to vote, for instance).

6. This problem occurs with most attempts to establish personhood as a moral category distinguishing human beings from other animals. As human beings differ from other animals only at certain stages of their lives, there will always be the so-called "marginal" cases, that is, those cases our general commitment to a concept such as personhood will not automatically cover.

7. Even authors who explicitly reject the species-membership argument frequently choose those features as bestowing moral significance upon their holders that are typically possessed by humans. In that sense, almost everyone is a kind of speciesist or anthropocentrist when it comes to selecting the features (such as moral agency) worth protecting.

8. If we regularly implanted animal embryos into the wombs of human females so that animals were born to them, then being born by humans may not suffice to establish the sort of kinship Scanlon (1998, 185) presumably seeks to invoke.

9. This does not imply that it is necessary or even desirable to make such a distinction in the first place. It would be less problematic because animals do not, for the most part, necessarily depend on humans (they do not need humans for their well-being) and thus, do not inevitably belong to our social universe. To the extent they belong to our social universe, they do this by our choice. So even if we morally distinguish between humans and animals, insofar as we make animals dependent on us, our moral obligations to them may be substantial.

10. Matthew Liao (2010, 164), for instance, has argued that being genetically human can provide the basis for human moral status.

11. This last claim is at least arguable. Unlike the newborn, embryos are still physically shielded from everyone but the woman carrying them (and perhaps some others who communicate with them in a limited way by touch and sound through the woman's belly) and are therefore presumably not yet part of a generally shared social universe.

12. David Boonin (2003) offers a similar argument when he says that "the implication that whether or not a fetus is a baby depends on whether the woman wants it to be a baby is, clearly, unacceptable, as is the implication that this is true of the question of whether or not it has the same right to life as you or I" (p. 278).

13. I thank an audience at the University of Santa Barbara and especially Matthew Hanser for pressing me on this point.

14. Although it would be morally wrong for a random person to destroy embryos for just any reason, it is unclear whether there should be punishment for such an act

and, if so, what the punishment should be. We certainly stand under some obligation to try to prevent such events from occurring. If someone chose to destroy embryos that a woman was waiting to have implanted, however, the woman should be entitled to some form of compensation for the life of a future person lost (to her).

15. Assuming that we have obligations to future persons in the first place (i.e., because they are persons, their time of birth is arbitrary from a moral point of view, and our actions affect them profoundly), defining a minimal threshold below which we ought not to bring people into this world is a way of getting around the so-called "Non-Identity Problem." The latter arises because it is impossible to harm particular (future) persons who do not exist through certain actions if their existence depends on the action in question (and if harming is understood as making someone worse off than they would otherwise be). Therefore, defining a threshold (in whatever way we choose to do so) helps spell out our obligations to future persons quite generally and regardless of who in particular will happen to be born. I have much more to say about the Non-Identity Problem and how to get around it in chapter 6.

16. It must be noted that Habermas's (2003) arguments against the reification of human embryos were formulated in the context of a rather specific political occasion, namely the German parliamentary debates on whether the import of human embryonic stem cells is permissible under the Law for the Protection of the Embryo. The reason Habermas spoke out so vehemently against these technologies was because he feared that they may evoke a change in our attitude toward human life. It was not his primary intention to up- or downgrade the moral status of embryos.

17. Let me briefly mention three alternative readings of potentiality and show why they would not be of much help either. First, potentiality could indicate as little as that the embryo is a *necessary precondition* for born life in the same way that a woman's uterus is a necessary precondition (Schöne-Seifert 2003, 174). It would be hard to derive any normative implications from this form of potentiality. Second, on a slightly stronger account, potentiality could imply a *possibility*. This indicates that it is logically conceivable that an embryo will develop into a person. However, even this is not specific enough. It would have to include a variety of sperm and egg cells, all of which may also eventually develop into individuals capable of moral agency, and even somatic cells that could, through reproductive cloning, be reprogrammed to develop into new persons. Third, on a slightly stronger account still, potentiality may imply a *probability*. This means that a fertilized egg will, in all likelihood and if no adverse circumstances occur, develop into a born person. This, of course, is not necessarily true. Many things can happen to fertilized egg cells and many of them never even end up implanting in the womb. It is thus more probable that fertilized eggs perish. Therefore, probability is not a good way to describe what connects embryos to persons.

18. This could mean that everyone belonging to a species, the typical member of which develops higher-order faculties, is properly "disposed" in a morally relevant way. Such a reading, however, would collapse the disposition argument into the species-membership argument. A species-membership argument implies that all embryos should be treated as persons just because they belong to the human species. By contrast, it must matter to the disposition argument whether or not an instance of human life actually has the disposition to develop those features on the basis of which human dignity is conferred.

19. There might, for instance, be a reason to limit the number of future persons if we knew that there were not enough resources left on earth to guarantee each future person a minimally decent standard of living.

20. I have more to say about why we, as a society, may be obliged to support individuals with their reproductive wishes in chapter 6.

CHAPTER 2

1. Stem cell research is prohibited in principle, although there are significant exceptions. I say more about these below (section 4). PGD used to be prohibited in all cases other than if a couple wanted to perform sex selection to prevent having a child with a sex-linked disease. However, the scope of permissible uses of PGD has been broadened somewhat. Doctors can now perform PGD when there is reason to believe that a genetic abnormality will lead either to the death or the serious impairment of offspring. I say more about this below (section 3).

2. *Gesetz zur Verhütung erbkranken Nachwuchses,* Reichsgesetzblatt (RGBl) 1933, 1: 529. In 1933 it was not a modification of §218 StGB, which liberalized abortion for those women with medical reasons, but ironically (and in some ways perplexingly), it was the Law for the Prevention of Genetically Diseased Offspring that allowed sterilization of the gonads, including the inside of a womb (i.e., which could contain a fertilized egg) under certain conditions.

3. According to part 16 of the Criminal Code of the German Reich (*Strafgesetzbuch für das Deutsche Reich*), put into effect in 1872 and called "Crimes and Misdemeanors against Life" (*Verbrechen und Vergehen wider das Leben*), §218 StGB punished abortion with up to five years of penitentiary and, in the case of mitigating circumstances, with no less than six months in prison (RGBl. 1871, 167). The same punishments were given to third persons aiding the abortion by any means, either by actually performing it, by merely advising the pregnant woman, or by giving her the necessary medications or instruments. However, there was §54 StGB, also referred to as "emergency provision," which generally allowed mitigating circumstances for both the delinquent and the person aiding the illegal act, if he or she thereby saved his or her own life or that of a relative in life-threatening circumstances. This rather strict "treatment" of abortion was modified by a decree of May 18, 1926. In it, § 218 StGB was reformulated to the extent

that the severity of punishment was decreased and "regular" forms of abortions were sentenced "only" with prison, retaining the penitentiary for cases in which someone attempted to perform an abortion on a woman who had not given her consent and for cases in which someone practiced abortions for monetary gain (*gewerbsmäßig; RGBl. 1926, I 239*). The fact that penitentiary was no longer the standard means of punishing abortion shows that abortion was not seen as a capital offense (this implies a crime that normally incurs the death penalty) anymore.

4. The death sentence was abolished in 1949 by Article 102 of the Basic Law.

5. After the war, there was a six-month grace period in which women could have abortions if they claimed to have been raped by a member of the allied forces. Other than that, the difficult situation for women continued. Abortion in general continued to be treated as the killing of the "bodily fruit" and punished as a misdemeanor with up to five years in prison. Several federal states preserved the 1935 version of the Law for the Prevention of Genetically Diseased Offspring, which allowed the possibility of abortion for medical reasons. Other German states (for instance Bavaria) considered as authoritative a decision of the Federal High Court for Criminal Justice (*Bundesgerichtshof in Strafsachen*) of January 15, 1952 (BGHSt 2, 111), which used the conditions named in the Nazi law for the permissibility of medical reasons as minimum preconditions for the permissibility of abortion.

6. On April 5, 1971, a group of 343 women, including Simone de Beauvoir, outed themselves as having had abortions in the "manifesto of the 343" published in the French *Nouvel Observateur* (no. 334). On June 6 of the same year, 374 German women declared "*Wir haben abgetrieben!*" (We have had an abortion!) on the title page of the German weekly magazine *Stern* (vol. 24, issue 24). In a spring 1974 edition of another weekly magazine *Der Spiegel*, the front-page article was on the activism of both women and doctors who joined together for the first time in a combined fight to liberalize abortion. In an initiative called *Letzter Versuch* (Last Attempt), activists from 80 German women's movements took to the streets throughout West Germany, supported by 12 doctors who declared they would perform abortions the following weekend and 329 doctors and medical assistants who publicly declared in *Der Spiegel* (November 1974, 30 f.) that they had illegally performed abortions and would continue to do so. They pronounced that: "We doctors and medical assistants are no longer willing to be complicit in the deaths of hundreds and the mutilation of thousands of woman annually! (. . .) Abortion is not an act of mercy, it is a right!" (my translation). What they all wanted at the very least was a solution that allowed women to decide for themselves whether to have an abortion or not within the first trimester (*mindestens die Fristenlösung*). Some wanted to go even further and decriminalize abortion altogether. *Der Spiegel* also announced in the subsequent issue (December 1974, 19–22) that the following Monday a documentary would be shown on a public television show

called *Panorama*, which was going to explain the suction method (removal of the embryo through suction). But the film was never aired due to the protests of the churches, the Christian Democratic party, its Bavarian sister party, the Christian Social Union, and some medical officials. If an abortion were to be shown on television, it should at least be portrayed as something terrible and horrific done in legal surroundings (i.e., a doctor's office), whereas this film showed an illegal abortion (obviously carried out in a private home) that was completely unproblematic, fast (five minutes in total, of which two and a half were depicted), and successful. In an interview, the woman was asked how she had felt after the procedure. She said she had felt fine and reported having gone to the theater that same evening. The film was intended to end the hypocrisy entailed in pretending to hold up an outdated morality that was ill equipped to deal with reality, a reality in which every day women were having illegal abortions, suffering (and dying) from unprofessional help.

7. There is a controversy over whether indications should be thought of as excusing or as justifying reasons—in other words, whether having an indication of some sort merely excuses an action that remains wrong or actually renders a person's action justified in the sense of giving this person a right to perform it.

8. BT Drucksache 7/561, May 15, 1973.

9. The legal procedure by which this was done is called "abstract norm control," which allows a third of the members of Parliament, the federal government, or a state government to petition the Constitutional Court to see if any given law is consistent with the Constitution. This procedure is "abstract" since it does not arise in the course of normal litigation.

10. Given the constitutional protections of embryos, one might wonder, however, whether there can be any "good" reason to destroy them (Jerouschek 1989, 282). From the embryo's perspective, rape is certainly not an obvious case because it is not the embryo's fault that anything happened and, surely, if embryos are protected as separate citizens even from the woman carrying them, it cannot matter how any particular embryo was created (Dworkin, 1994, 32). Certainly, exempting from punishment abortions performed for eugenic reasons (i.e., because the child will be born with a disability) is highly controversial. Women are, after all, not allowed to kill their disabled children at any other point in their lives.

11. This can be taken in one of two ways: first as emphasizing that there might be pregnancies that women cannot be expected to bear. This reading is what seems to inspire some to praise the decision as showing the extreme sensitivity with which the court approached the issue of pregnancy (Glendon 1987, 33). However, it is probably more accurate to consider it, second, to be insulting and misplaced for a court to decide what can be expected of women under "normal" circumstances.

12. Before January 2010 abortions that took place after the twenty-third week of pregnancy did not require women to undergo a consultation or to wait at least three

days between any medical diagnosis and an abortion. However, this was changed to avoid situations in which women terminate their pregnancies out of shock after they have been told that their child has a genetic abnormality (*Gesetz zur Änderung des Schwangerschaftskonfliktgesetzes*. BT Drucksache 447/09 May 22, 2009).

13. This claim is somewhat qualified by the notorious episode of the so-called "witch hunt" of Memmingen in 1988 and 1989. The case concerned a doctor who was performing abortions in Memmingen (Bavaria). His patient records were confiscated under dubious circumstances, and he was charged for performing abortions without having sufficient indications. Every one of his patients whom he had performed an abortion on since 1980 was questioned with the result that 279 women and 78 men were charged with having committed punishable acts or with having aided in the performance of a punishable act. The doctor himself was sentenced to two and a half years in prison and three years occupational ban. This was revised down to one and a half years of suspended sentence in the last instance.

14. That abortion is no longer anything like the hotly contested topic it continues to be in the United States has been taken to indicate that the Constitutional Court was quite successful (more successful, that is, than the U.S. Supreme Court was with its abortion decision) "in shaping the direction of the overall debate as well as securing the prominence of the specific cluster of ideas that they affirmed" (Ferree et al. 2002, 128).

15. Jeff McMahan comes to the same conclusion (namely, that it is worse to injure an embryo that will be born than to kill an embryo) but for different reasons. According to McMahan, a fetus has very weak present interests in its own future. These interests can therefore sometimes be overridden by women who may have much stronger interests in wanting to abort. However, once we can expect an embryo to be born and grow into an adult who may suffer from injuries inflicted on him or her prenatally, then the fetus's anticipated future interests frequently outweigh whatever interests a woman might have in inflicting prenatal injury (McMahan 2006, 631f.).

16. A cell is totipotent if it has the potential to develop into every cell of the human body.

17. Potentially, and I suppose intentionally, this definition covers all stem cells derived from embryos. However, this has always been hotly contested by stem cell supporters. They claim that stem cells from blastocyst-stage embryos are no longer totipotent, for they can develop into any tissue of the body but one: the placenta. They are thus only pluripotent and, as such, are taken (by stem cell research supporters) not to fall under the protection of the ESchG.

18. Originally, the reason for this was to avoid situations of divided motherhood. This was thought to be bad for the resulting child. There are certainly people who hold the view that it is essential for children's well-being that they grow up

among their biological kin (Velleman 2008, although he would also object to divided fatherhood, which is permitted in Germany). However, there is ample evidence to show that children who grow up in nontraditional family contexts do very well (Richards et al. 2012).

19. One such challenge emerged in 2010 when the case of a woman came before a court who wanted to become pregnant with the prenuclei stage cells (also referred to as pre-embryos) from her late husband which they had created and frozen prior to his death. As already mentioned, while embryos cannot be frozen and stored other than in exceptional circumstances according to the ESchG, pre-embryos can (they are "merely" considered to be gametes according to § 8 (3) ESchG). Initially, the clinic where these pre-embryos were frozen declined the woman's wish to obtain them by pointing to § 4 (1) 3 of the ESchG. This is the prohibition against impregnating a woman with sperm of a deceased man. The Court decided against the clinic and in favor of the woman with the argument that it was no longer only sperm that the couple had frozen but (nine) pre-embryos. Therefore, no one was forced to "use" the sperm of a dead man to fertilize an egg (thereby violating § 4 (1) 3 of the ESchG) since the sperm had already been "used" to begin the fertilization process while the man was still alive (OLG Rostock 2010, Rndnr. 37). With this decision the court respected a woman's wish to become pregnant even under not entirely traditional circumstances. A cynical reader might point out, however, that this decision did not do much to challenge the conventional picture of a heterosexual family. The kind of single motherhood it thereby facilitated hardly breaks with a tradition where women are frequently expected to raise their children in the absence of their men who are either predominantly engaged with their work, at war, or otherwise absent.

20. In July 2011 the German parliament decided to amend the ESchG to generally prohibit PGD but to allow exceptions in cases in which there is the danger that parents will transmit a serious genetic disorder to their offspring.

21. I rejected this kind of argument in chapter 1, claiming instead that the potential of both embryos in vivo and embryos in vitro to develop into persons is the same in that it equally depends on whether there is a woman willing to carry them to term.

22. For a discussion about why it is appropriate to treat embryos in different situations differently (and why this does not reflect an attitude that values various embryos differently), see Herzog (2001) and Kollek (2002, 204–209). For an explanation for why the legislator has been much stricter about embryos in vitro see Isensee (2002, 44). Isensee suggests that this is a form of compensation, that is, a way to relieve the guilty conscience produced by the *de facto* rather liberal abortion ruling.

23. This still leaves open the question of creation, that is, whether there should be any restrictions on who should be permitted to create embryos in vitro. I have not

said much about this here, but I certainly do not think so. If we allow all persons who can have children without medical assistance to go ahead and reproduce, we have no grounds for refusing persons who depend on reproductive help the right to try. This should hold regardless of whether a person is seeking to build a traditional family or to raise his or her child as a single parent or together with a same-sex partner, for instance. For a more detailed account of my views, see Karnein (2012).

CHAPTER 3

1. The reader might wonder why the approach offered in this book, which puts so much emphasis on the importance of independence, would not also endorse viability as the cut-off point after which there is a legitimate state interest to protect the life of the fetus. The reason that viability is not the point at which I consider there to be a legitimate state interest is that my emphasis is on actual and not potential independence. As long as the embryo is, as a matter of fact, still symbiotically tied to a woman, she cannot be forced to do anything against her will to secure the survival of her fetus.

2. Sandel's (1982) criticism is interesting in the following regard: On the one hand, he worries that a politics that prides itself on bracketing contentious questions about the good life creates a moral void "that opens the way for narrow, intolerant moralisms" (p. 24). On the other hand, he argues that *Roe* is not neutral because it clearly favors those who do not think the embryo is a person from the moment of conception. Here Sandel contradicts himself: If he thinks *Roe* creates a moral void, then he must also think that the ruling genuinely *is* neutral. Because Sandel thinks that *Roe* is not neutral, he does not have to worry about there being a substantial void.

3. Among the latest attempts of states to undermine the central holdings of *Roe* are various so-called "personhood" initiatives that seek to change state legislation to include the fertilized human egg in the category of "person." Colorado was the first state that voted on the initiative (where it was twice defeated, first in 2008 and then again in 2010), followed by Mississippi in 2011 (where it was also defeated). As of the writing of this book similar initiatives are continuing to gather force in other states.

4. In June of 1989, for instance, in *Webster v. Reproductive Health Services*, a newly constituted court was asked to determine the constitutionality of Missouri's restrictions on abortion, all of which the court upheld with the explanation that they were not violating the basic principles set out in *Roe*. The restrictions included allowing a preamble stating that human life begins at conception, prohibiting governmental institutions and employees from performing abortions except in cases in which the life of the mother is threatened, ordering physicians to perform a viability test on the woman if she is twenty or more weeks pregnant, and prohibiting the allocation of funds for abortion counseling.

Roe was even more thoroughly reconsidered by the Supreme Court in 1992, in *Planned Parenthood of Southeastern Pennsylvania v. Casey*. At issue here were five provisions of the Pennsylvania Abortion Control Act of 1982. It required a woman's informed consent, which meant that the woman had to be provided with information material at least twenty-four hours before the procedure, written permission for an abortion by parents of a minor (but including a judicial bypass procedure), and a written statement married women had to supply declaring that they had informed their husbands. The Act provided a definition of "medical emergencies" that would suffice to circumvent the previous requirements. Finally, it demanded that facilities providing abortion services report certain statistics. Only the provision about having to notify the husband was declared unconstitutional. The *Casey* Court essentially affirmed *Roe* since it held that it was a woman's right and liberty to terminate her pregnancy before viability. "The woman's right to terminate her pregnancy before viability is the most central principle of *Roe v. Wade*. It is a rule of law and a component of liberty we cannot renounce" (*Casey* 1992, 871). At the same time, the *Casey* court also took some further steps in allowing states to put substantial limits on abortion. This stands in some contrast to the general mood of the country, which was as liberal as never before and, until now, as never after. According to the Gallop Poll, the number of pro-choice supporters peaked in June 1992, with 34 percent of Americans saying abortion should be permitted in all cases and only 13 percent saying abortion should be banned completely (Gallup Poll 2003, 204). In form and content, the *Casey* court took a serious second look at the possible state interest in potential life. It concluded that the trimester solution was theoretically flawed and practically unworkable. "A logical reading of the central holding of *Roe* itself, and a necessary reconciliation of the liberty of the woman and the interest of the State in promoting prenatal life, require, in our view, that we abandon the trimester framework as a rigid prohibition on all pre-viability regulation aimed at the protection of fetal life. The trimester framework suffers from these basic flaws: in its formulation, it misconceives the nature of the pregnant woman's interest. And in practice, it undervalues the State's interest in potential life, as recognized in *Roe*" (*Casey* 1992, 873). Even prior to viability, the *Casey* court endorsed a series of restrictions (see above). "Though the woman has a right to choose to terminate her pregnancy before viability, it does not at all follow that the State is prohibited from taking steps to ensure that this choice is thoughtful and informed. Even at the earliest stages of pregnancy, the State may enact rules and regulations designed to encourage her to know that there are philosophic and social arguments of great weight that can be brought to bear in favor of continuing the pregnancy to full term (. . .). It follows that States are free to enact laws to provide a reasonable framework for a woman to make a decision that has such profound and lasting meaning" (*Casey* 1992, 872). The *Casey* court limited state restrictions on abortion by stating that any legal provision is invalid as soon as its purpose or effect constitutes an "undue burden" for the woman, that is, places substantial obstacles in the way of a woman looking to abort her previable fetus. However, this standard is problematic, because it is now up to the subjective evaluation of judges to decide what constitutes an "undue burden." This concept was also immediately criticized by the dissenting judges for being much too vague and for being as flawed and unworkable as the trimester solution.

5. In addition to individual states banning late-term abortions, on November 5, 2003, President George W. Bush signed the Partial Birth Abortion Ban Act. Partial birth abortion is not a medical term but is used for a procedure called intact dilation and extraction (D&X). This is a method performed after the sixteenth week of gestation (second trimester) when the fetus is too developed to be extracted from the womb through vacuum suction. A similar ruling in Nebraska was deemed unconstitutional because it did not include an exception to allow the procedure if the health of the pregnant women was in danger and thus was judged to put an undue burden on women's choice to have an abortion (*Stenberg v. Carhart* 2000). The federal law, however, was upheld by the Supreme Court in *Gonzalez v. Carhart* (2007) with no exceptions; that is, the procedure can be banned even in cases in which the health of the woman is at stake.

6. It is striking that at a time at which abortion was generally condemned (even by notable leaders of the woman's suffrage movement such as Elizabeth Cady Stanton and Mary Wollstonecraft), only killing but not severely injuring a fetus was harshly condemned.

7. For a list of state homicide laws see National Conference on State Legislatures (2010).

8. Colorado, Iowa, and North Carolina.

9. It is easier to list the (far fewer) states that have neither fetal homicide laws nor increased penalties for crimes committed against pregnant women. These are: Connecticut, Delaware, District of Columbia, Hawaii, Missouri, Montana, New Hampshire, New Jersey, New Mexico, New York, Oregon, Vermont, and Wyoming.

10. Florida, Georgia, Michigan, Mississippi, Nevada, Rhode Island, Washington, and Wisconsin punish the intentional killing of a quick fetus as manslaughter; Georgia punishes the crime as feticide.

11. Indiana, Maryland, and Tennessee have statutes that include the viable fetus. Massachusetts has interpreted legislative intent as including the viable fetus in its criminal statute.

12. For the expression of a similar worry see McMahan 2006, 625.

13. With regard to abortion, the Act states that someone engaging in an abortion procedure with the consent of the woman may not be prosecuted, nor may the pregnant woman herself.

14. Even if the woman was subject to a criminal offense on her way to the abortion clinic, additional punishment for the killing of her fetus would be in order as others took it upon themselves to end a life that only she had a right to end.

15. In 2008 the South Carolina Supreme Court reversed its sentence with the explanation that McKnight had not been given a fair trial (*McKnight v. State* 2008).

16. For instance, in *Raleigh Fitkin-Paul Morgan Memorial Hospital v. Anderson* (1964), the court ordered blood transfusions over the objections of a Jehovah's Witness in her thirty-second week of pregnancy, to save her life and that of the fetus. In *Jefferson v. Griffin County Hospital Authority* (1981), the court ordered that a cesarean section be performed on a woman in her thirty-ninth week of pregnancy against her will (she had religious reasons to oppose the surgery) to save both the mother and the fetus. These cases are problematic in the sense that they force women to have children in situations in which the alternative is not having children in an injured state but rather not having children at all. According to the position advocated in this book, prior to birth women should always be free to decide not to have children if having them would require these women to undergo medical procedures they prefer to avoid.

17. In *Taft v. Taft* (1983) the court decided that a four-month-pregnant woman could not be forced to undergo a "purse-string" operation against her wishes—although this operation was not classified as particularly major and there was some evidence that the woman would miscarry if she did not have this procedure. However, consider *Jamaica Hospital, in re* (1985). Here the court ordered a Jehovah's Witness to have a blood transfusion to save the life of her nonviable, eighteen-week-old fetus, although she objected to this transfusion on religious grounds. The court found that the state's interest in the as-yet unviable fetus outweighed the patient's interest. But again, according to the PDP, a woman does have a right to let her fetus die. She may not harm a fetus that will be born—at least, if not harming the fetus is a real option for her.

18. The difference in number between live births and babies born is due to the circumstance that ARTs often lead to multiple births. For annual ART reports see http://www.cdc.gov/art/ARTReports.htm.

19. The Dickey-Wicker Amendment prohibits the use of federal funds for "(1) the creation of a human embryo or embryos for research purposes; or (2) research in which a human embryo or embryos are destroyed, discarded, or knowingly subjected to risk of injury or death greater than that allowed for research on fetuses in-utero" (H.R. 2880, Sec. 128, 34).

PART II

1. See Skinner (2002) and Pettit (1997) for ways in which more familiar types of domination (i.e., between contemporaries) are described. One might object to my using the term "domination" for intergenerational relationships given that there is no obvious institutional remedy to the problem, that is, one that would enable future persons to participate in selecting or actively contest the choices of those living in the present. Moreover, it is of course also true that some amount of power assertion is inevitable and necessary in all intergenerational relationships. However, just because some amount is unavoidable does not imply that we should not be careful about aggravating the asymmetry between persons of different generations.

2. It is arguable to what degree a concern with domination also includes a concern with people's positive right to actively and creatively structure their lives. That being as it may, the principal focus relevant here is that persons should be free to leave situations that are bad for them and opt out of cooperative schemes that do not adequately track their interests.

3. Marilyn Friedman (2008, 256), for instance, maintains that those worried about domination (she is specifically concerned with Pettit's arguments) should appreciate that some members of asymmetrical relationships actually benefit from the asymmetry. Thus, the scope of domination should be narrowed to refer only to actual instances of domination and not also include merely possible ones.

CHAPTER 4

1. A variety of scholars share this view. See, for instance, John Harris (2007, 26) and Julian Savulescu (2007, 532). Both Harris and Savulescu go further than this, however. They maintain that there is an obligation to engage in radical enhancement to improve the lives of children and to advance the human species.

2. Robertson (2003) is against genetic alterations that diminish a child's capacities, so one might think he would be opposed to the first couple lowering their child's IQ. However, his definition of what constitutes an act of illegitimately diminishing a child's traits through genetic manipulation is such that it refers only to a genetic intervention "that aims to reduce or remove capabilities that would otherwise have made the child normal and healthy" (p. 480). Based on this definition, lowering an IQ to 130 cannot count as a diminishment of the sort that is illegitimate, as 130 is a perfectly sufficient IQ for leading a normal and healthy life.

3. A further way to illustrate the difference between selection and design is this: Suppose a woman has a strong wish to fall in love with a pirate and no one else. She has two ways to achieve this: She can either make her love for her current partner (or whoever else she meets) conditional on him becoming more like a pirate, or she can sail the seas in search of somebody who already is a pirate. While she will not treat the person she wants to make into a pirate with the

appropriate amount of respect for who he is, there is nothing (morally) to prevent her from going out (of her way) to look for one.

4. Similarly, Ludwig Siep (2003), who thinks that the human body in its genetically unaltered form is a valuable "common heritage" and, as such, an essential condition of the modern social and legal order, argues that "what we have a right to do and what we value depends on the constitution and abilities of our body. If we change it to a considerable degree—which might be the outcome even of small-scale interventions—our abilities and our values will change and this in turn may have a deep impact on our social life" (p. 175).

5. From a Kantian perspective at least, the equal moral status of persons follows directly from being capable of moral agency. Thus, as long as the capacity for human agency could be guaranteed, having equal moral status would merely be a logical consequence and not subject to whether different individuals felt like treating each other as equals. That motivation is lacking in many already today. This having been said, however, a future in which there are a number of different human natures might certainly create considerable obstacles when it comes to people's motivation to treat very different kinds of persons as equals and thus, for realizing justice as "the first virtue of social institutions" (Rawls 1971, 3). This concern alone provides sufficient reason for trying to prevent such an outcome.

6. Genotype refers to an organism's entire genetic make-up, including that part of the genetic information that is not expressed and therefore not visible to the outside world. So in the case of a recessive genetic disorder, the illness may not be expressed phenotypically (the individual seems perfectly healthy), but it may be passed on to the next generation (because the individual is a carrier nevertheless).

7. None of these restrictions, it might be noted, respond in any way to the concerns about the limits of justice when it comes to questions about altering human nature.

8. The reverse will predictably occur as well. There will be cases in which children rebel against parental or social value judgments and, as a result, violently want to reject them. For them, being genetically imprinted with precisely these values will turn out not only to have been the moral wrong I want to claim it is but, in addition, a subjectively experienced disaster: How do we expect them to ever be able to distinguish between who they would have been and who they have become due to their parents' genetic intervention? Moreover, how can we expect them to productively "reject" the genetic hand they were dealt (intentionally) by their parents? I have more to say about this in the next chapter.

CHAPTER 5

1. Naturally conceived children presumably do not know about the various (sometimes surely eugenic) considerations involved in their parents choosing each other as mating partners, for instance.

2. This argument has been made more forcefully by David Velleman (2008). For Velleman, successful identity formation critically hinges on knowing about one's origins and on not being deceived about them. He argues that it amounts to a personal need to associate with biological relatives. For a critical discussion of this approach, see Karnein (2012).

3. Even if it were possible to insert an "off switch" that genetically altered persons could use once they were old enough to evaluate their traits in light of who they are and want to be, it is unclear whether this problem could really be solved. It would certainly be hard for genetically manipulated persons to imagine themselves without the genetic manipulation.

4. If genetic manipulation became widely available, nonmanipulated children unhappy with their lot could of course wish that their parents had altered them in some way. However, this concern would still be of a different quality than that of genetically manipulated persons. The latter were not accepted for who they would have turned out to be (without being genetically interfered with), while the former are wishing that their parents had acted on their guesses about what would be "best" for their children (instead of just accepting them the way they came into this world). But whatever their parents' "best" guesses would have been, they are likely not to be the ones the children now have in mind. Thus, nonmanipulated children would easily come to understand that wishing they had been genetically manipulated by their parents is an idle fantasy that, had some alteration indeed previously occurred, would probably not have been of the specific kind they are longing for.

5. This claim is highly controversial. Rainer Forst (2007, 92), for instance, maintains that there cannot be external reasons for engaging in morality. Rather, it is itself a moral duty to do so. Be that as it may, it is certainly true that in this particular case, namely when the question is about whether and to what extent we are allowed to make use of new reprogenetic technologies, there is no reason to leave the realm of morality to argue for or against their application. Habermas himself, for instance, names several ways in which the new technologies can be employed that express the appropriate amount of respect for persons (see section 1). This shows that there are ways to control the new technologies with our existing moral vocabulary and without necessarily undermining it.

6. I am using "arbitrary" here differently from elsewhere in the text, namely to indicate events that are only marginally controllable by humans.

CHAPTER 6

1. Parfit (1984) calls this a "Same Number Choice" (p. 356). He thereby refers to the fact that whatever we decide to do before conception will affect the identities but not the number of people living in the future. In contrast, we would be confronted with a so-called "Different Number Choice" if we were to discuss various

possible energy policies, for instance. Depending on which one we pursue, it is likely that an entirely different set of people will live because having more or less light and hot water available at different times of the day will affect people's procreative behavior (creating future persons of different identities and numbers).

2. Despite all the structural similarities, there is a further difference between the two cases: Whereas the woman with the temporary medical condition does not destroy an embryo—whatever her decision with regard to the date of her conception might be—prospective parents employing PGD do exactly that (if there are no women willing to carry the leftover embryos to term). However, as I argued in the first part of this book, there is no obligation to bring persons into existence if there are no women willing to be pregnant with them, and thus the prospective parents commit no wrong.

3. Parfit (1984) calls these "Same People Choices" (p. 356).

4. This raises another interesting question, namely whether this woman, who is presumably considering natural conception, could be forced to create her embryo in vitro so that the genetic manipulation can take place. Given that the hormonal stimulation and egg retrieval involved in assisted reproduction profoundly affect a woman's physical integrity, she cannot be compelled to do this. This would be different if her embryo was in vitro to begin with (since ensuring that her future child will develop into an adult who can lead a minimally independent life would then involve tampering only with her embryo, not with her).

5. I thank an anonymous reviewer for alerting me to this possible misunderstanding.

6. Again, I thank an anonymous reviewer for alerting me to this further possible misunderstanding.

7. Sometimes people may choose not to take care of themselves, such as men in cultures in which women—mothers and wives—regularly take care of them throughout their lives. Here, although it may indeed become questionable whether such men could presently maintain themselves on their own, they could, given their mental and physical abilities, at least be expected to learn how to (if they had to because there was no alternative to their providing for themselves, for instance). Moreover, although independence of the sort I am advocating may not be something people always choose to live by, what independence is and who those persons are who are not capable of leading independent lives, even if they wanted or had to, will remain recognizable.

8. The case Shiffrin (1999) has in mind is that of a child who "suffers from a serious, somewhat debilitating, untreatable, painful, congenital condition" whose life is, all things considered, worth living and therefore, a benefit to her. Nevertheless, Shiffrin argues that the child still should be able to seek compensation for the afflictions that are inseparably part of this benefit (p. 120). However, Shiffrin's reevaluation of the morality of procreation could apply not only to the child with the "serious, somewhat debilitating, untreatable, painful, congenital condition" but to all children who are faced with what Shiffrin describes as the essential predicament of being born.

9. This may appear to be like saying that because no one is responsible for the fact that smoking causes cancer, whoever smokes is not morally responsible for the cancer for which her smoking was causally responsible. My answer to this would be yes and no. As long as people have an honest choice between whether or not to smoke, they can be held causally as well as morally responsible. If, however, there turns out to be a large corporate (in the case of smoking) or social (in the case of procreation) interest that demonstrably skews the range of options or the desirability of not smoking versus smoking or procreating versus not procreating, then the primary moral responsibility may jump ship.

10. The case might be different in societies, cultures, or religions (e.g., Manicheanism) that explicitly discourage procreation. Such discouragement may gain further momentum due to growing concerns over climate change and an increasing awareness of the problem of overpopulation.

11. Ghengis Khan left his genetic mark on 0.5 percent of the world's male population, which translates into roughly 16 million descendants living today (Zerjal et al. 2003). This is impressive. But what good is this to Ghengis Khan?

BIBLIOGRAPHY

Allaire v. St. Luke's Hospital, 184 IL 359 (1900).

Apel, Karl-Otto. 1976. *Das Apriori der Kommunikationsgesellschaft*. Vol. 2, Transformation der Philosophie. Frankfurt am Main: Suhrkamp.

Asch, Adrienne. 2002. Prenatal Diagnosis and Selective Abortion: A Challenge to Practice and Policy. In *The Double-Edged Helix: Social Implications of Genetics in a Diverse Society*, ed. Joseph S. Alper et al., 123–150. Baltimore, MD: The Johns Hopkins University Press.

Birnbacher, Dieter. 2006. *Bioethik zwischen Natur und Interesse*. Frankfurt am Main: Suhrkamp.

Bonbrest v. Kotz, 65 F Suppl 138 (DDC 1946).

Boonin, David. 2003. *A Defense of Abortion*. Cambridge, UK: Cambridge University Press.

Brighouse, Harry, and Adam Swift. 2006. Parents' Rights and the Value of the Family. *Ethics* 117:80–108.

———. 2009. Legitimate Parental Partiality. *Philosophy & Public Affairs* 37 (1): 43–80.

Brody, Jane. 1970. Abortion Law Gaining Favor as New Statutes Spur Debate. *New York Times*, November 29, 52.

Buchanan, Allen, Dan W. Brock, Norman Daniels, and Daniel Wikler. 2000. *From Chance to Choice: Genetics and Justice*. New York: Cambridge University Press.

Bush, George W. 2001. Appendix B. Remarks of the President George W. Bush on Stem Cell Research, August 9, 2001. In *Monitoring Stem Cell Research: A Report of the President's Council on Bioethics, edited by President's Council on Bioethics (U.S.)*, 183–187. Washington, D.C.: U.S. Government Printing Office 2004. Also available from: http://usgovinfo.about.com/blwhrelease16.htm.

———. 2004. Remarks on Signing the Unborn Victims of Violence Act of 2004. April 1, 2004. In *Public Papers of the Presidents of the United States, George W. Bush, 2004, Bk. 1: January 1 to June 30, 2004*, 497–498. Office of the Federal Register: Washington, D.C.: Government Printing Office 2007. Also available from: http://georgewbush-whitehouse.archives.gov/news/releases/2004/04/20040401-3.html.

Byrn v. New York City Health & Hospital Corp., 31 NY 2d 194, 286 NE2d 887 (1972).

Cherry, April L. 2004. Roe's Legacy: The Nonconsensual Medical Treatment of Pregnant Women and Implications for Female Citizenship. *Journal of Constitutional Law* 6 (4): 723–751.

Dworkin, Ronald. 1992. Unenumerated Rights: Whether and How *Roe* Should Be Overruled. *University of Chicago Law Review* 59: 381–432.

———. 1994. *Life's Dominion. An Argument about Abortion, Euthanasia, and Individual Freedom.* New York: Vintage.

———. 1996. Politics, Death, and Nature. *Health Matrix* 6: 201–218. Case Western Reserve University, Cleveland.

———. 2000. *Sovereign Virtue: The Theory and Practice of Equality.* Cambridge, MA: Harvard University Press.

Eser, Albin. 2001. Vorbemerkungen zu den §§ 211 ff. In *Strafgesetzbuch, Kommentar,* 26th ed., ed. Adolf Schönke and Horst Schröder, 1727 München: C.H. Beck.

Feinberg, Joel. 1979. Abortion. In *Freedom and Fulfillment: Philosophical Essays,* by Joel Feinberg, 37–75. Princeton, NJ: Princeton University Press 1992.

———. 1980. The Child's Right to an Open Future. In *Freedom and Fulfillment. Philosophical Essays,* by Joel Feinberg, 76–97. Princeton, NJ: Princeton University Press 1992.

———. 1984. *Harm to Others: The Moral Limits of the Criminal Law.* New York: Oxford University Press.

Ferree, Myra Marx, William Anthony Gamson, Jürgen Gerhards, and Dieter Rucht. 2002. *Shaping Abortion Discourse. Democracy and the Public Sphere in Germany and the United States.* Cambridge, UK: Cambridge University Press.

Forst, Rainer. 2007. *Das Recht auf Rechtfertigung. Elemente einer konstruktivistischen Theorie der Gerechtigkeit.* Frankfurt am Main: Suhrkamp.

Friedman, Marilyn. 2008. Pettit's Civic Republicanism and Male Domination. In *Republicanism and Political Theory,* ed. Cecile Laborde and John Maynor, 246–268. Oxford, UK: Blackwell.

Gallagher, Janet. 1995. Collective Bad Faith: "Protecting" the Fetus. In *Reproduction, Ethics, and the Law. Feminist Perspectives,* ed. Joan C. Calahan, 343–379. Indianapolis: Indiana University Press.

Gallup. 2003. July 24. Abortion. In: *The Gallup Poll. Public Opinion 2002,* ed. by George Gallup, 204–207. Wilmington, DE: Scholarly Resources.

Glendon, Mary Ann. 1987. *Abortion and Divorce in Western Law: American Failures, European Challenges.* Cambridge, MA: Harvard University Press.

Gonzales v. Carhart, 550 US 124 (2007).

Griswold v. Connecticut, 381 US 479 (1965).

Grobstein, Clifford, et al. 1985. Frozen Embyos: Policy Issues. *New England Journal of Medicine* 312 (24): 1585–1588.

Günther, Hans-Ludwig, Jochen Taupitz, and Peter Kaiser. 2008. *Embryonenschutzgesetz: Juristischer Kommentar mit medizinisch-naturwissenschaftlichen Einführungen.* Stuttgart: W. Kohlhammer.

Habermas, Jürgen. 1994. *Justification and Application: Remarks on Discourse Ethics.* Cambridge, MA: MIT Press.

———. 2001. *The Postnational Constellation: Political Essays.* Cambridge, MA: MIT Press.

———. 2003. *The Future of Human Nature*. Cambridge, UK: Polity Press.

Hanser, Matthew. 1990. Harming Future People. *Philosophy & Public Affairs* 19: 47–70.

Harman, Elizabeth. 1999. Creation Ethics: The Moral Status of Early Fetuses and the Ethics of Abortion. *Philosophy & Public Affairs* 28 (4): 310–324.

Harris, John. 2007. *Enhancing Evolution. The Ethical Case for Making Better People*. Princeton, NJ: Princeton University Press.

Herzog, Felix. 2001. Präimplantationsdiagnostik—im Zweifel für ein Verbot? *Zeitschrift für Rechtspolitik* 34 (9): 393–397.

Holzapfel, Michael. 2002. The Right to Live, the Right to Choose, and the Unborn Victims of Violence Act. *The Catholic University of America Journal of Contemporary Health Law & Policy* 18: 431–466.

H.R. 2880. Public Law 104–99 (The Balanced Budget Downpayment Act, I), Jan. 26, 1996; 110 STAT. 26–47. Available from: http://www.gpo.gov/fdsys/pkg/PLAW-104publ99/pdf/PLAW-104publ99.pdf.

Isensee, Joseph 2002. Der grundrechtliche Status des Embryos. In *Gentechnik und Menschenwürde: An den Grenzen von Ethik und Recht*, ed. Otfried Höffe, Ludger Honnefelder, Josef Isensee, and Paul Kirchhof, 37–78. Köln: DuMont.

Iser, Mattias. 2008. *Empörung und Fortschritt. Grundlagen einer kritischen Theorie der Gesellschaft*. Frankfurt am Main: Campus.

Jamaica Hospital, in re, 128 Misc.2d 1006, 491 NYS 2d 898 (Sup Ct 1985).

Jefferson v. Griffin County Hospital Authority et al., 247 GA 86, 274 SE 2d 457 (1981).

Jerouschek, Günther. 1989. Vom Wert und Unwert der pränatalen Menschenwürde. *JuristenZeitung* 44: 279–285.

Jonas, Robert E., and John D. Gorby. 1976. West German Abortion Decision: A Contrast to *Roe v. Wade*. Translation of BVerfGE 39, 1. *Marshall Journal of Practice and Procedure* 9: 605.

Kamm, Frances. 1992. *Creation and Abortion: A Study in Moral and Legal Philosophy*. Oxford, UK: Oxford University Press.

———. 2005. Moral Status and Personal Identity: Clones, Embryos, and Future Generations. *Social Philosophy and Policy* 22 (2): 283–307.

Kant, Immanuel. 1797. The Metaphysics of Morals. In *Immanuel Kant. Practical Philosophy*, ed. Mary J. Gregor, 353–603. Cambridge, UK: Cambridge University Press 1996.

Karnein, Anja. 2012. Parenthood—Whose Right is it Anyway? In *Reproductive Donation: Bioethics, Policies and Practices*, ed. Martin Richards, Guido Pennings, and John Appleby. Cambridge, UK: Cambridge University Press.

Kaufmann, Armin. 1971. Tatbestandsmäßigkeit und Verursachung im Contergan-Verfahren. *JuristenZeitung* 26 (18): 569–576.

Kollek, Regine. 2002. *Präimplantationsdiagnostik. Embryonenselektion, weibliche Autonomie und Recht*. Tübingen: Francke.

Kumar, Rahul. 2003. Who Can Be Wronged? *Philosophy & Public Affairs* 31 (2): 99–118.

Ladwig, Bernd. 2007. Das Recht auf Leben—nicht nur für Personen. *Deutsche Zeitschrift für Philosophie* 55 (1): 17–39.

Liao, Matthew. 2010. The Basis of Human Moral Status. *Journal of Moral Philosophy* 7 (2): 159–179.

Locke, John. 1690. *Two Treatises of Government*, ed. Peter Laslett. Cambridge, UK: Cambridge University Press.

Lüttger, Hans. 1983. Geburtsbeginn und pränatale Einwirkungen mit postnatalen Folgen. Bemerkungen zu BGH-3 StR 25/83 vom 22. 4.1983. *Neue Zeitschrift für Strafrecht* 11: 481–485.

McKnight v. State, 78 SC 33 (2008); 661 SE 2d 354.

McMahan, Jeff. 1993. The Right to Choose an Abortion. *Philosophy & Public Affairs*, 22 (4): 331–348.

———. 2006. Paradoxes of Abortion and Prenatal Injury. *Ethics* 116: 625–655.

National Conference on State Legislatures. 2010. Fetal Homicide Laws. Washington, DC: National Conference of State Legislatures. Available from: http://www.ncsl.org/default.aspx?tabid=14386.

Norris, Michele L. 1991. Cries in the Dark Often Go Unanswered: For Drug-Addicted Mothers, Treatment Is Hard to Find, Even Harder to Stick With. *The Washington Post*, July 2, A1.

Paltrow, Lynn M., with Hillary Fox, Julie Petrow, Suzanne Shende, Teresa Scott, Charlotte Levine, Laura Solinger, Jo Ann Citron, and Kathryn McGowan. 1992. *Criminal Prosecutions against Pregnant Women. National Update and Overview.* Reproductive Freedom Project. New York: American Civil Liberties Union Foundation.

Parfit, Derek. 1973. Rights, Interests and Possible People. In *Bioethics. An Anthology*, ed. Helga Kuhse and Peter Singer, 2d ed., 108–112. Oxford, UK: Blackwell.

———. 1984. *Reasons and Persons*. New York: Oxford University Press.

Pemberton v. Tallahassee Memorial Regional Medical Center, Inc., 66 F. Supp. 2d 1247 (1999).

Pettit, Philip. 1997. *Republicanism: A Theory of Freedom and Government.* Oxford, MA: Clarendon Press.

Planned Parenthood of Southeastern Pennsylvania v. Casey, 505 US 833 (1992).

Quante, Michael. 2007. *Person*. Berlin: de Gruyter.

Raleigh Fitkin-Paul Morgan Memorial Hospital v. Anderson, 42 NJ 421, 201 A2d 537 (1964).

Rau, Johannes. 2001. Wird alles gut? Fortschritt nach menschlichem Maß. Berliner Rede. May 18. Available at http://www.bundespraesident.de/SharedDocs/Reden/DE/Johannes-Rau/Reden/2001/05/20010518_Rede.html.

Rawls, John. 1971. *A Theory of Justice*, rev.ed. Cambridge, MA: Harvard University Press.

Renzikowski, Joachim. 2001. Die strafrechtliche Beurteilung der Präimplantationsdiagnostik. *Neue Juristische Wochenzeitschrift* 50 (38): 2753–2758.

Richards, Martin, Guido Pennings, and John Appleby, eds. 2012. *Reproductive Donation: Bioethics, Policies and Practices*. Cambridge, UK: Cambridge University Press.

Roberts, Dorothy E. 1991. Punishing Drug Addicts Who Have Babies: Women of Color, Equality, and the Right of Privacy. *Harvard Law Review* 104 (7): 1419–1482.

Robertson, John A. 1994. *Children of Choice: Freedom and the New Reproductive Technologies.* Princeton, NJ: Princeton University Press.

———. 2003. Procreative Liberty in the Era of Genomics. *American Journal of Law & Medicine* 29: 439–487.

Roe v. Wade, 410 US 113 (1973).

Sachs, Benjamin. 2011. The Status of Moral Status. *Pacific Philosophy Quarterly* 92: 87–104.

Sacksofsky, Ute. 2009. Das Frauenbild des Bundesverfassungsgerichts. In *Querelles. Jahrbuch für Frauen-und Geschlechterforschung 2009*, Vol. 14, ed. Beate Rudolf, 191–215. Göttingen: Wallstein.

Sandel, Michael J. 1982. *Liberalism and the Limits of Justice.* 2d ed. New York: Cambridge University Press.

———. 2004. The Case Against Perfection. *Atlantic Monthly* 293 (3): 50–62.

———. 2007. *The Case Against Perfection: Ethics in the Age of Genetic Engineering.* Cambridge, MA: Harvard University Press.

Savulescu, Julian. 2007. Genetic Interventions and the Ethics of Enhancement of Human Beings. In *The Oxford Handbook of Bioethics*, ed. Bonnie Steinbock, 516–535. Oxford, UK: Oxford University Press.

Scanlon, Thomas. 1998. *What We Owe to Each Other.* Cambridge, MA: Harvard University Press.

Schöne-Seifert, Bettina. 2003. Contra Potentialitätsargument: Probleme einer traditionellen Begründung für embryonalen Lebensschutz. In *Der moralische Status menschlicher Embryonen: Pro und contra Spezies-, Kontinuums-, Identitäts-und Potentialitätsargument*, ed. Gregor Damschen and Dieter Schönecker, 169–186. Berlin: de Gruyter.

Sherley et al. v. Sebelius et al., U.S. District Court for the District of Columbia, Civ. No. 1:09-cv-1575(RCL) (2010).

Shiffrin, Seana. 1999. Wrongful Life, Procreative Responsibility and the Significance of Harm. *Legal Theory* 5: 117–148.

Siep, Ludwig. 2003. Normative Aspects of the Human Body. *Journal of Medicine and Philosophy* 28 (2): 171–185.

Silver, Lee M. 1997. *Remaking Eden. How Genetic Engineering and Cloning will Transform the American Family.* New York: HarperCollins.

Skinner, Quentin. 2002. A Third Concept of Liberty. *London Review of Books* 24 (7): 23–25.

Smith v. Brennan, 31 NJ 353 (1960).

State v. McKnight, 352 SC 635 (2003); 576 SE 2d 168.

Steinbock, Bonnie. 2011. *Life Before Birth: The Moral and Legal Status of Embryos and Fetuses.* 2nd edition. New York: Oxford University Press.

Stenberg v. Carhart, 530 US 914 (2000).

Stern, Susan. 1997. *Working Women in Contemporary Germany: Roles, Attitudes and a Handful of Success Stories*. Bonn: Basis-Info 9.

Sterne, Laurence. 1760. *Tristram Shandy*, ed. Howard Anderson. New York: Norton.

Taft v. Taft, 388 MA. 331 (1983); 446 NE 2d 395.

Thomson, Judith Jarvis. 1971. A Defense of Abortion. *Philosophy & Public Affairs* 11 (1): 47–66.

Velleman, David. 2008. Persons in Prospect. *Philosophy & Public Affairs* 36 (3): 221–288.

Webster v. Reproductive Health Services, 492 US 490 (1989).

Whitner v. State, 328 SC 1 (SC 1997); 492 SE 2d 777.

Wilkerson, Isabel. 1991. Woman Cleared After Drug Use in Pregnancy. *The New York Times*. April 3, A15.

Zerjal, Tatiana et al. 2003. The Genetic Legacy of the Mongols. *The American Journal of Human Genetics* 72 (3): 717–721.

Zypries, Brigitte. 2003. Vom Zeugen zum Erzeugen? Verfassungsrechtliche und Rechtspolitische Fragen der Bioethik. Rede der Bundesministerin der Justiz beim Humboldt-Forum der Humboldt-Universität zu Berlin, October 29. Available from http://pdf.zeit.de/reden/wissenschaft/Bioethik_031030.pdf.

INDEX